Punishment and Madness

Governing Prisoners with Mental Health Problems

The imprisonment of offenders with mental health problems is one of the most dismaying, unsettling and controversial aspects of contemporary penal practice. It is also an enduring and longstanding problem, with prison reformers from John Howard onwards disapprovingly noting the presence of the 'insane' in penal institutions.

The focus of this book is on responses to the imprisonment of offenders with mental health problems from the 1980s to the present. This period has seen a major transformation in the social fabric – the shift to 'late modernity' – which in turn has had a massive impact on crime and punishment. The aim of this book is to investigate the impact of this transformation on the governance and treatment of prisoners with mental health problems. Specifically, its concern is to understand how such prisoners have come to be viewed increasingly as sources of 'risk' requiring 'management' or containment, rather than as people suitable for therapeutic responses.

The book draws on primary research carried out by the author, including interviews with key informants involved in the field during this period, such as former cabinet ministers, senior civil servants, campaigners and academics.

Toby Seddon is Senior Research Fellow in the School of Law at the University of Manchester.

Punishment and Madness

Governing Prisoners with Mental Health Problems

Toby Seddon

Routledge·Cavendish
Taylor & Francis Group
a GlassHouse book

First published 2007 by Routledge-Cavendish
2 Park Square, Milton Park, Abingdon, Oxon OX14 4RN

Simultaneously published in the USA and Canada
by Routledge-Cavendish
270 Madison Ave, New York, NY 10016

A Glasshouse book

*Routledge-Cavendish is an imprint of the Taylor & Francis Group,
an informa business*

© 2007 Toby Seddon

Typeset in Times New Roman by
RefineCatch Limited, Bungay, Suffolk
Printed and bound in Great Britain by
TJ International, Padstow, Cornwall

British Library Cataloguing in Publication Data
A catalogue record for this book is available from the British Library

Library of Congress Cataloging in Publication Data
Seddon, Toby.
  Punishment and madness / Toby Seddon.
    p. cm.
    ISBN 1–904385–90–7 (pbk.) — ISBN 1–904385–63–X
(hardback) 1, Mentally ill offenders—Great Britain. 2. Mentally
ill prisoners—Great Britain. 3. Prisons—Great Britain. I. Title.
  HV8742.G72S43 2006
  365′.460941—dc22   2006020254

ISBN10: 1–904385–90–7(pbk)
ISBN10: 1–904385–63–X (hbk)

ISBN13: 978–1–904385–90–5 (pbk)
ISBN13: 978–1–904385–63–9 (hbk)

For Poppy, Sam and Molly-Eva

Contents

Tables

Acknowledgements

This book started out some years ago as research for my PhD. I am extremely grateful to Frances Heidensohn for her expert and patient supervision and for her continuing interest in my work. I thank too all my interviewees for their time. Nikolas Rose and Geoffrey Pearson gave me an (intellectually) bruising but invaluable 'mini-viva' at the half-way stage of the PhD, and David Downes and Richard Sparks were sympathetic but demanding examiners at the 'real' viva. Richard's searching questions in particular made me re-think some of my approach during the process of turning the thesis into this book.

The original intellectual genesis for the research was reading David Garland's *Punishment and Welfare*, which for me remains a landmark book to which I continue to return. Garland's subsequent work has also deeply influenced my own developing thinking, as will be apparent in the pages that follow. My substantive interest in mental health issues was ignited by a short period in the late 1990s working at Revolving Doors Agency, a small mental health charity which continues to do innovative and important work with some of the most vulnerable members of our society. I would like to thank former colleagues there for introducing me to some of the complex issues faced by practitioners in the field. Parts of Chapter 2 in this book started life as a briefing paper I wrote for the Agency, designed to summarise the research literature and feed in to the development of new initiatives for prisoners. I have been delighted to watch from a distance as those initiatives have come to fruition and flourished. I am also grateful to the Centre for Criminal Justice Studies in the School of Law at the University of Leeds for appointing me to a Senior Research Fellowship in 2004. The Fellowship was invaluable in giving me the time to write this book.

At Cavendish, Beverley Brown showed an initial interest in the book for which I am very grateful. Subsequently, Colin Perrin has been a calm, patient and supportive editor. The readers' reports – from Véronique Veruz and Jill Peay respectively – provided constructive and insightful feedback on the draft of the manuscript.

Last but definitely not least, Sally has been an invaluable and unfailing support, putting up with all those evenings when I sat in front of the computer working on my thesis and then later on this book. On top of all that, she also designed the cover!

Chapter I

Introduction

Punishment, prisons and madness

> Many of the bridewells are crowded and offensive, because the rooms
> which were designed for prisoners are occupied by the insane. Where these
> are not kept separate they disturb and terrify other prisoners. No care is
> taken of them.
>
> (Howard, 1777)
> [Eighteenth century prison reformer John Howard]

> I have reason to believe that the proportion of convicts afflicted with men-
> tal and bodily diseases and infirmities is greater than would be found in any
> other section of the community.
>
> (Dr RM Gover, medical director of Millbank Prison and
> subsequently national prison medical inspector in the
> late nineteenth century, quoted in Wiener, 1990:314)

> The stench of the slop out and unwashed humanity hangs in the air. In the
> first cell there is a naked and contorted body lying on the floor next to a
> torn mattress, faeces are daubed on the wall and food lies underfoot [. . .]
> In the next a man in strip conditions paces, mumbling to himself and
> occasionally shouting at his private demons [. . .] I am simply waiting for a
> disaster to happen.
>
> (Needham-Bennett, 1995:516 – A doctor working in a
> London prison in the 1990s)

I. BACKGROUND AND CONTEXT

The imprisonment of offenders with mental health problems has long been
one of the more dismaying and unsettling aspects of penal practice and one
which has aroused considerable controversy over the years. Walker (1968:30)
observes that when the first prisons started to be built in the thirteenth century, they became an 'obvious place for the violent lunatic'. Certainly, by the
sixteenth and seventeenth centuries there is evidence that the Bridewells and
houses of correction were used to confine some of the 'more dangerous or

troublesome lunatics' (Scull, 1993:16). By the eighteenth and nineteenth centuries, prison reformers like John Howard and Elizabeth Fry noted with disapproval the presence of the insane within penal institutions.

This emergence of institutional responses to insane offenders clearly has a long history. Foucault (1967) famously describes in *Madness and Civilization* the origin of what he terms the 'Great Confinement', the point in the middle of the seventeenth century at which confinement (whether in the Hôpital Général, the workhouse or the prison) came to be designated as the natural abode for madness, criminality, poverty and idleness. He notes that the consequent 'presence of madmen among the prisoners' became a source of indignation (1967:225). Walker and McCabe (1973:1) observe that in the eighteenth century, the 'natural repository for the lunatic who had committed a felony [. . .] was the local gaol or house of correction'. To a lesser extent, they were also to be found in other institutions, like the workhouses and private madhouses (Walker and McCabe, 1973:1). Insane offenders were thus dispersed across these various institutions, although there was a particular reliance on penal establishments.

In the nineteenth century, some 'special' provision for this group was established for the first time. Following the Criminal Lunatics Act of 1800 and a House of Commons Select Committee report in 1807, a new wing at Bethlem Hospital was opened in 1816 for what were then called 'criminal lunatics'. Half a century later, Broadmoor, the first entirely separate institution for 'criminal lunatics', was opened in 1863. Despite this separate provision, as both Walker and McCabe (1973) and Murphy (1996) note, only a small number of 'lunatics' and the disordered were removed from penal establishments and it remained an acknowledged problem for the prison system (Grounds, 1991a; Sim, 1990; Walker and McCabe, 1973; Garland, 1985:7–8).

Into and throughout the twentieth century, the problem remained (Goring, 1913; Roper, 1951; Epps, 1951, 1954; Woodside, 1962; West, 1963; Robinson et al, 1965; Bluglass, 1966; Gibbens, 1967; Gibbens, 1971; Faulk, 1976; Gunn et al, 1978). Even by the 1990s, offenders with mental health problems could still be found in great numbers in the prison system (Gunn et al, 1991; Singleton et al, 1998). The recently established DSPD (Dangerous and Severe Personality Disorder) units (two of which are sited in prisons, two in Special Hospitals) will add another probable location for some of this group. These questions of how to deal with offenders who are also suffering from mental health problems, of how to decide who should be treated and who should be punished, who should be sent to one form of institution and who should be sent to another, are thus part of a longstanding and controversial debate over 'dividing practices'.

The focus of this book is on more recent times: specifically, the last quarter of the twentieth century. In general terms, the period from the 1970s to the present has witnessed massive economic and structural change accompanied by the 'rapid unravelling of the social fabric of the industrialized world'

(Young, 1999:vi). Signifying the enormity of these changes, Hobsbawm (1994) has described the last three decades of the century as the 'crisis decades', whilst others have characterised this period as the shift from modernity to late modernity (Young, 1999; Garland, 2001). Fundamental changes in the economy, modes of production, the labour market, women's employment patterns, the family, communities, patterns of leisure, the role of the state and so on have totally altered the contextual landscape in Britain (and elsewhere). This shift to late modernity has also seen related and equally dramatic changes in crime and 'incivilities' as well as in the crime control and penal spheres (Garland, 2001). A 'crisis of penal modernism' (Garland, 1990a) has been reached in which the penal-welfare strategies established at the start of the twentieth century have unravelled and to a great extent been sidelined, only to be replaced by a re-configured crime control field characterised by its 'volatile and contradictory' nature (O'Malley, 1999). As Rose (2000:183) puts it, a common contemporary view of penal commentators is that 'current control practices manifest, at most, a hesitant, incomplete, fragmentary, contradictory and contested metamorphosis'.

In a nutshell, the principal and overarching question explored in this book is whether these profound social, economic, cultural and penal transformations have also led to a re-configuring of the 'dividing practices' applied to offenders with mental health problems. To put it another way, the question is whether and how these 'dividing practices' have been shaped by the shift from modernity to late modernity. Focusing on the 1980s and 1990s – the decades in which the impact of this shift has been most apparent in other areas – the book looks specifically at the government of prisoners with mental health problems. The 'problem' for investigation is how this group of prisoners, who had since the 1930s been seen as at least potentially suitable for treatment or therapeutic responses, came to be viewed increasingly as sources of 'risk' requiring 'management', containment or control.

Such a project inevitably involves making some assumptions. Above all, it presumes that the categories of 'madness', 'badness', 'dangerousness', 'risk' and so on are not the fixed, transparent and self-evident ones that they are sometimes taken to be. Were that the case, this investigation would be unnecessary and surplus to requirements. In fact, as will be shown, these categories are historically contingent, deeply problematic and not well understood aspects of the social and penal realms. Although not directly explored here, it should also be noted that they are *culturally* contingent too, as Downes (1988:88–99) illustrates, for example, in contrasting the extent of psychiatrisation in penal policy between the Netherlands and England and Wales in the 1950s and 1960s.

As with many other areas of social life, over time these categories, and the institutional responses to the people who fall within them, manage to create a certain self-evident and 'taken-for-granted' status which tends to limit and inhibit thinking. The difficult and deep questions about these categories and about the 'dividing practices' in which they are implicated are rarely raised. The critical project of this book is to tackle some of these questions by 'shaking this false self-evidence' as Foucault puts it (1991a:75).

This idea – that there is a 'false self-evidence' to contemporary arrangements and practices that are in fact historically contingent – is an underpinning assumption of this book. Chapter 2 explores this in much more detail, by tracing the historical context from the eighteenth century onwards. For present purposes, a brief overview here of some of the key strategic phases in this field during the twentieth century provides some useful introductory scene-setting by focusing on the changing contours of penal-welfare strategies. The major policy measures and reports of the century are set out in Table 1.1.

Table 1.1 Major policy measures and reports 1895–1999

Year	Measure
1895	Gladstone Report
1898	Inebriates Act
1908	Royal Commission report on the care and control of the feeble-minded
1913	Mental Deficiency Act
1927	Mental Deficiency Act
1939	East–Hubert report
1957	Percy Commission on law relating to mental illness and mental deficiency
1959	Mental Health Act
1974	Glancy working party report on security in NHS psychiatric hospitals
1975	Butler Committee report on Mentally Abnormal Offenders
1975	White Paper *Better Services for the Mentally Ill*
1983	Mental Health Act
1986	House of Commons Social Services Select Committee report on the Prison Medical Service
1987	DHSS/Home Office Working Group report on 'mentally disturbed prisoners'
1990	Efficiency Scrutiny of the Prison Medical Service
1990	Home Office Circular 66/90 on provision for mentally disordered offenders
1991	Woolf report on prison disturbances
1992	Reed Review on services for mentally disordered offenders
1994	Ritchie inquiry report into the care and treatment of Christopher Clunis
1996	HM Chief Inspector of Prisons report *Patient or Prisoner?*
1999	Prison Service/NHSE report on the Future Organisation of Prison Health Care
1999	Proposals for dealing with people with Dangerous and Severe Personality Disorders

There are, broadly speaking, four discernible phases of strategic development in this area in the twentieth century:

- The establishment of penal-welfarism (the first two decades of the century);
- The 'mentally disordered offender' as the paradigm for all offenders (the 1920s and 1930s);
- The era of rehabilitation (the post-war period up to the 1960s);
- The unravelling of penal-welfarism (from the 1970s to the 1990s).

The main features of these four phases are summarised in Table 1.2. This summary is inevitably crude – as the subsequent chapters will show, the 'phases' are actually more complex and less discrete than it suggests – but it is used here as a presentational device to aid the textual exposition below and in Chapter 2.

Table 1.2 'Master' changes in twentieth-century strategy

	Phase One (1890s–1914)	Phase Two (1920s–1939)	Phase Three (1945–1960s)	Phase Four (1970s–1990s)
1. General penal strategy	Establishment of penal-welfarism.	Penal-welfarism.	Penal-welfarism.	Unravelling of penal-welfarism. Strategy re-configuring.
2. Strategic response to prisoners with mental health problems	Clear out MDOs from the prisons and into new specialist institutions (eg inebriate reformatories).	Psychotherapy and psychiatry in prisons to prevent re-offending.	Expansion of prison psychotherapy and psychiatry. More diagnostic than therapeutic work.	Risk management. Routing offenders into treatment outside prison.
3. Main locations for interventions	New specialist institutions (eg inebriate reformatories). Residuum in prison.	Increasingly in prison.	In prison.	In prison. In hospital/ community for those diverted or transferred (1990s).
4. Conception of the 'problem'	Source of national degeneracy.	All crime as a 'medical' problem – the 'mad' and 'bad' as an extreme on a continuum.	Mental ill-health as ancillary 'care' need in prison and as potential impediment to rehabilitation and resettlement.	Sources of risk. Prison management problems. Prison suicide problems.
5. Main form of response	Specialist treatment for different groups.	Psychotherapy and psychiatry.	Psychiatric diagnosis.	Management and containment.

Source: adapted from Cohen, 1985:16–17.

The first phase, during the first two decades of the century, which was set in train by the Gladstone report on prisons in 1895, was focused on the 'clearing out' of various categories of mentally abnormal offenders from the prison system in order to enable it to operate more effectively on 'responsible' criminals (Gunn et al, 1978:10–14; Garland, 1985). Hence, the Inebriates Act of 1898 and the Mental Deficiency Act of 1913 sought to facilitate the removal of 'inebriates', 'idiots', 'imbeciles', the 'feeble-minded' and 'moral imbeciles' out of prisons and into specialist institutions. Whilst the implementation of this policy suffered mixed fortunes – for example, the reformatory system for 'inebriates' had been totally abandoned by 1921 (Gunn et al, 1978:13; Radzinowicz and Hood, 1986:307–15) – the aspiration to focus the prisons on dealing solely with 'fully responsible' criminals was clear. Much of the debate in this period was closely linked to concerns with the 'problem' of national degeneracy posed by the defective, unfit and weak-minded (Garland, 1985:142–52; Wiener, 1990:351–8). Indeed, the unravelling of Victorian penal policy, which was built on the central notion of deterrence, in the last few decades of the nineteenth century was partly linked to emerging tensions between the deterrent requirements of prison discipline and the growing anxiety that not all prisoners were mentally fit enough to withstand such discipline (Wiener, 1990:313–18). According to Garland's influential account (1985), this phase marks the establishment of modern penal-welfare strategies in place of the Victorian penal complex which had been dominant since the 1860s.

In the second phase of development, in the 1920s and 1930s, ideas about the psychological and psychoanalytical treatment of offenders began to flourish on a broader front. Indeed, the 'mentally disordered offender' arguably became the paradigm for all offenders in this period, as the claims of psychological medicine as a 'cure' for crime reached a high point. The most enthusiastic supporters of this position, such as Grace Pailthorpe and Maurice Hamblin-Smith, argued that all crime had 'mental' origins and hence could be 'cured' by psychological or psychoanalytical techniques (Pailthorpe, 1932; Garland, 1997a:39). Other influential figures of the time, like Norwood East, Medical Director on the Prison Commission in the 1930s, also supported a psychological approach to crime but believed that it was properly applicable only to a minority of offenders, roughly 20 per cent of the prison population (East and Hubert, 1939). This period thus saw a continuation and development of penal-welfarism.

In the third phase, the post-war decades saw the consolidation and expansion of psychiatric work in prisons, with a particular focus on diagnosis rather than treatment (Gunn et al, 1978:23–4). The establishment of a psychiatric prison, originally recommended in an important report by East and Hubert (1939) on their work in Wormwood Scrubs in the mid-1930s, finally happened in 1962 with the opening of Grendon Underwood prison. During the 1950s and 1960s, it thus became accepted that treatment or therapeutic responses to offenders could be effectively implemented within prisons, a marked contrast with the position at the start of the century. Indeed, more broadly, in many accounts the post-war period is defined as the era of rehabilitation (Bean, 1976). The period from 1945 to the mid-1960s thus saw the high water-mark of penal-welfarism and correctionalist crime control, in which its framework of assumptions, logics and objectives provided the underlying structure and pattern of the system, fixing the contours of the penal and welfare complexes. Outside the penal system, from the 1950s, a series of developments in mental health policy marked a significant shift away from institutional responses to mental illness, with the long decline in the population of the mental hospitals in England and Wales beginning in 1955 (Barham, 1992). There was also considerable optimism at this time in many quarters about the future scope and achievement of psychiatry, driven in part by the apparent therapeutic potential of emerging new drug treatments (Barham, 1992:11–12).

Bringing this picture up to date, the fourth phase of development is, in essence, the focus of this book, but a brief sketch here of some of its main features may be useful. By the 1970s, some of the premises and practices of the post-war decades were starting to come under critical scrutiny. One of the most explicit and trenchant critiques was Martinson's (1974) infamous claim about rehabilitative interventions that 'Nothing Works' (see also Brody, 1976). By the 1980s and 1990s, some novel elements within policy and strategy, falling outside the penal-welfare framework, had started to emerge. These included a strong focus on the 'administration of risk' and the management of exclusion (Rose, 1996a), as well as a concern for increasing the efficiency and effectiveness of systems and processes by utilising tools and techniques borrowed from the private sector. Other elements apparent in this phase, however, pointed to a more confused picture. For example, the revived humanitarianism in the Woolf report on prison disturbances (and the Reed Review of services for mentally disordered offenders), a new emphasis on human rights and a general concern with identifying mentally disordered offenders and routing them into treatment were also all part of the picture in the 1990s. Thus, whilst penal-welfarism was clearly unravelling from the mid-1970s, the re-configuring field was unsettled, fragmentary and inconsistent in the last two decades of the century.

More recent policy developments in the field illustrate well this complex picture of a re-configuring field. The ongoing pilot programme concerning Dangerous and Severe Personality Disorders, for example, exemplifies the new 'risk thinking'. Indeed, within this programme, the trigger for intervention is when an individual, because of their personality disorder, poses a significant risk of serious harm to others. On the other hand, the phased transfer between 2004 and 2006 of responsibility for commissioning mental health services from prisons to local Primary Care Trusts embodies a mixture of progressive humanitarianism with neo-liberal managerialism (Prison

Service/NHSE, 1999; Department of Health/Prison Service/Welsh Assembly, 2001). These developments also raise the question of whether we are now seeing the start of a new fifth 'phase' of strategy in which 'advanced liberal' forms of government are becoming predominant (see Rose, 2000) or, alternatively, in which a 'culture of control' has become the new strategic paradigm (Garland, 2001). This important question will be returned to in Chapters 6 and 7.

What this brief overview of twentieth century policy and strategy shows is that the apparently 'self-evident' responses to prisoners with mental health problems, rather than being fixed and constant, are actually subject to shifts and change over time. Putting it in the most concrete way, exactly which mentally vulnerable offenders are considered as most suitable for prison rather than other institutions can and does change from one period to the next. As an official in the Home Office Mental Health Unit put it in an interview conducted in 1999 in the early stages of the research on which this book is based:

> I know for a fact there are a lot of prisoners who in 1984 would have been categorised as psychopaths but aren't now because the psychiatric profession doesn't want them.

This then marks the sphere of inquiry for the book and introduces some of the background context. By choosing this area for study, it was hoped to achieve a number of objectives. First, as will become evident from Chapter 2, this subject area has been dominated in the twentieth century by research from within what Nikolas Rose has termed the 'psy' disciplines (Rose, 1985). Consequently, there are a whole series of questions and issues that are relatively unexplored from a broader social science perspective. The book can therefore make a significant contribution to substantive knowledge in this area.

Second, it can contribute to the broader project of attempting to understand the nature of the emerging new penality in late modernity which is one of the major challenges for contemporary criminology (see, for example: Sparks, 1996; Garland, 1995, 2001; Young, 1999; O'Malley, 1999; Rose, 2000; Pratt, 2000a). The 'dividing practices' examined in the book run across the fault lines between the penal and welfare complexes and, consequently, it provides a particular insight into the changing relationship between these domains. It throws into sharp relief questions of the appropriate balance between punishment, treatment, management and control, all of which underpin the penal-welfare nexus. The book aims to inject some empirically based and specific findings into this rich and fertile criminological debate.

Third, at the most general level, this study should reveal something about the social world in the late twentieth and early twenty-first centuries and about how social order is constructed today. As Garland (1990a; Garland

and Young, 1983) has argued, the penal and social realms are interdependent and shape each other, so investigating penal issues inevitably sheds some light on broader social ones. Specifically, this study can help illuminate the linkages 'between the penal realm and problems of state sovereignty and legitimation' (Sparks, 2000a:141; Garland, 1996), advancing our understanding of the 'place of the penal realm within contemporary statecraft' (Sparks, 2000a:141).

Set in this context, it should be apparent that the book seeks to address a series of research questions at different levels, ranging from the general, abstract and theoretical to the specific, concrete and substantive. The research attempts to tackle all these questions by direct and close reference to empirical material. Its closest 'cousin' in terms of research intent and analytical approach is perhaps Garland's (1985) *Punishment and Welfare*, although this book has a much narrower focus, in terms of both subject area and time period covered. The empirical nature of the research is an important feature. It is, in Cohen's (1985:9) words, a study which 'uses theory rather than being about theory'.

2. RESEARCH QUESTIONS AND KEY THEMES

Research questions

As described above, the central and overarching research question is whether and how the 'dividing practices' applied to offenders with mental health problems have been shaped by the shift in the last quarter of the twentieth century from modernity to late modernity. Addressing this involves posing two major questions, one historical and the other sociological. The historical question asks how change in this field came about during this period and why this change took the form it did. It seeks to understand the transformative forces that shaped and reconstituted this field during these decades. The sociological question asks about the nature of the relationship between these changes in the penal sphere and wider transformations in the social, economic and cultural realms.

The analysis sets about answering these main questions, and a series of subsidiary ones, by a close and detailed empirical examination of an approximate 20 year period starting from the mid-1980s. This empirical scrutiny, or, to put it another way, this engagement with historical methods, is, however, primarily analytical rather than archival (Garland, 2001:2). In other words, the aim is not to write a comprehensive history of this period in the manner of conventional narrative history, but rather to uncover the 'conditions of existence' on which changes in the field during this period depend. It is in this sense a 'history of the present' (Foucault, 1977:31) which aims 'not to think historically about the past but rather to use that history to rethink the present' (Garland, 2001:2). By understanding the social and cultural conditions on which the transformations in the last two decades of the twentieth century depend, a deeper understanding of present-day practices (and their underpinning 'conditions of existence') is possible.

The scope and limits of the empirical enquiry are worth spelling out here. The book covers England and Wales only. In terms of subject area, as described above, the focus is on those 'dividing practices' that route individuals into prisons, rather than on the field of 'mentally disordered offenders' as a whole. Such a tight geographical, historical and subject focus may seem excessively narrow and may raise the question of whether such a study is likely to be of much significance. As Garland (2001:vii–viii) observes, there is an inevitable tension and dilemma for researchers between focusing on the general (which carries the danger of over-simplification) and on the particular (which brings the risk of lack of significance or wider generalisability). However, it is argued that as an area of scholarship, research on penality in the late twentieth century has recently come to be dominated by generalising studies hypothesising about the overall organising structures and patterns of contemporary crime control and related areas (for example: Garland, 1995, 2001; Rose, 2000; Pratt, 2000a; Sparks, 1996, 2000a). Garland's (2001) work *The Culture of Control* exemplifies this tendency with its focus on the whole range of social responses to crime in both the UK and the USA across a period of three or four decades. Similarly, Rose's (2000) analysis examines the broad field of rationalities and technologies for the government of human conduct. Without questioning at all the intellectual insight and stimulation generated by these general accounts, the gap in knowledge is increasingly about the variation, difference and complexity within these broader patterns. It is suggested that this book can act as a case study which can refine and revise these more general and abstract findings in the literature. To put it another way, there are now enough general accounts available for it to become valuable in terms of knowledge advancement to start testing these out with some specific and focused empirical research.

Alongside the main research questions, a series of subsidiary questions are also investigated here. One of the most important of these is the question of the links between structure and agency. This has been one of the abiding debates within sociology and recent social theory has made some interesting contributions. Giddens' (1984) theory of structuration, for example, has stimulated great debate within social theory in general (Held and Thompson, 1989) as well as within the field of criminology (Vaughan, 2001; Sparks, 1997:421–4; Farrall and Bowling, 1999). Bourdieu's (1996) notions of *habitus* and *field* also provide a challenge to the dualism of structure and agency which has started to have influence within criminology (Sparks, 1997:423–4; Zedner, 2002:358–60). On the other hand, within the 'governmentality' analytic, another recent influence on sociology and criminology, it is not at all clear that agency has any place at all (for example, Rose, 2000). The investigation in this book, which seeks to understand and explain change in the penal sphere, goes to the heart of this debate about structure and agency. In essence, it raises questions of to what extent (if at all) individuals (policy-makers, politicians and so on) influence and affect change. This issue has been handled very differently within the penal history literature, ranging from Rock's (1996) micro-sociological approach to Foucault's (1977) 'structural' account in *Discipline and Punish*. Others have adopted a middle position: for example, Downes (1988) in his comparative study of post-war penal developments in the Netherlands and in England and Wales, and similarly, albeit within a very different theoretical framework, Garland (1985) in *Punishment and Welfare*.

Closely related to this are questions about the cultural and expressive aspects of penality. This study is not simply a matter, on the one hand, of understanding the strategic structural shifts, and, on the other, of paying attention to the immediate press of political tactics and the role of individual agents. There are expressive and emotive aspects too, as Garland has argued (1983, 1990a, 1990b). Indeed, the issues of 'dangerousness' and 'risk' that have long surrounded the area of offenders with mental health problems have lent particular 'heat' and passion to debates and policy-making in this field over many years (see Pearson, 1999). Considering this expressive dimension goes in turn to a set of questions about representations. If 'dividing practices' are partly a means of controlling and managing risks and threats, then from what risks do we particularly desire protection? As Sparks (2001a) argues, to understand this question requires reference to the role of communications media in circulating and exchanging knowledge and beliefs. He suggests that this is crucial to any attempt to understand the relation between politics and penal politics. To put it another way, these questions about culture and representations are essential for grasping how structural forces or factors become mobilised within the political arena (2001a:196).

Aside from these theoretical questions, there are a number of substantive ones that have been addressed in this research. What mental health services is it appropriate or necessary to provide in prison? How should they be funded and who should provide them? What should be the relationship between prison-based services and those provided by the NHS (both in other institutions and in the community)? To what extent should there be specialist provision in the prison system (such as Grendon)? Which prisoners should be diverted or transferred from prison? Where and how should the most 'dangerous' prisoners be treated or managed? These are important questions which go to the heart of many of the contemporary policy debates.

Theoretical and methodological approach

The essence of the approach adopted in this book is summarised well by McCallum (2001:36):

Rather than presupposing the continuous figure of the mentally ill person, or the criminal, or the historically inevitable tension between these two in the dualism of 'bad or mad', it is suggested that the study of particular problem populations must account for the way in which categories of person are 'made up' and become known in order to be governed.

The dualism referred to between the 'bad' and the 'mad' is often deployed in this field (eg Verdun Jones, 1989; Prins, 1980; Wilczynski, 1997), but, as will be shown in later chapters, it offers a somewhat over-simplified and imprecise formula for the 'dividing practices' actually involved. The approach used here is a more critical one that seeks to problematise the ways in which we think about, know and 'make up' categories of people in order to govern their conduct. In broad terms, this kind of analysis draws closely on the work of Foucault and especially the 'governmentality' approach associated with some of his late writings (Foucault, 1991b; Burchell et al, 1991; Rose and Miller, 1992; Rose, 1996b; O'Malley, 2001).

The governmentality approach in fact provides the first of three building blocks for historical explanation which are employed here. What it reveals are the *'conditions of possibility'* for new strategies: that is, the invention of 'ways of thinking' that make them possible. The second explanatory building block investigates the sensibilities and mentalities that make new strategies desirable: that is, it reveals their *'conditions of desirability'*. Included here are the questions of culture and representations referred to earlier. Together these first two elements reveal the 'conditions of existence' for strategic change. The third and final building block examines how these conditions of existence come to be translated at particular moments in particular contexts into particular events and courses of action. In other words, it explains how these conditions come together in *specific contingent circumstances* to shape or define practical events and actions. This is an important part of the approach. As Downes (1988:56) argues, 'a good explanation would also suggest the processes whereby so-called "causes" are mediated through the human agencies [. . .] who accomplish their apparent effects' (see also Garland, 1990a:128). Putting all three elements together allows for a comprehensive and critical social analysis of historical change.

It is perhaps worth clarifying here the relationship between this theoretical framework and Foucault's work. There has been some debate about whether governmentality analysis is compatible with more sociological approaches. In an interesting review essay on Garland's *The Culture of Control*, Voruz (2005) argues strongly that it is not and suggests that Garland's selective use of the Foucauldian project significantly undermines its radical critical potential. The crux of Voruz's argument centres on the way in which Garland uses Foucault's genealogical approach as a precursor to making judgements about preferred directions for future penal policy, a controversial move from a

Foucauldian perspective (Foucault, 1991a:84; Dean, 1994:213–16; O'Malley, 2001). For his part, Garland (1997b) himself has set out a detailed and convincing argument for the value and indeed necessity of supplementing the insights of the governmentality analytic with sociological analysis. In particular, he argues that governmentality studies miss some critical aspects of penality – notably the cultural, expressive and symbolic dimensions that play an important part in shaping the penal sphere (see also: Garland, 1983, 1990a, 1990b; Sparks, 2001b) – that can be best addressed using sociological tools. The theoretical framework described above thus follows Garland in viewing governmentality as a useful but partial theoretical lens which can be fruitfully extended and developed by drawing on other more conventional sociological perspectives.

The analysis presented in this book draws on empirical material from two main sources: documents and face-to-face interviews. The former includes a wide range of material from government or 'official' documents (such as White Papers, inquiry reports, parliamentary proceedings) to 'pressure group' papers (such as press releases and reports from penal reform campaigning groups) to academic material (journal papers, monographs, conference proceedings). To supplement these documentary sources, 20 face-to-face interviews were conducted with senior people who had been closely involved or interested in policy-making towards 'mentally disordered prisoners' during the period under study. The achieved sample included a broad mix of former cabinet ministers, senior civil servants, campaigners and academics.

Key themes

Running through the book are two key themes:

- 'Dividing practices';
- The concept of 'risk' and risk management.

Looking at the first of these, the notion of 'dividing practices' is a pivotal concept in the book. Developed by Foucault, the concept forms a central part of some of his most important works, such as *Madness and Civilization*, *The Birth of the Clinic* and *Discipline and Punish*. In these works, Foucault explores how 'dividing practices' serve as political strategies which categorise, separate, normalise and institutionalise populations:

> The subject is either divided inside himself or divided from others. This process objectivizes him. Examples are the mad and the sane, the sick and the healthy, the criminals and the 'good boys'.
> (Foucault, 1982:208)

Rabinow defines the term as follows:

Essentially 'dividing practices' are modes of manipulation that combine the mediation of a science (or pseudo-science) and the practice of exclusion – usually in a spatial sense, but always in a social one.

(Rabinow, 1984:8)

As a conceptual tool, the idea of 'dividing practices' goes to the nub of a series of critical issues. As Rose (1999a:31) states, 'to govern is to cut experience in certain ways', and the ways in which populations and individuals are categorised, defined, distinguished and divided are therefore of central significance to any analysis of how human conduct is governed. McCallum's (2001) *Personality and Dangerousness*, which traces the history of the category of 'anti-social personality disorder', shows how the category is constructed as a means of knowing certain groups of the 'disorderly' in order that they can be governed. Thus, he describes such acts of categorising as separating practices which are administrative acts of population management (2001:36). Similarly, the concept of 'dividing practices' links some of the main issues explored in this book: of 'madness', 'dangerousness', 'risk' and 'badness', of sorting the 'high-risk' from the 'low-risk', and of determining whether offenders end up in prison or elsewhere. The wider significance, however, of the idea of 'dividing practices' is that it is linked to broader theoretical questions of the relations between power, knowledge and subjectivities which form part of the theoretical framework for this research (Foucault, 1982). As Foucault puts it in *Discipline and Punish*, each individual under the disciplinary 'gaze' is 'made up' as a 'case' which 'at one and the same time constitutes an object for a branch of knowledge and a hold for a branch of power' (1977:191). In other words, there are interconnections between, first, the modes of objectifying, categorising and distinguishing human subjects; and, second, the social and human sciences which provide the language and discursive resources for these modes of 'knowing' human beings and making them subjects; and, third, the modes of controlling, containing and regulating the subjects thus classified. The concept of 'dividing practices' brings together these three interconnected areas.

An important point is the idea that 'dividing practices' and the categories on which they are based are not transparent and fixed; rather, they are historically contingent and contested. Consequently, in looking at how these categories are used at different times, the ultimate objective is not to uncover or reveal their 'real essence' or 'truth'. This is an important distinction to make, as, even within the radical anti-psychiatry movement in the 1960s, debate took place at the level of disputing the 'truth' of madness itself (Rose, 1990). For example, R.D. Laing (1960:181) in *The Divided Self* observes that 'what is meant precisely by good, bad and mad we do not yet know', that 'yet' implying that one day in the future we might. In contrast, in this book, the analytical focus is on uncovering or revealing 'regimes of truth' relating to these categories. To put it another way, the aim of the project is to understand and reveal how particular ways of using or defining these categories come to be seen as 'true' and how this truth-status, and its associated authority and legitimacy (cf Sparks, 1994), is accomplished. It is worth making clear too that the importance and significance of these kinds of 'regimes of truth' is that they impact on how individuals are regulated, controlled and responded to. This is not an abstract or esoteric question; indeed, it is arguable that this type of analytical approach goes right to the heart of the most pressing and urgent pragmatic questions of what happens to people and why this is so. As Foucault (1991a:79,85) explains:

> My problem is to see how men govern (themselves and others) by the production of truth [. . .] My general theme isn't society but the discourse of true and false, by which I mean the correlative formation of domains and objects and the verifiable, falsifiable discourses that bear on them: and it's not just their formation that interests me but the effects in the real to which they are linked.

Thus this book will not bring us any closer to knowing more precisely what the categories of 'madness', 'badness' or 'dangerousness' mean. Indeed, such a project would arguably be epistemologically naïve (Rose, 1990). It will, however, illuminate the changing ways in which these categories are defined and used in order to govern human conduct, allowing a better understanding of the 'effects in the real' with which these categories and their associated 'dividing practices' are connected.

The second key theme concerns the concept of risk and risk management practices. Notions of 'risk' have relatively recently come to be seen as crucially important for understanding our present, both within criminology (Feeley and Simon, 1992; Sparks, 1997:424–6; Leacock and Sparks, 2002; Loader and Sparks, 2002:92–5) and more broadly in social theory (Beck, 1992; Douglas, 1992; Garland, 2003). As Giddens (2000:39) puts it, 'this apparently simple notion unlocks some of the most basic characteristics of the world in which we now live.' Sparks (1997:432) has identified understanding the concept of risk and risk management practices as one of the 'central theoretical problems for contemporary criminological enquiry'. Work by Beck (1992), Douglas (1992), O'Malley (2004) and others has opened up an exciting and theoretically-informed research agenda to which criminology could potentially make a significant contribution. In the field of 'mentally disordered offenders', 'risk' has increasingly in the 1980s and 1990s come to the forefront of debates of politics, policy and practice. As Peay (2002:747) observes, 'current policy in mental health and crime in England and Wales [. . .] is permeated by perceptions and attributions of risk'. This whole area is explored throughout this book in the attempt to understand how notions and discourses of risk and risk management fit within the changing and developing strategic 'mix' in this field from the mid-1980s onwards. The book can therefore potentially make an empirically based contribution to this important theoretical debate.

3. OVERVIEW OF THE BOOK

As noted above, the central argument of this book is that as a result of the social, economic and cultural transformations that have taken place in the last three decades of the twentieth century, the ways in which 'dividing practices' are applied to 'mentally disordered offenders', and in particular the ways in which prisoners with mental health problems are governed, have also started to be transformed. The book is divided into seven chapters.

Chapter 2 provides an analytical overview of the history of the place of penal establishments in the management of the 'insane' in Britain from the late sixteenth century onwards. The particular focus is on the presence of the 'insane' within the prison system. The purpose of this historical chapter is to provide the broader context for the investigation of more recent times that is the main interest of the book. This historical perspective casts doubt on a number of commonplace assertions often made today. For example, the idea that the contemporary problem of the presence of the mentally unwell in prison is in large part a consequence of the post-war closure of the large mental hospitals and the underfunding of community care is belied by the fact that this phenomenon pre-dates the hospital closure programme by centuries. The historical overview also raises several of the key issues in the field. The following four chapters all pick up and follow different strands of the agenda set out for the first time here.

Chapters 3, 4, 5 and 6 are the core of the book and consist of the analysis of the empirical material. The basic argument of these central chapters is as follows. Each period covered by these chapters – the 1980s, early 1990s, mid-1990s, late 1990s to the present – saw a 'headline' shift in penal strategies, towards neo-liberalism, humanitarianism, 'penal populism' and risk management respectively. However, strategies throughout this period were actually more multi-faceted and complex, with no single 'logic' or rationality achieving prominence. The introduction or re-emergence of new elements actually involved the overlaying of these novel aspects within a complex 'strategic mix' in which traces of older elements remain. Strategic development is not a process of wholesale replacement or succession of one strategy by another. As Garland (1985:155) puts it, the social realm is:

A multi-layered mosaic, the product of layer upon layer of organisational forms, techniques and regulatory practices, each one partial in its operation, each one dealing with the residues and traces of previous strategies as well as its contemporary rivals and limitations.

Accordingly, the aim of these chapters is to map and explain the changing balance of elements within the multi-stranded 'strategic mix'. It is argued that the evident volatility of strategies during this period is an indication that penal strategies were going through a major re-configuration following the unravelling of penal-welfarism and the 'crisis of penal modernism' first evident in the 1970s (Garland, 1990a), but without settling clearly into a new penal paradigm.

Turning then to the specific content of each of these four central chapters, the 'headline' shift in Chapter 3, which focuses on the 1980s, is the emergence of neo-liberalism in the wider context of the then dominance of New Right politics in the Thatcher administration. Following a third general election victory in 1987, a wide-ranging radical neo-liberal programme was set in motion, with major reforms planned in the areas of education, trade union law, housing, the legal profession and the National Health Service, not to mention further privatisations of state utilities and the introduction of the community charge (the 'poll tax'). In the field of prisons and mental health, neo-liberalism is certainly evident as a strong and new feature of strategy. An emerging focus on 'risk management' and strategies of containment rather than treatment is also evident. Nevertheless, despite this, it is clear too that there is far from a wholesale paradigm shift by the late 1980s, with, for example, elements from penal-welfare strategies strongly persisting alongside these novel 'ways of thinking'. It is certainly not possible to describe neo-liberalism in this field during this period as anything other than a new strand within a multi-faceted strategy.

The 'headline' shift in Chapter 4, which looks at the early 1990s, is the revival of humanitarian and progressive approaches, signified first by the Woolf report on prisons and then by the Reed Review of services for mentally disordered offenders. Yet the managerialism of the late 1980s remains a significant feature, notably in the Reed Review itself, which firmly continues the 'way of thinking' set out in the late 1980s. It is thus evident that the emergence at this point of a 'new' element to strategy actually constitutes an overlaying of another strand within a complex strategic 'mix' rather than the replacement of existing elements.

The 'headline' shift in Chapter 5, which examines the mid-1990s, is the sudden re-emergence of punitive responses and the politicisation of punishment, captured in Bottoms' (1995) phrase 'penal populism'. Following so quickly after the progressive moment of Woolf and Reed, this again was an unexpected shift which seemed to reset completely the co-ordinates for the direction of penal strategy. The influence of this shift on the field of prisons and mental health was perhaps not as marked as the two previous 'headline' shifts. Other elements are also strongly evident in mid-1990s strategy. Managerialism and a focus on the administration of risk are very prominent, and the humanitarianism of the Woolf/Reed era persists too in certain forms.

The 'headline' shift in Chapter 6 is the further rise to prominence of risk thinking and risk management practices as central to strategy in the late 1990s and into the new century. Again, whilst there is substantial evidence of this shift, other elements remain important and it is hard to view the focus on risk management as the emergence of an entirely new paradigm.

Chapter 7 concludes the book and attempts to bring together the main arguments. It considers how the preceding chapters shed light on some of the enduring conundrums and critical issues in the field of mental health, crime and punishment. It also sets out an agenda for future research in this field and comments on the likely prospects of current policy and legislative proposals being discussed at the time of writing in late 2005.

Chapter 2

A brief history of imprisoning the 'mad'

This book is about the government of prisoners with mental health problems during the last 20 years. There is of course a much longer history to this intersection between punishment and 'madness', and in this chapter an overview of this history is presented. It takes as its starting point the period in the late sixteenth century when institutional confinement started to become a central feature of responses to a range of social problems, including madness, criminality and vagrancy (Foucault, 1967). It then traces how the presence of the 'insane' within the penal elements of this institutional network has been a continual feature ever since.

The purpose of this historical review is to set the wider context for the book and to anticipate some of the central and fundamental issues, themes and questions with which it engages. For example, why are those considered to be 'insane' or mentally unwell consistently to be found within penal institutions? Setting out the historical context also offers a sense of perspective on the extent to which the issues we face today, and our responses to them, are as novel and contemporary as we may think. More than this, though, it lays bare the extent to which our ways of seeing or thinking about the problem, and our corresponding responses to it, vary over time. What may seem a 'natural' or 'self-evident' view at one particular time can be replaced by an entirely different perspective at another.

The exposition that follows divides the broad historical time frame covered into six periods:

- The 'Great Confinement' (1555–1750);
- The birth of the modern prison (1750–1830);
- Victorian penality (1830–1895);
- The emergence of penal-welfarism (1895–1914);
- The rise of prison psychology and psychiatry (1914–1945);
- The era of rehabilitation (1945–1979).

This type of broad periodisation is, of course, open to criticism for being too schematic, or for over-simplifying what are in fact less distinct and 'messier' transitions over time. Nevertheless, it is useful as a presentational framework for this historical overview.

1. THE 'GREAT CONFINEMENT': 'MADNESS' IN THE HOUSES OF CORRECTION

Prisons of one kind or another have a very long history (Muncie, 1996:159). Pugh (1968), for example, states that in England the practice of imprisoning defendants awaiting trial dates back to the ninth century (see also Dunbabin, 2002). However, their use as a form of punishment, rather than simply as a 'holding' facility, began to come to prominence in England only in the second half of the sixteenth century, when the houses of correction or bridewells were established. The original Bridewell opened in London in 1555 in an old royal palace and by the 1630s every shire had its own house of correction (McDonald, 1981:7).

The birth of this system of penal institutions was one part of a more general move in this period towards the use of institutional confinement as a response to social problems. The first workhouses were established in the 1630s, and from the 1660s private madhouses for the insane began to pro-liferate (McDonald, 1981:11). In *Madness and Civilization*, Foucault (1967) describes this movement as the 'Great Confinement'. Some historians have argued that Foucault significantly overstates the scale and spread of this development, especially for the English case (see: Porter, 1987, 1990; Scull, 1993; cf Gutting, 1994). The expansion of confinement in Britain as a legit-imate and mainstream response to certain problem social groups certainly appears to have taken a somewhat slower turn than Foucault suggests, it being only in the middle of the eighteenth century that the spread of work-houses, asylums and madhouses became really significant and substantial (Scull, 1993). Nevertheless, the rise of institutionalisation in the seventeenth century did mark a significant shift in patterns of social control.

There is evidence that right from the start of this movement to confinement, the 'mad' were to be found in penal institutions. Scull (1993:16) observes, for example, that the houses of correction 'served as houses of confinement for the more dangerous or troublesome lunatics'. However, McDonald (1981:7) suggests that in the seventeenth century the incarceration of lunatics in the bridewells was 'regarded as an exceptional and undesirable expedient' and, in a similar vein, Roy Porter (1987:119) argues that we should be careful not to exaggerate the extent to which 'lunatics' were confined in the bridewells during this period (see also Scull, 1993:25).

Through the course of the eighteenth century, though, it was increasingly becoming the case that the 'natural repository for the lunatic who had com-mitted a felony [. . .] was the local gaol or house of correction' (Walker and McCabe, 1973:1). By the second half of that century, it had clearly become a feature of prisons. The philanthropist and prison reformer John Howard (1777) observed, for example, in his classic work *The State of Our Prisons* that:

> Many of the bridewells are crowded and offensive, because the rooms which were designed for prisoners are occupied by the insane. Where these are not kept separate they disturb and terrify other prisoners. No care is taken of them.

The fact that evidence for this phenomenon dates right back to the origin of the prison as a punitive institution implies that the two may be connected in a fundamental way. In this vein, Foucault (1967:225–6) asserts provocatively that the 'presence of madmen among the prisoners is not the scandalous limit of confinement but its truth; not abuse but essence'. In other words, it is not evidence of a malfunctioning of the system; on the contrary, it is an intrinsic part of its very nature. This claim goes to the heart of the question of why this movement towards confinement occurred in Britain (and elsewhere) during this period from the late sixteenth century through to the mid-eighteenth century.

There is some consensus on the answer to this question. Foucault (1967:49) argues that:

> Confinement [. . .] constituted one of the answers the seventeenth century gave to an economic crisis that affected the entire Western world: reduction of wages, unemployment, scarcity of coin.

He suggests that it was for this reason that ostensibly different categories of people – the 'mad', the criminal and the poor – came to be viewed and defined as a unified group to whom the appropriate response was confinement (1967:45). Scull (1993:29) argues similarly that:

> The main driving force behind the rise of a segregative response to madness (and to other forms of deviance) can [. . .] be asserted to lie in the effects of a mature capitalist market economy.

In brief, the argument is that the development of English capitalism and a market economy, founded on a system of wage labour, brought to prominence the question of fitness and willingness to work. The logic of these economic considerations was that the unproductive segments of the labour force should be separated from those in employment. The 'mad', the 'deviant', the poor and the infirm therefore belonged in this sense to a single definitional category (the 'idle') and so were amenable to a single common response (confinement as a 'condemnation of idleness' (Foucault, 1967:46)). It is in this way, as noted above, that Foucault is able to describe (1967:225–6) the presence of the 'insane' within prisons as the 'essence' of confinement rather than evidence for its malfunctioning or abuse. In line with their underpinning rationale, the regime within the houses of correction centred on enforced labour – Spierenburg (1991) describes them as 'prison workhouses' – both to inculcate the discipline of labour and also for economic advantage.

2. 'MADNESS' IN THE EARLY MODERN PRISON

In the last quarter of the eighteenth century, a decisive shift took place in the penal system, as a period of significant reform ushered in the modern prison (Foucault, 1977; Ignatieff, 1978). Although, as discussed above, the initial move to confinement had occurred much earlier, it was only now that imprisonment started to supplant public rituals of physical punishment such as branding, whipping and hanging and began to become the pre-eminent penalty for serious crime. Existing penal institutions were developed during this period and new ones were also built. The first national penitentiary, Millbank, opened in 1816. Outside the penal sphere, other institutions – workhouses, hospitals, charity asylums and private madhouses – also expanded during this period, together adding up to a major consolidation of the network of social control institutions and of the principle of segregative responses to social problems (Scull, 1993:18–19).

Within the emerging modern prison, the presence of the 'insane' remained a significant problem (Grounds, 1991a; Sim, 1990; Walker and McCabe, 1973). For example, Elizabeth Fry (quoted in Shaw and Sampson, 1991:106) described a visit to Newgate prison in 1817 during which she came across a prisoner who had become 'quite mad' and could not be restrained even by a 'strait waistcoat'. Despite the expansion of the network of asylums and madhouses, the 'mad' were still to be found in the modern prison, just as they had been in the houses of correction (Walker and McCabe, 1973).

Prison reform during this period covered many areas, as the authorities sought to develop a 'well ordered, disciplined, clean and properly managed form of confinement' (Matthews, 1999:16). One significant element of particular relevance here was the passing in 1774 of 'An Act for Preserving the Health of Prisoners in Gaol and Preventing Gaol Distemper', a move ostensibly prompted by John Howard's investigations at this time and which led to the eventual establishment of the Prison Medical Service (Gray, 1973:130). Although not explicitly focused on mental ill-health at this point – the impetus for the 1774 Act was actually primarily related to the need to prevent the spread of typhus from prisons to the community – prison doctors obviously did have contact with insane and 'disturbed' prisoners (Gunn et al, 1978:4). It is significant, though, that the idea of 'contagion' and the public protection function are embedded in the origins of the Prison Medical Service. These are key concepts that will be returned to throughout this book.

The reasons for this period of 'reform' and for the emergence of the modern prison have been the subject of considerable debate. In the Whig tradition of history, this development was viewed as the outcome of the work of philanthropic and religious individuals of conscience, such as John Howard, Elizabeth Fry and others (Gibson, 1971; Ramsay, 1977; Radzinowicz, 1978; Radzinowicz and Hood, 1986). Within these narratives of progress, reform was a humanitarian enterprise motivated by revulsion at the 'squalid neglect' of prisoners and the cruelty of physical punishments (Ignatieff, 1983:75). From this perspective, the 1774 Act and the emergence of the Prison Medical Service are simply elements within this wider reform programme and hence considered as essentially benevolent and progressive (Gunn et al, 1978: 1–33; Smith, 1984; Topp, 1977; Gray, 1973).

Others offer a more critical and radical account, locating the motor for reform in the wider social and economic transformation taking place during this period, as the Industrial Revolution saw a shift away from a primarily rural agricultural economy to a more urban manufacturing one (see Muncie, 1996:173–80). Morgan (2002:1119), for example, describes modern prisons as a 'product of the industrial age'. Within these radical or revisionist histories, Rusche and Kirchheimer (1939) and Melossi and Pavarini (1981) adopt an orthodox Marxist approach focusing on the relationship between prison reform and the economic demands of the new industrial capitalism, whilst Foucault (1977) and Ignatieff (1978) offer more complex accounts. Ignatieff places particular importance on the religious and philosophical beliefs of reformers and analyses how these were mediated through the new class relations of the industrial economy. For Ignatieff, reform was not simply the result of the benevolent intentions of the reformers, but rather also functioned as part of the wider imposition of discipline and control in the new social order that accompanied the Industrial Revolution. In *Discipline and Punish*, Foucault (1977) also builds his account on a materialist analysis linking the emergence of the modern prison with the new economic relations of industrial capitalism. He argues that the prison's rise to prominence at this time is part of a broader emergence of disciplinary power within schools, asylums, hospitals and so on.

Sim's (1990) account of the emergence of the Prison Medical Service draws closely on the ideas of Foucault and Ignatieff in arguing that 'discipline, regulation and exclusion [. . . are . . .] integral to the genesis of medicine' in prisons (1990:5). In other words, for Sim the apparently 'progressive' reform of introducing medicine into the prison system is actually part of a system for disciplining the 'idle' rather than the result of any 'benevolence towards sickness' (Foucault, 1967:46). He argues therefore that responses to health issues during this period were primarily driven by the requirements of prison discipline and management (Sim, 1990:11–40). For example, there was a common concern among prison doctors and governors that 'difficult' inmates were feigning insanity and this was usually 'tested' by strict disciplinary measures such as electric shocks, cold baths or the administration of medicines (Sim, 1990:15). He (1990:14–22) catalogues a series of examples from the early nineteenth century of this kind of disciplinary practice being exercised under the authority and guidance of prison medical staff.

Within the network of disciplinary power, practices within different institutions can be seen to share similar functions. For example, just as prison doctors were charged with protecting the public from contagion right from the origins of prison medicine in the 1774 Act, so their counterparts in the asylums took on a similar public protection role from the mid-eighteenth century as public fears of madness grew (Foucault, 1967:199–220). According to Gunn and colleagues (1978:5), in the late eighteenth century, the fledgling prison medical service was not greatly concerned with the provision of *treatment* for prisoners with mental health problems. The primary function of prison doctors during this period in relation to mental health was limited to diagnosis (Gunn et al, 1978:5). For example, a diagnosis of insanity might remove liability to capital punishment for an unsentenced prisoner. Thus, the practice of prison medicine in the emerging modern prison was strictly circumscribed in its objectives and inextricably linked with the exercise of disciplinary power.

3. 'MADNESS' AND THE VICTORIAN PENAL SYSTEM

During the course of the nineteenth century, and particularly from the 1830s onwards, the prison system was increasingly rationalised and centralised, culminating in the 1865 and 1877 Prison Acts, which brought prisons under the control of central government for the first time. At the same time, the goal of reforming individual prisoners was gradually diminishing in importance, to be replaced by a growing emphasis on deterrence and repression (Muncie, 1996:182–8). Central to this shift was a concern that punishment should be more certain and, above all, more uniform (see Garland, 1985:36–53).

The prison lay at the heart of the Victorian penal system and constituted the principal and standard form of punishment. A central concern was with prison discipline, and a key organising principle was the notion of less eligibility. As prison was considered as a freely chosen market option, it was essential to minimise its attractions through a harsh disciplinary regime – minimum diet, close supervision and so on (Garland, 1985:46). Indeed, even within John Howard's reform programme, the idea of 'less eligibility' was a key benchmark in determining the limits of prison reform (Aikin, 1772:79–81).

At a discursive level, there was a clear correspondence between the reasoning subject of Victorian political economy and the rational actor of classical criminology. Bringing these elements together was the idea of individualism, which was the dominant ideology of the Victorian period

(Garland, 1985:41–2). Hence, within penality the emphasis was on deterrence, uniformity and the doctrine of less eligibility.

The Victorian prison, now lying at centre stage in the penal system, continued to host significant numbers of 'insane' offenders. Ignatieff (1978:9), writing about Pentonville prison in the mid-nineteenth century, quotes from a doctor's report on an inmate who was observed to be 'depressed in spirit and strange in his manner and conversation'. Mayhew and Binney (1862) noted in relation to Pentonville that during the first eight years of its operation as a new model prison (1842 to 1850) it received over ten times more 'lunatics' than would have been expected from the proportion in the general population. In a similar vein, William Guy, medical superintendent at Millbank prison between 1856 and 1869, calculated that the convict population was 34 times more liable to insanity than the general population (Guy, 1869).

During this period, there were two other significant institutional developments. Firstly, there was the enormous expansion of the public asylum system (Scull, 1993; Murphy, 2003). Barham (1992:66) aptly describes the nineteenth century as the real 'heyday of the institutionalisation of the insane' in Britain. The County Asylums Act of 1808 gave local authorities permission to build asylums for pauper lunatics. The Lunacy and County Asylums Acts of 1845 then made it an obligation to provide adequate accommodation for this group and this marked a significant step. As an illustration of the scale of expansion that followed, between 1844 and 1870 the number of certified pauper lunatics trebled from around 16,000 to just over 48,000 (Barham, 1992:68). To house this expanding population, not only did the number of asylums increase but also the average capacity of each institution grew larger. By the end of the century, some of the London asylums housed as many as 2,000 patients (Barham, 1992:68). Victorian asylums had become by this point vast warehouses for largely incurable lunatics. In 1870, for example, fewer than 8 per cent of inmates were considered by asylum superintendents to be 'curable' and the number of people discharged from the institutions was very low (Barham, 1992:68). Whilst in the first half of the century the asylum was intended as a curative and humanitarian enterprise, during the second half it increasingly became a custodial one. In a parallel with prison doctors, asylum doctors were accused by critics of exercising essentially disciplinary and management functions under the cloak of medical treatment (Scull, 1993:290–1). The use of tranquillising drugs and the manipulation of dietary intake took place in nineteenth-century asylums (Scull, 1993:291) just as they did at the same time in prisons (Sim, 1990:26–7). Medical practitioners were thus at the centre of institutional control practices.

Why did this enormous expansion of the asylum estate not transform the problem of the 'insane' appearing in prisons? As Scull (1993:372) argues, the rise in admissions to asylums was largely the result of a fundamental shift in the make-up of the asylum inmate population, away from obvious cases of lunacy to a much broader and 'heterogeneous mass of physical and mental wrecks'. These 'wrecks' included chronic alcoholics, epileptics, syphilitics, the senile, the brain-damaged, the malnourished, the 'simple-minded', women exhausted by repeated childbirth and 'those poor worn-out souls who had simply given up the struggle for existence' (Scull, 1993:372). In other words, the asylums in the Victorian period became dumping grounds for the troublesome and inadequate who would previously have been largely cared for by their families.

The second significant development during this period was the establishment of separate and specialist institutions for what were termed 'criminal lunatics'. The first of these, Broadmoor, opened in 1863. Its origins can be traced back over 60 years to the passing in 1800 of the Criminal Lunatics Act (following the attempted assassination of George III at Drury Lane Theatre by James Hadfield), which provided for the compulsory detention of dangerous insane offenders in certain circumstances (Moran, 1985). In 1807, a House of Commons Select Committee was appointed (following further agitations by, among others, the prison reformer Sir George Onesiphorus Paul). It recommended, *inter alia*, the creation of a separate establishment outside the prison system for 'criminal lunatics'. The Committee's argument was that the containment of the insane in prison not only made their recovery near to impossible but also made general prison management much more difficult. The immediate response to the Committee's report, however, was restricted to the building of a new wing at Bethlem for criminal lunatics, which opened in 1816 with a capacity of 60. Demand quickly outstripped supply, resulting in an expansion of Bethlem's capacity and the building of an extension for criminal lunatics at Fisherton House, a private madhouse near Salisbury. The system of institutional provision for 'criminal lunatics' continued to grow during the following decades, culminating in the opening of Broadmoor as the first entirely separate institution for this group.

It might be thought that the advent of Broadmoor and this new provision would have entirely transformed the intersection between punishment and 'madness'. However, as both Walker and McCabe (1973) and Murphy (1996) note, this separate provision only ever removed from the prisons a small number of 'lunatics' and the disordered: namely, those who were deemed the most dangerous and unmanageable. Other elements of provision at this time (such as the private madhouses, the workhouses and particular institutions like Tukes' Retreat near York) also received only a small number of criminal lunatics (Walker and McCabe, 1973). Thus, even in the late Victorian period from the 1860s to the 1890s, when Broadmoor had opened, mentally disordered individuals who had committed imprisonable offences were still primarily contained by the ordinary prisons (Garland, 1985:7–8).

This raises the question of why such separate provision should emerge at this time as the apparently 'self-evident' solution to the 'problem' of criminal lunatics, whilst in fact dealing only with a very small minority of this group. As noted above, Victorian penality was in general characterised by uniformity of treatment, with imprisonment as the mainstay of the penal system. Special institutional provision for criminal lunatics was thus unusual at this time in strategic terms. The development was driven by essentially pragmatic concerns. Managing prisons was made very difficult by the presence of a small number of the most dangerous and troublesome 'lunatics'. 'Warehousing' this small group in their own separate institutions was a straightforward practical response that still fell within the logic of Victorian penality. The establishment of Broadmoor and similar provision was thus primarily about making the prisons more manageable, rather than about providing 'criminal lunatics' with 'special' treatment or care. It is thus unsurprising that Broadmoor was designed by Sir Joshua Jebb, the architect who had been responsible for Pentonville and Holloway prisons, as a core part of its purpose was the secure containment of difficult and dangerous offenders.

In the second half of the nineteenth century there was another strand of debate concerning the punishment of criminals suffering from mental disorder which proved to be highly significant (Wiener, 1990:313–21). Wiener observes that 'in 1869 insanity and weak-mindedness were first discussed in the reports of convict medical officers; thereafter, the subject was a perennial one' (1990:314). The reason for this developing concern, he argues, was 'the emerging tension between the needs of deterrence and moralization and the fear that the human material in the prisons was too weak' (1990:315). In other words, the logic of Victorian penality – based on deterrent prison regimes and uniformity of treatment – did not easily sit with the recognition of the mental (and physical) fragility of some prisoners. This issue was, in part, the beginning of the debate about the 'problem' of national degeneracy, which was to achieve increasing prominence by the end of this century. The 1879 Penal Servitude Commission examined this question at length and recommended that 'insane', 'weak-minded' and 'imbecilic' prisoners should be removed from prison and placed in separate institutions. This recommendation foreshadowed developments at the start of the twentieth century, discussed below, in which the 'clearing out' of different categories of the mentally vulnerable from the prison system began to be put into practice.

The debate about national degeneracy had a significant gender dimension. In the second half of the nineteenth century, women made up an increasing proportion of the 'lunatic' population and by the end of the century were in the majority across all types of asylum (Zedner, 1991:268; Showalter, 1985). As will be discussed below, concerns about 'mentally defective' or 'feeble-minded' women procreating and weakening the national 'stock' were to become central to the penal transformation that was about to occur at the turn of the twentieth century.

4. 'MADNESS' AND THE EMERGENCE OF PENAL-WELFARISM

David Garland (1981, 1985) has argued that a fundamental transformation in overall penal strategy occurred in Britain at the start of the twentieth century, in response to wider structural changes which were occurring in the transition from liberal free-market capitalism to monopoly capitalism. His thesis is that between 1895 and 1914 the Victorian 'classicist' penal approach described above – based on individualism, free will and less eligibility – was transformed as a new 'penal-welfare' complex emerged. The new penality was based on principles of individualisation, assessment, classification, categorisation and normalisation; these laid the foundation for a broadly welfarist approach which was to persist for well over half a century.

Garland (1985) argues that, although reformatory aims had been a significant element in the prison system since at least the early 1800s (Foucault, 1977; Ignatieff, 1978; Forsythe, 1991, 1995; Muncie, 1996:161), this took on a wholly different character at the start of the twentieth century. In the nineteenth century it had primarily concerned the moral atonement and education of prisoners, with the process of reformation attending 'upon the visitation of God's Grace or the return of true reasoning' (Garland, 1985:79). It was based on 'individualism', in the sense of the individual being both the unit of analysis and the point of intervention, but, with its classical conception of the responsible individual subject, it insisted on uniformity and equality of treatment. In contrast, reform in the early twentieth century was concerned with behaviour modification and human transformation through the use of 'positive techniques of intervention' (1985:79). It was based on 'individualisation', meaning that it claimed to treat or respond to individuals according to their varying needs or characteristics. Thus, it was characterised by differential rather than uniform treatment.

According to Garland (1985) the report in 1895 of the Departmental Committee on Prisons (the Gladstone Report) was one of the early signs of the emerging new penal-welfare strategy. It promoted the whole notion of reformative treatment for prisoners and also placed the concepts of classification and differential treatment at the centre of penal strategy. A critical departure in the report was the idea that prison was not necessarily suitable for all types of offender. Following Gladstone, a series of reports by the Prison Commissioners between 1900 and 1913 also began to doubt the efficacy of the prison for various sub-groups of the prison population (for example, inebriates, the 'feeble-minded', vagrants and 'habituals') in a way that would have been unthinkable in the preceding Victorian period. Garland (1985:60) quotes several penologists at this time, such as Garafalo, Morrison, Carpenter and Saleilles, endorsing this emerging critique of imprisonment.

Significantly then, within the logic of the new strategy, the prison was no longer central in importance; it was just one end of a long continuum of sanctions. Garland (1985:238–44) suggests that it actually constituted the 'deep-end' of this continuum, serving primarily a 'warehousing' function, despite its usual positive presentation in terms of prevention or reformation. Several categories of the disordered, notably inebriates and the 'feeble-minded', were now in principle to be dealt with outside the prison system.

Just as the earlier 'Great Confinement' saw a close interconnection between the functions of the asylums, madhouses and houses of correction, within penal-welfarism issues of mental health and the emerging new discipline of psychiatry were quite central to many of the developments in this period. Charles Goring's classic study, carried out between 1903 and 1908 and published in 1913 as *The English Convict*, illustrates some important aspects of this and is worth dwelling on here.

Goring's research involved the observation and measurement of large numbers of prisoners and the statistical analysis of the resulting data. It marked a major step forward for the emerging positivist criminological science which was concerned with observation, classification and the gathering of 'positive' data on criminals in order to uncover the causes of criminality. The classificatory techniques of this new science were important in strategic terms, as they facilitated the categorisation and differentiation of offenders which was a hallmark of penal-welfarism. The prison was critical here as it acted as a practical 'surface of emergence' for the individualising, differentiating discourse of criminology (Foucault, 1977; Garland, 1985:82–3, 1997a). In other words, it provided a site for the development of the new knowledge by making possible in studies like Goring's the long-term observation, measurement and cataloguing of imprisoned criminals. This mirrored the way in which the formation of the national network of lunatic asylums after the 1845 Lunacy Acts had provided the 'surface of emergence' for the development of the new discourse of psychiatry (Garland, 1985:81). Criminology and psychiatry shared also a reliance on the positivist scientific method.

In substantive terms, Goring's research found evidence for close links between criminality and factors such as insanity, 'feeble-mindedness' and inebriety. Specifically, he estimated that between 10 and 20 per cent of his sample could be classed as 'mentally defective', compared to just 0.45 per cent of the general population. His use of concepts like 'feeble-mindedness' was significant in two respects. Firstly, as Garland (1985:81, 1997a:27) has shown, the early criminology at the turn of the twentieth century drew extensively on the recently emerged independent discipline of psychiatry, which had developed between the 1840s and the 1880s from the earlier specialisms of 'alienism' and 'psychological medicine'. Thus categories like 'moral insanity' and 'feeble-mindedness' were taken from psychiatry and used by people like Goring in the development of the new criminological science. This borrowing of concepts had benefits for psychiatry too, in terms of reproducing, repeating and reinforcing its terms. It also opened up the judicial domain as an area for psychiatry's expansion, a development which eventually led to the new sub-discipline of forensic psychiatry (Garland, 1985:81–2; Foucault, 1978). Second, at a strategic level, Goring's (1913) finding of a 'high and enormously augmented association of feeble-mindedness with conviction for crime' was central to the positioning of his study as evidence supporting the eugenic programme (Garland, 1985:179–80; Beirne, 1988:331–4). As Garland (1985:179) observes, it is revealing that Goring's research was 'conducted under the auspices of Karl Pearson's biometric laboratory', which was the 'scientific nerve centre of the eugenic movement'. Eugenic terms and ideas were central to the new penological discourse.

This links back to the debate about national degeneracy described above, which took place over the course of the second half of the nineteenth century. In relation to the penal system, the concern was whether certain types of prisoners were fit enough to withstand the demands of prison discipline (Wiener, 1990:313–21). This concern served to undermine the principle of uniformity in Victorian penality and led to the idea of differential treatment of offenders which was to be a central element of the new penal-welfare strategy. Thus, for example, in the landmark Gladstone Report it was questioned whether weak-minded prisoners should be in prison at all and argued that 'they should be sent to some special institution in the nature of an asylum' where they could be placed under 'special observation and treatment'. This was picking up the earlier recommendation of the Penal Servitude Commission in 1879, discussed above. The Report made similar recommendations for other groups, proposing for example that inebriates should receive 'special medical treatment' in reformatories (a measure enacted by the Inebriates Act of 1898).

The Gladstone Report also identified female prisoners as a 'special' group requiring 'special' attention. As noted above, concerns had developed during the course of the nineteenth century about 'mentally defective' and 'feeble-minded' women breeding and weakening the population. The influential Royal Commission on the Care and Control of the Feeble-Minded, which reported in 1908, supported the view that 'feeble-minded women were more fecund than normal women' (quoted in Sim, 1990:141); in 1906, Aylesbury Prison was established as an institution specially for 'weak-minded' women. This close connection for female offenders between madness and criminality – which was to become a 'ubiquitous theme in criminology' (Carlen, 1983:64; see also Morris, 1987:55–6 and Sim, 1990:129–76) – is thus linked with the eugenic strands within penal-welfarism. Zedner (1991, 1995) notes that the new institutions for inebriates and the 'feeble-minded' became disproportionately filled by women. Again, this makes sense from a eugenic perspective, as the institutional incapacitation of 'defective' women was a means of preventing the reproduction of the 'inferior' classes. Zedner suggests too that the regimes within these institutions were characterised by intensive surveillance and claustrophobic attempts to maintain ideal standards of femininity in order to address the alleged problems of promiscuity and excessive reproduction. It has been argued that this has since become a common phenomenon: that is, that whenever women are the subjects of 'special' penal treatment, this tends to result in repressive and infantilising regimes (Heidensohn, 1997:781; see also Forsythe, 1993, and Sim, 1990:129–76; cf Allen, 1987).

So what was the overall impact of the emergence of penal-welfarism on the problem of the presence of the 'insane' in the prison system? In principle, the decentring of the prison within penal strategy should have served to reduce the problem. The establishment of inebriate reformatories from 1901 onwards, and particularly the new institutions for the 'mentally defective' set up following the Mental Deficiency Act 1913, should have had a major effect on prisons, in terms of clearing out substantial numbers of the insane, defective and disturbed. However, in practice prisons did not always find it easy to rid themselves of as many 'defectives' as they wished, and the residual problem in prisons continued to be significant (Walker and McCabe, 1973). As will be seen below, later attempts to clear out the 'residuum' from prisons faced similar difficulties. Thus, at this stage there was only a limited reduction of the problem, whilst at a discursive level the connections between punishment and 'madness' continued to develop through the close linkages between psychiatry and the new criminological science. As will now be discussed, the role of the 'psy' sciences would be of continuing significance in the development of penal strategy and prison practice in the early decades of the twentieth century.

5. THE RISE OF PRISON PSYCHOLOGY AND PSYCHIATRY

The inter-war years saw several important developments. The essential strategy discussed above, of classification and differentiation, with the prison at one end of a continuum of sanctions, was largely unchanged during this period. There was, however, a renewed interest in the residual group of mentally disordered offenders who did not end up in any of the new institutions but remained in prison. Indeed, in practice, some parts of the new institutional system were abandoned – for example, by 1921 the inebriate reformatories had been closed down, restoring the alcoholic offender as 'a mainstay of the prison population' (Gunn, 1985:137). Prisons had in any case retained large numbers of 'defective' and 'disordered' inmates (Walker and McCabe, 1973) and the logic of the new strategy (categorisation for treatment purposes) did not in principle exclude 'special' provision within prison. During this period, it was this area that saw most of the new developments.

One prerequisite for these developments was an explicit recognition that 'mental disorder' covered a broader range of conditions than just insanity or 'defectiveness' (that is, those categories covered by the Lunacy and Mental

Deficiency Acts which qualified inmates for transfer out of prison). This view, and the accompanying belief that such prisoners were not suitable for the standard prison disciplinary regime, quickly became influential in the 1920s (Fox, 1934:110). In line with the logic of the strategy, this group was subject to numerous typologies, and a bewildering number of categories were applied to them: for example, subnormality, psychopathy, neuroticism, congenital mental deficiency, imperfectly developed insanity, senility, mental weakness after insanity, weakmindedness due to alcoholism, weakmindedness of undefined origin and so on (Fox, 1934:110; East, 1949).

This trend of focusing on the prison population became sufficiently clear and widespread throughout the system that Sir Lionel Fox, Secretary of the Prison Commission, felt able to write in 1934:

> Considerable advances have been made since the war in the treatment of problems connected with mental disease among prisoners; indeed, it would seem that today the investigation and recognition of mental states [. . .] have come to form the most important part of the Medical Officers' duties.
>
> (1934:108–9)

A specific and significant instance was the work of Norwood East and Hubert in Wormwood Scrubs prison. In 1934, they established a long-running experiment involving the investigation and psychological treatment of prisoners deemed to be likely to respond to such therapy. The resulting report, published as *The Psychological Treatment of Crime* (East and Hubert, 1939), recommended, *inter alia*, the establishment of a special prison to provide psychological treatment to certain types of prisoners (this proposal eventually led to the opening of Grendon Underwood prison in 1962). Such was the optimism and enthusiasm for this type of approach to prisoners that some attempted to extend its application beyond just the psychologically or mentally abnormal. For example, Grace Pailthorpe's (1932) five-year study in Holloway prison concluded that most crime was linked to mental conflict and could be treated by psychoanalysis. Indeed, in this period, it is arguable that the 'mentally disordered offender' became the paradigm for all offenders, as optimism in psychological, psychiatric and psychoanalytic responses to crime rapidly rose. It is interesting and not insignificant too that, although Pailthorpe's work was taken up by enthusiasts as the potential basis for a new approach to crime in general (Garland, 1997a:39), her research was carried out on women prisoners. As discussed above, the idea that there was a special connection for women between madness and criminality already had a long history by the early twentieth century.

This burgeoning interest in the psychotherapeutic treatment of disordered prisoners within the prison was spearheaded by a number of influential prison doctors, including Norwood East, Hubert and Hamblin-Smith. From a Whig perspective, these doctors were 'pioneering' prison practitioners exploring new approaches with their 'patients'. In strategic terms, the development can be seen as an extension of the underpinning penal-welfarist idea of differentiation for the purposes of individual treatment. Indeed, Garland (1985:83) argues that the project of 'differentiation' existed 'ready-made in the context of the prison' in the sense that the clearest demarcation of the criminal from the non-criminal was provided by prison walls. The work of these 'pioneers' also made a substantial and significant contribution to the development of criminology during this period. Garland (1997a:40), for example, describes the work of Norwood East, a psychiatrically trained prison doctor and for a time Medical Director on the Prison Commission, as representing the mainstream of British criminology in the 1920s and 1930s. The prison thus continued to act as a 'surface of emergence' or, as Garland (1985:82) puts it, a 'kind of experimental laboratory' for the development of this new knowledge.

There are thus close connections during this period between penal strategy, the developing discourse of criminology and practice within prisons, with the punishment–'madness' nexus lying at the heart of developments. The extension and expansion of the role of the new 'psy' sciences within criminological discourse and prison practice during this period is particularly significant. Nikolas Rose (1985, 1999b) has argued more generally that the psy disciplines and psy expertise which emerged most strongly in the early twentieth century have had a 'key role in constructing "governable subjects" ' and, in turn, a 'very significant role in contemporary forms of political power, making it possible to govern human beings in ways that are compatible with the principles of liberalism and democracy' (1999b:vii). In the context of prisons in this period, it can be seen quite clearly how psy expertise helped to produce new categories of prisoner – the 'weakminded', the 'subnormal', the 'neurotic' – that could then be governed through particular technologies and practices (for example, Norwood East's psychological treatment in Wormwood Scrubs prison) that appeared both legitimate and entirely compatible with the 'real nature of humans as psychological subjects' (Rose, 1999b:viii).

6. 'MADNESS' IN THE ERA OF REHABILITATION

The post-war period saw the heyday of penal-welfare strategies with its 'most vigorous developments in the 1950s and 1960s' (Garland, 2001:34). It is often described in conventional penological accounts as the 'era of rehabilitation', as the concern with individualised treatment reached a high point (Bean, 1976). Garland (2001:35–6) highlights the key elements of this era as the primacy of the rehabilitative ideal as an organising principle and the centrality of professional (social) expertise to judgements about sanctions and treatment.

In relation to mental health in the prison system, building on the pre-war trend, specialist provision within prisons expanded. Grendon prison opened in 1962, a belated result of the 1939 East–Hubert report. Its initial objectives were threefold (Snell, 1962):

• The investigation and treatment of mental disorders generally recognised as calling for a psychiatric approach;
• The investigation of offenders whose offences in themselves suggest mental morbidity;
• An exploration of the psychopath and methods for their treatment and management.

Under the leadership of its founding medical superintendent, Dr William Gray, Grendon operated in the 1960s and 1970s as a therapeutic community (Gunn et al, 1978). A number of smaller specialist units were also established in the prison estate: for example, Parkhurst C wing in 1970 and Glen Parva Borstal in the early 1970s. More broadly, the Prison Medical Service – which remained in place despite the introduction of the National Health Service in 1948 – expanded its psychiatric services in the immediate post-war years and into the 1950s. Most of the work, however, was diagnostic. Gunn (1985:129) observes, for example, that in 1957 only 200 male prisoners received psychotherapy, whilst 5,000 were remanded in prison custody for psychiatric reports. Morris and Morris (1963:194–205) also observed in their study of Pentonville in the late 1950s that the actual provision of mental health care or treatment within the prison was highly limited.

Outside the prison, some important developments began in the 1950s. The Percy Commission report in 1957 and the resulting 1959 Mental Health Act marked a significant shift in the provision of psychiatric care. The new policy was based on an optimistic view of the potential of psychiatry, notably with the emergence of new therapeutic drugs. The long process of decline in the mental hospital population began in 1955 (Barham, 1992:11); such was the optimism of the times that some predicted that eventually the long-stay population would virtually disappear (Tooth and Brooke, 1961). It was anticipated that the 1959 Act would help the prisons by allowing the transfer of more of the mentally disordered into hospitals. In fact this did not happen; indeed, levels of prison transfers slowed down during the 1960s and into the early 1970s (Orr, 1978; Gunn et al, 1978:26–9; Gunn, 1985:131). In 1961, 179 sentenced men were transferred to hospital, but by 1976 this number was down to 30 (Gunn, 1985:131). In the mid–1970s, the Glancy (DHSS, 1974) and Butler (Home Office/DHSS, 1975) reports both recommended substantial increases in the capacity of secure psychiatric units, but the actual level of expansion fell significantly short of their targets.

This relationship, and the overlap, between the populations of the mental hospitals and the prisons was particularly debated in the post-war period, especially as the process of decarceration from the former began in the late 1950s. Lionel Penrose had famously argued on the basis of comparative European statistics that there was an inverse relationship between the number of mental hospital patients and the number of prisoners (Penrose, 1939). Penrose's law, as it became known, was an attractive idea to critics of decarceration, as it implied that the closing of the mental hospitals, rather than being a progressive step, simply tended to shift those patients into the prison system. Gunn (2000) notes, however, in a perceptive analysis that although at an aggregate level Penrose's law appears to be a robust finding (for example, Biles and Mulligan, 1973), there is little or no evidence that at an individual level the same people move between the institutions. The mentally disturbed found in post-war prisons were much more likely to be circulating between hostels, periods of homelessness and occasional short hospital episodes, rather than being former long-stay mental hospital patients (Jones, 1992:3). Gunn (2000) raises the interesting hypothesis that the apparent empirical support for Penrose's law at an aggregate level, although not evidence for a direct relationship between the mental hospital and prison populations, may be related to changing public and professional attitudes towards mental disorder and perceptions of dangerousness. This resonates with Sparks' (2001a) argument noted in Chapter 1 about the need to understand how public anxieties about particular sources of risk are mobilised in penal politics. Arguments about Penrose's law returned to prominence in the 1980s and 1990s in the context of debates about the alleged failures of the 'care in the community' policy and its connection with the 'crisis' of the mentally disturbed in prison, and these will be examined in the chapters that follow.

One striking feature of the immediate post-war decades is the proliferation of small-scale prison-based research on the mental health of prisoners. Several studies were published between the 1950s and the 1970s (Roper, 1951; Epps, 1951, 1954; Woodside, 1962; West, 1963; Robinson et al, 1965; Bluglass, 1966; Gibbens, 1967; Gibbens, 1971; Faulk, 1976; Gunn et al, 1978) and no doubt many unpublished ones were also carried out. The basic findings of this body of work are summarised in Tables 2.1 and 2.2. Broadly, they paint a fairly consistent picture of the mental health of British prisoners during this time: high levels of mental disorder (especially personality disorders, alcoholism and neuroses) and low levels of psychosis. Precise rates of identified mental disorder vary widely, reflecting the use of different diagnostic categories, different sampling procedures and the different prisons studied. Even for the same diagnostic categories there is a variation in usage and interpretation. A good example of this is the term 'subnormal'. Epps' (1951) study of Borstal females used a measure of intelligence which defines 'subnormal' as equivalent to the bottom 25 per cent of the general population. Bluglass (1966), in contrast, combined intelligence measures with clinical assessments of social functioning, leading to a definition of 'subnormal' applicable to less than 5 per cent of the general population. Taking these studies as a whole, there is

Table 2.1 British studies of mental disorder in male prisoners 1950s–1970s

Main author	Sample details	Main findings
Roper 1951	1,100, sentenced	12% neurosis 8% psychopathy 3% intellectually defective
West 1963	100, long-term sentenced	9% previous hospitalisation 10% current or previous psychosis
Robinson 1965	566, sentenced	31% psychiatric diagnosis 24% subnormal
Bluglass 1966	300, sentenced	46% psychiatric disorder 2% psychosis 2% neurosis 13% psychopathic 11% alcoholism 3% subnormal
Gibbens 1967	200, sentenced to Borstal	0.5% psychosis 27% mentally abnormal
Anthony 1973	Borstal	50% psychopathic traits 33% past suicide attempts
Gunn 1978	629, sentenced	31% psychiatric diagnosis 2% psychoses 9% neurosis 13% alcoholism 22% personality disorder

Table 2.2 British studies of mental disorder in female prisoners 1950s–1970s

Main author	Sample details	Main findings
Epps 1951	300, sentenced to Borstal	1.3% schizophrenia 21% neurotic
Epps 1954	100, sentenced recidivists from 1951 Borstal sample	Personality and neurotic disorders more common amongst recidivists
Woodside 1962	139, sentenced	42% psychiatric history 9% subnormal
Gibbens 1971	638, mix of sentenced and remand	*Sentenced* 15% mental illness 7% alcoholism *Remand* 26% mental illness 4% alcoholism

broad agreement that around 30 per cent of prisoners had a mental health problem of some kind. The most common diagnoses were alcoholism, personality disorders and neuroses. Alcoholism was more common for males and neuroses more common for females. For psychoses, the prevalence figure ranges from 3 per cent down to 0.5 per cent which is similar to the level found in the general population. This literature also illustrates some other important and relevant points.

First, it is striking that all of these studies adopt a psychiatric or psychological perspective rather than a sociological one. In the post-war decades, sociological research in Britain directly focusing on prisons and mental health was in fact almost non-existent. Looking at the 1960s and 1970s, Cohen and Taylor's (1972) work on long-term prisoners, for example, examined the strategies inmates adopted for psychological survival and only mentioned in passing those outside their sample whose survival strategies failed and who did deteriorate mentally. Beyond this, British sociological work in this area is restricted to the Morrises' Pentonville study, which contains a short chapter on health (1963:192–206) which includes some discussion of mental abnormality, together with some passing references elsewhere in the book to examples of distressed or disturbed prisoners failing to cope with the regime (1963:165). Even the international literature is slim. Goffman (1961), for example, focuses primarily on the mental hospital rather than the prison in his investigation of the characteristics of total institutions. Scull (1977) too looks at the shared roles and functions of the mental health and penal systems in a modern capitalist state but does not look at mental health *within* the penal or prison system.

This is partly the result of pragmatic issues of access in an era when prisons were still shrouded in secrecy. Few social researchers were allowed to 'set up their anthropological huts on British prison landings' (Morgan, 1997:1177, quoting from Morris and Morris, 1963). In contrast, psychiatrists and medical officers already working within prisons will not have had these problems of access. At a political level, there may also have been some suspicion within the Home Office about sociologists, who may have been felt more likely to extend their gaze beyond narrow health matters, turning their critical eye on policies, regimes and staff (Matthews, 1999:92). The infamous experience of Cohen and Taylor in the 1970s is a good example of this kind of suspicion, and indeed the Morrises were required to remove from their book a chapter describing a riot in Pentonville which had not been publicly reported. More fundamentally, the nature of the research carried out in this period was connected with the continuing importance of psy expertise within prisons and the number of diagnostic personnel working with prisoners in the system. Hence, many of these studies were conducted by prison medical officers (for example, Roper, 1951; Epps, 1951, 1954) or prison social workers (Woodside, 1962).

A second striking feature of this literature is that it focuses almost exclusively on the sentenced population. This is despite the fact that the practice of remanding people in prison custody for psychiatric assessment began as far back as the 1880s and continued to represent a substantial proportion of the psychiatric work actually carried out with prisoners (Grounds, 1991a). This apparent gap in the research becomes more intelligible when set in the context of the basic strategy of penal-welfarism: that is, classification for the purpose of individualised treatment. Thus, as noted above, prison medical officers and social workers had a clear interest in studying the sentenced population as part of their everyday practice. In contrast, for the remand population providing treatment services was much more problematic, as remand prisoners usually spend shorter and more unpredictable periods of time in prison. Planning programmes was therefore practically very difficult. In this sense, it is unsurprising that there was far less interest in this period in studying remand prisoners, compared with the sentenced population. As will be seen later, it is only at the end of the 1970s, as penal-welfarism begins to unravel, that significant research attention starts to turn to the remand process and the remand population, as, for example, in two important papers by Paul Bowden (1978a, 1978b). At this point, remand prisoners become viewed as sources of difficulty in management terms and, accordingly, come much more to the forefront of research, policy and practice from the early 1980s.

A third important aspect concerns gender. It has already been noted in this chapter that the tendency to see a closer connection between madness and criminality for female offenders has a long history, and, more specifically, that the consequent 'special' penal treatment for women formed part of penal-welfare strategies right from the start of the twentieth century. The studies summarised in Table 2.2 all purport to show that women prisoners have exceptionally high rates of psychiatric disorder (see also Eysenck and Eysenck, 1973). Various explanations for this have been offered from a number of different perspectives. Some have argued that the 'pains of imprisonment' are felt more acutely by women, thus putting them under more strain and pressure (Ward and Kassebaum, 1965; Heidensohn, 1975; Casale, 1989; Mandaraka-Sheppard, 1986; Carlen, 1985a). Others have suggested that the regimes for women are harsher, again resulting in increased pressure on women (Carlen, 1983, 1985a, 1985b). Another explanation is the 'residuum' argument: that since there are so few women in prison compared with men, those that are there must be 'mad'. There are also Lombrosian arguments based on the notion that women are inherently 'different' and much more subject to biological swings and influences. Yet another view is the version of the 'chivalry' hypothesis presented by Allen (1987), who suggests that violent offences by women are more readily explained in psycho-medical terms.

It can be questioned, however, whether this apparent gender difference actually exists. There is a considerable literature which argues generally that psychiatry's definitions of mental health are based on male norms, with the result that women are likely to be assessed as mentally unhealthy simply because they are women (Chesler, 1974; Busfield, 1983; Morris, 1987:53–4; Smart, 1976). Morris (1987:56) suggests further that, even if the research studies do show that levels of psychiatric disorder are high amongst women in prison, research on male prisoners indicates similarly high psychiatric morbidity.

Despite these kinds of critique, the idea did persist in this period to the extent that in the 1970s the redevelopment of Holloway prison was planned along the lines of a hospital (Rock, 1996). An important question then is why this notion proved so resilient when, as Maden (1996:21) notes, rigorous empirical support for it was at best ambiguous. One explanation sometimes given is that the relative rarity of female offending inevitably leads to female offenders (and prisoners) being perceived as 'abnormal', on the assumption that the unusual is by definition 'unnatural' (Smart, 1976; Morris, 1987). A different type of argument is that women's place within the family and their reproductive role make female 'deviance' much more of a threat to the social order. Hence, the 'sick' model of female criminality legitimates special forms of treatment to normalise women into their 'proper' domestic roles (Sim, 1990; Smith, 1962). Thus, it is argued more broadly that women are subject to more pressures to conform throughout society (Heidensohn, 1996) and therefore the psychiatrisation of female criminality is simply the formal and severe end of a wider continuum. It is also a good example of what feminist criminologists have termed 'double deviance', in the sense that 'special' measures against female offenders are driven by a perceived double transgression, against the criminal law and against gender norms (Heidensohn, 2002:504).

7. CONCLUSION

This brief survey of a 400 year period of history has necessarily and inevitably been selective and schematic. Its purpose has been to set the historical context for the rest of the book and to identify some of the central and enduring themes in this field. Five key points are worth pulling out and summarising here, as a contextual framework for the rest of the book.

(1) The presence of the insane or mentally disturbed within penal institutions is a phenomenon which goes back right to the origin of the confinement project in the late sixteenth century. It has continued ever since.
(2) There are strong and close connections between the discourses of modern criminology and psychiatry, which both emerged in the nineteenth century. The asylum and the prison were central 'surfaces of emergence' for these discourses, which also underpin the practice of prison psychiatry in the twentieth century.

(3) The idea that there is a particularly close link between madness and criminality for female offenders also has a long history and has been used to justify 'special' treatment and regimes for women.

(4) The proportion of mentally disturbed prisoners appears to have been fairly stable between the 1950s and 1970s. There were relatively high rates of disorder (approximately 30 to 40 per cent) but low rates of psychosis (broadly similar to rates in the community).

(5) The post-war policy of decarceration from the mental hospitals does not seem to be a direct or major influence on the situation in prisons during the same period.

All five points share one underlying theme, which can serve as a conclusion to this chapter. The intersection between punishment and madness, as played out in the prison system, is deep-rooted, long-standing and fundamental. This suggests, echoing Foucault (1967), a hypothesis that can be posed as a provocative question for investigation in the rest of this book: the 'problem' of mentally disturbed prisoners is not an aberration or a malfunctioning of systems (which can therefore be solved by reforming those systems); rather, it is intrinsic to the whole project of using institutional confinement as a method of punishment.

Chapter 3

The New Right and managerialism, 1980–1990

> The answer to some of the problems in the prison medical service is better trained doctors combined with adequate accessible psychiatric services in the community.
>
> (Professor John Gunn, quoted in Edwards et al, 1985:1698)

> Present management structures do not seem to us to facilitate the effective functioning of the PMS [Prison Medical Service].
>
> (Efficiency Scrutiny of the Prison Medical Service, Home Office, 1990a)

This chapter examines the 1980s, a period during which some novel features appeared to start to emerge in the terrain being examined in this book. The two quotations above suggest something of the flavour of this apparent shift: by the end of the 1980s, the key to improvements in this field was more likely to be sought in altering administrative and management arrangements rather than in addressing clinical or treatment issues.

By way of introduction, and to set the context for the analysis that follows in the rest of the chapter, the first section provides an overview of some aspects of the social, political, economic and penal context in England and Wales in the 1980s. It also describes some general features of the New Right political project, which began in 1979 with the election of the first Thatcher government. The main section of the chapter then analyses how all this impacted on the 'dividing practices' aimed at offenders with mental health problems, with specific and particular reference to prisoners.

I. CONTEXT: BRITAIN IN THE 1980s

There is an unusual consensus about this period in Britain (and indeed, more widely in the Western democracies). Writers and analysts from a wide range of perspectives all agree that, after some decades of relative stability, in the last quarter of the twentieth century enormous shifts took place in the social, economic and cultural spheres. The historian Eric Hobsbawm (1994), for example, charts these shifts in his history of the century, *Age of Extremes*. Writing about what he terms the 'Crisis Decades' from the 1970s to the 1990s, he states:

> The history of the twenty years after 1973 is that of a world which lost its bearings and slid into instability and crisis.
>
> (1994:403).

Similarly, Jock Young (1999:vi) describes the aim of his book, *The Exclusive Society*, as to trace 'the rapid unravelling of the social fabric of the industrialized world in the last third of the twentieth century.' From a very different theoretical vantage point, 'governmental' analyses have described the emergence during this period of 'advanced liberal' societies, which are characterised by a new range of strategies, rationalities and techniques of government (Rose, 1999a). Others have described this transformation as the shift from modernity to late modernity (Young, 1999; Garland, 2001).

As might be expected, although there is agreement that massive change occurred during this period, there is less consensus about exactly what these changes have involved and why they have come about. Nevertheless, there are some reasonably widely accepted aspects of the transformation which serve as a useful starting point (for a particularly concise and lucid account, see Garland, 2001:78–87). These can divided into four main areas: the economy and the labour market; the family; mass media and communications; and the role of the state. Briefly summarising the points of broad agreement, in relation to the *economy*, the British economy became much weaker during these decades, with periods of recession accompanied by wage and price inflation. It also came to be characterised by widening inequalities and the social exclusion of 'non-profitable' groups. The manufacturing base significantly reduced in size as the service sector increased. The impact of all this on the *labour market* was dramatic. The restructured labour market saw major shifts in types of employment (away from manufacturing; towards service industries), levels of employment (as unemployment increased) and the nature of that employment (as job security in particular reduced significantly). For the latter, there was also a gender dimension, as increasingly the male 'bread winner' bringing home the family income was replaced by part-time insecure female labour. Changes in the tax and benefits system tended to reinforce these new patterns, increasing inequalities and consigning sections of the population to poverty.

Arrangements relating to the *family* changed enormously, with soaring divorce rates, rising numbers of people living alone (that is, not as a couple or part of a larger family) and increasing numbers of single-parent (largely single-mother) families. The latter brought with it new problems of child poverty. Indeed, these changes in the family were also marked by widening inequalities. On the one hand, the expansion of single-parent families tended to lead for many to problems of poverty. On the other, increasing education and employment opportunities for middle-class women created a new set of 'two-income' households. Again, these inequalities were reinforced by the tax and benefits system.

Developments within the *mass media and communications* were also significant, with the rapid growth of television, the information technology 'revolution' and, towards the end of the century, the rise of the internet dramatically 'shrinking' the world. The impact of these developments on social relations was enormous. No longer were sensibilities and perspectives primarily based in and linked to small group identities and locales. The new visibility and transparency of events and the emphasis the new media tended to place on the intimate and emotive aspects of them transformed expectations, cultural sensibilities and the relations between groups.

Within all of this, the *role of the state* changed too, as the national government pulled back from being the ultimate guarantor of security and provider of welfare services. Importantly, in all these areas, the transformations were not exclusive to Britain but were witnessed at the same time across the Western world (although of course not always evenly in different parts of the world) (Hobsbawm, 1994).

At a political level, in Britain, the Thatcher administration which came to power in 1979 did so very much in the context of these changes (Gamble, 1988). Its brand of free-market neo-liberal economics and associated social policy sought to address, respond to and change these transformations as they were happening. There was a particular emphasis on 'rolling back the state', deregulating the labour market and freeing up the economy ('neo-liberalism'). There was also a populist reactionary dimension to social policy which deprecated, *inter alia*, undeserving recipients of state welfare benefits, the break-up of the traditional family and the breakdown of 'law and order' ('neo-conservatism').

This New Right political order was developed in Britain primarily by the Thatcher administrations during the 1980s. The influence of neo-liberal market thinking was evident in a number of areas during this period. What Hutton (1995) terms 'marketisation' affected fields as diverse, and previously unused to market forces, as pensions, housing, education and health. Taking the New Right 'reforms' of health care as an example, the NHS was viewed as a state-run monopoly provider which by definition must be inefficient. The 'solution' was to re-invent it as a market by creating a split between providers or producers (for example, hospitals) on the one hand and purchasers (for example, health authorities) on the other.

A key aspect of this new political project was the decline of faith in 'social' experts and 'social' responses, a decline Rose (1996c) has characterised as the 'death of the social'. This social expertise was of course one of the foundations of the welfare state, which was by the 1980s becoming severely discredited. Within the neo-liberal political rationality, it was viewed as an expensive system which served to undermine individual responsibility and generate unnecessary dependence on the state. The sustained economic growth and full employment of the 1950s and 1960s, which had provided the buttressing economic foundation for welfarism, had long gone by the 1980s. Welfare itself thus came to be seen as a problem rather than a solution.

Another important feature of the 1980s, and one linked to the spread of 'marketisation', was the borrowing of resources, language and techniques from the private sector – auditing, performance indicators, management information systems, budget control and so on (see Rose, 1993). Garland (2001:188–92) has termed this a shift from a 'social' to an 'economic' style of reasoning.

The emergence of a distinctively new emphasis on risk and risk management was a nascent dimension of the 1980s which was less visible at the time but in retrospect has come to be seen as an absolutely central element of the new 'political vocation' of 'advanced liberal' or neo-liberal strategies for governing conduct (Rose, 1996a). Early sightings of the rise of risk came in some groundbreaking papers in the middle of the decade (Floud, 1982; Reichman, 1986; Simon, 1987, 1988; it was also anticipated in Stan Cohen's (1985) *Visions of Social Control*). As will be seen below and in the chapters that follow, this aspect of the new governmental configuration had a major impact on how offenders with mental health problems were perceived and responded to.

At the same time as, and related to, these massive structural and political shifts, crime levels also rose significantly. Garland (2001:90) notes, for example, that recorded crime in England and Wales rose tenfold between 1950 and 1994. This was an unexpected development. It had been anticipated that the post-war development of the welfare state, the gradual spread of economic prosperity and the rise in the standard of living in the 1950s and 1960s would reduce crime. Instead, the opposite happened; crime rates rose substantially. The rise in recorded crime continued throughout the 1980s, increasing from just over 2.5 million in 1980 to over 4 million by 1990 (Matthews and Young, 1992:1). These trends were taken as supporting evidence for the New Right critique of the welfare state as partly responsible for undermining the social fabric and contributing to the breakdown of law and order.

The criminal justice and crime control field also underwent a significant re-configuring during the same period (Rose, 2000; Garland, 2000, 2001; Young, 1999). The old penal-welfare strategy, which had held sway for most of the twentieth century, began to break down in the 1970s, a process Garland (1990a) has termed the 'crisis of penal modernism'. Its central organising principle, the rehabilitative ethic, came under full frontal attack by the growing view that in fact 'Nothing Works' (Martinson, 1974). The re-configured crime control field that emerged during the last two decades of the century following this unravelling of penal-welfarism has been strikingly volatile, contradictory and ambiguous (O'Malley, 1999). This has made it difficult for commentators to pin down the essence of the new field; it has been variously described as actuarial (Feeley and Simon, 1992, 1994), as postmodern (Pratt, 1998, 2000a), as 'advanced liberal' (Rose, 2000) and as embodying a new late-modern 'culture of control' (Garland, 2001). Nevertheless, some defining characteristics can be discerned. A high-profile feature of contemporary crime control has been the morally charged, expressive and punitive discourses towards crime that have dominated, particularly in the 1990s. These have been given effect in a range of punitive initiatives, but most notably in the massive expansion of the use of imprisonment. Yet, at the same time as this emphasis on 'spectacular' punishment, some rather different developments have also emerged as central characteristics of the field. First, there has been the rise of restorative justice thinking and practices (Braithwaite, 1999). Second, at the local level, the development of multi-agency crime prevention partnerships has been a major change on the ground (Crawford, 1997). Third, the rise of managerialism, with its associated techniques of audits, target-setting and performance management, has sought to transform criminal justice agencies by creating new regimes of efficiency and value for money modelled on the private sector. Indeed, the private sector itself has increasingly contributed directly to the performance of certain criminal justice and policing functions that had previously been the subject of state monopolies. The use of contractual instruments to govern crime and 'deviance' has also been observed across diverse areas of social life (Crawford, 2003). Fourth, and in sharp contrast to the rise of punitive discourses noted above, there has been what Loader and Sparks (2002:87–8) have called a 'de-centring of the criminal justice state', in which efforts have been made to emphasise the limits of the sovereign state in controlling crime (Garland, 1996, 2001). Taken together, these developments suggest that whilst it is clear that there is a new field of crime control and punishment, its precise nature has been much harder to grasp and identify. The analysis below and in the following three chapters will explore this further.

Garland (2001), in *The Culture of Control*, has attempted to develop an argument that pulls together these accounts of late-modern transformations in the social, economic, cultural, political and criminal justice arenas. He argues that:

> The political, economic and cultural supports that had previously underpinned modern crime control were increasingly eroded by late modern social trends and the intellectual and political shifts that accompanied them. These trends, in turn, posed novel problems, gave rise to new perceptions, and shaped a variety of practical adaptations, out of

which gradually emerged the crime control and criminal justice practices of the present period.

(2001:77)

Underpinning his argument is the idea that contemporary crime control is driven by two conflicting impulses – the desire to assert the sovereign power to punish and the dispersal of crime control functions to agencies and networks that lie 'beyond the state' – and that this tension is the source of its 'volatile and contradictory' nature.

Another important part of the context for this chapter concerns developments in mental health policy and, in particular, the policy of 'care in the community'. As noted in Chapter 2, the closure of the mental hospitals had begun in the mid-1950s. This was partly the result of optimism about the efficacy of new pharmacological treatments for mental ill-health which did not require institutional care to be effective. As Rose (1986:56–7) observes, however, this was only possible because of post-war developments in the welfare state. Social security benefit payments, public housing provision, the development of community social work and a comprehensive primary care system based around general practitioners all enabled the maintenance of mentally disordered and vulnerable individuals outside mental hospitals. In this sense, welfarism and community care were closely connected.

For this reason, community care was a highly significant policy issue for the Thatcher administrations in the 1980s. The difficulty was how to provide the social support deemed necessary to make community care effective in the face of the New Right critique of welfarism and the attempted re-configuration of welfare provision. It certainly proved to be a difficult political issue. For example, a report on community care completed in early 1979 by a Conservative Policy Group chaired by Cecil Parkinson was kept out of the public domain until the summer of 1981, when a summary was published (Parkinson, 1981) as a precursor to the publication that year of the *Care in the Community* Green Paper. Fundamentally, Parkinson's analysis of the problem – the failure to invest adequately in community-based resources and provision – was in some tension with the broader political goal of 'rolling back the state'. As will be seen below in this chapter, and in those that follow, a connection was also made during the 1980s between the problems of the community care policy and the 'crisis' of the presence of the mentally ill in prisons. The argument, drawing on Penrose's (1939) famous paper, was that by releasing patients from the mental hospitals but then failing to provide adequately for them in the community, the prison system became a *de facto* form of asylum for these individuals. The situation in prisons came to be seen during this decade as symptomatic of the failure to deliver care in the community.

This, then, is the backdrop to the analysis that follows in this chapter and the following three. As set out in Chapter 1, the problematic for this book is to understand and trace whether and how these wider transformations – the shift to late modernity – affected the 'dividing practices' aimed at offenders with mental health problems, and particularly the use of imprisonment.

2. PRISONS AND MENTAL HEALTH UNDER THE THATCHER ADMINISTRATIONS

As was seen in the previous chapter, the presence of the mentally disturbed in prisons has for a long time been perceived as a 'problem'. It certainly troubled some of the early prison reformers, like John Howard and Elizabeth Fry, and has continued to do so. Nevertheless, there have tended also to be parallel attempts to develop constructive responses or solutions to the problem. In some periods there has even been a certain feeling of optimism about it, notably in the twentieth century from the 1920s to the 1960s and, to a lesser extent, at the beginning of the nineteenth century. The 1980s, however, were largely not an optimistic time in this field. The collapse of faith in the penal-welfare project (Garland, 2001) – the 'death of the social' (Rose, 1996c) – left the issue of offenders with mental health problems particularly exposed to pessimism. If the social workers, psychologists and psychiatrists could no longer help the disturbed and vulnerable in the criminal justice system, then what could be done?

The example of Holloway prison for women makes this point well. As Paul Rock (1996) describes, at the end of the 1960s, at the high point of the era of rehabilitation, the redevelopment of Holloway was planned in terms of the new prison being more like a hospital. By the early 1980s, however, this rehabilitative vision had turned sour. In 1984, a major scandal erupted about the prison's C1 unit for 'disturbed' women. The late Chris Tchaikovsky, then Director of Women in Prison, described in interview how this came about:

> Some women came to see us – this started the C1 campaign – [. . .] and told us that a woman had put out her eye. Another woman had attempted to do the same and another woman who I was able to see had cut her breast [. . .] Now the woman who had cut her breast told me that she had cut it. She was actually on 23 and a half hour lock-up. Food was put through the hatch and in fact it was actually longer than that she was out literally for a very quick dip in the bath and you know nothing else just a wash. The rest of the time it was total bang-up. The training unit was closed there was no association whatsoever. So in fact she told me it was quite clear that she cut her breast I mean I would put it as 'in need of human contact' but that's not how she put it because she said she wanted to see someone, you know talk to someone [. . .] I got through to Nick Davies of The Observer [. . .] and on the Sunday they ran 'The Muppet House of Horror at Holloway'. Then all the rest of the press jumped on

[and] we were joined by MIND and NCCL [. . .] and we had a picket at the Home Office [. . .] and we did a 16-minute film with Clean Break for Newsnight [. . .] and Polly Toynbee went in there from The Guardian and [. . .] she wrote a really damaging article [. . .] And they set up the project review.

Toynbee's *Guardian* article about C1, published in October 1984, was particularly trenchant in its critique:

A prison 'psychiatric' wing is nothing more than a dumping ground, a containment for them. The atmosphere is punitive not therapeutic, the prisoners' mad outbreaks and attacks are regarded as punishable rather than treatable and the psychiatric care they can expect [. . .] is nothing more than a parody of proper treatment.

(quoted in Sim, 1990:173)

A project review committee was set up in December 1984 to review the whole of the regime at Holloway – not just the C1 unit – and its future development. Before the committee reported in July 1985, a highly critical report on Holloway by the Chief Inspector of Prisons was published (HM Chief Inspector of Prisons, 1985) in which, amongst many other things, the practice of using disciplinary proceedings against mentally disturbed prisoners was condemned. A revealing internal report on C1 was also 'leaked' at around this time which confirmed one of the campaigners' central claims:

C1 had the primary function of holding and caring for the most disturbed women received into Holloway. The phrase 'disturbed' was double-edged. It was seen as referring to both psychiatrically ill women AND those whose behaviour or mental state was clearly disturbed, as evidenced by the difficulties they presented the prison in the management of their persistently disruptive behaviour, but who were not considered to be suffering from mental illness.

(Stewart and Shine, 1984:1–2)

In other words, the unit was being used partly for the management and containment of behaviourally difficult inmates. Chris Tchaikovsky referred in interview to her own personal experience in C1:

The prison also used C1 as a – which it had done for years to my certain knowledge because they did it to me – used it as a unit to control problem prisoners, for people without any mental health problems. Because a) it would scare them, it was a very scary place to put people and b) to get them out the way essentially but mainly for the scariness of it.

The project review committee report released in July 1985 bluntly concluded that C1 was 'totally unsuitable for its task' (Prison Service, 1985:32), noting in particular the difficulties related to conflicts between nursing and disciplinary staff. This point was strongly made in interview by Colin Allen, who was Governor at Holloway between 1985 and 1989:

> There was inadequate health care being given, the discipline staff were more or less in control and therefore women who were very seriously disordered were actually being treated as if they were normal [. . .] I remember a woman very well who had tried to commit suicide over a hundred times, yet was being put on report, put on a charge for trying to kill herself. It was just desperate stuff.

The whole C1 'episode' is significant and illuminating in several respects. As discussed in the previous chapter, the notion that there are particular connections for women between madness and criminality has a long history. Therefore for women prisoners, the collapse of faith in the penal-welfare project raised in a particularly sharp form the question of how they should be dealt with. With trust in rehabilitative and welfarist approaches dissipating, control or disciplinary responses to 'disturbing' women became more domin-ant, as Colin Allen found in Holloway. The inherent ambiguity in the notion of 'disturbance' was thus brought to the surface, as Paul Rock noted in interview:

> In the idea of disturbance it seems to me there are those twin elements of saying that you know there is something that needs attention, as it were a psychiatric dimension on the one hand, and on the other hand there is this threat to discipline.

In terms of 'dividing practices', all this suggests a more complex process than simply one of sorting the 'mad' from the 'bad' as is conventionally described. 'Disturbed' women in Holloway posed a series of inter-related challenges around mental disorder, self-harm, threats to discipline and bizarre behaviour. Deciding where individual women should be located – in the C1 unit, on the medical wing, on the ordinary wings, or transferred out to hospital – was a difficult and far from clear-cut process. The scale of the problem faced by the prison was indicated by a study by Turner and Tofler (1986) carried out on a random sample of new receptions to Holloway over an eight-month period from September 1984 to April 1985. They found that just over one in three receptions had a history of psychiatric illness and/or a history of self-harming (244 women out of 708).

A central discursive concept within these 'dividing practices' is the category of 'personality disorder'. This is an important issue that will be returned to later in this chapter and in subsequent ones. Of relevance to this discussion of

Holloway is an interesting paper by Pat Carlen (1985b) in which she argues that the notion of 'personality disorder' is operationalised in a particular way for women prisoners. The category is inherently ambiguous and tautological, as it is defined in behavioural terms but at the same is used to explain those behaviours. Crucially, only those individuals whose disorder is deemed 'treatable' come within the ambit of the mental health legislation. As Carlen (1985b:619) suggests, the judgment of 'treatability' then becomes the mechanism through which other interests can be served:

> A whole range of other institutional, ideological and industrial interests could combine in determining the recommendations as to treatability or not.

Colin Allen described in interview his experience of this at Holloway:

> To me as a layman, as a non-medical person, there's this arbitrary distinction between treatability and non-treatability, between personality disorder and mental illness [. . .] there's a grey area and it very much depends on whether people are wanted or not [. . .] The Holloway experience was for me the biggest realisation of this arbitrary distinction, that what was really the case was that there was some kind of other agenda working here, which seemed to be able to pick and choose almost between who went and who didn't.

Carlen (1985b:620) argues that for women offenders the category of 'personality disorder' is used to justify, *inter alia*, the rigidity of the disciplinary regime and the heavy use of prescription drugs. There is an historical resonance here with the earlier examples discussed in Chapter 2 of using the alleged 'madness' of female offenders as justifications for 'special' regimes that in practice turned out to be more repressive (Zedner, 1991, 1995).

There is an interesting contrast to be drawn between C1 and the special unit for men in Parkhurst C wing, which was (re-)opened at the end of 1985 (the original C wing unit had operated between 1970 and 1979). Whereas C1 was intended to be for disturbed women, the Parkhurst C wing special unit was explicitly designed as a response to the problems posed by a small group of prisoners who presented serious control problems for prison management, with mental disturbance a secondary focus. The selection criteria for the unit were that the prisoner should have a history of, or present symptoms of, mental abnormality *and* should have persistently presented one or more of the following behaviours 'in an uncontrolled fashion' at more than one establishment: violence to staff or prisoners; repeated discipline offences; damage to prison property; behaviour generally giving cause for concern (including self-harm) (Evershed, 1991:90). In other words, whilst the two units may in practice have served fairly similar functions in managing 'difficult' prisoners, the unit for women was described as a psychiatric facility whilst the one for men was explicitly intended to serve management or control purposes. Again, this can be set in the historical context of the long-standing connection that has been made for women between madness and criminality. Ironically, research in the late 1980s in Parkhurst C wing found strikingly high levels of mental disorder, with 35 per cent of the men diagnosed as suffering from a serious mental illness at the time of interview (Coid et al, 1991). A similar picture was found by a study in the other two special units for difficult male prisoners in Lincoln and Hull prisons respectively (Coid, 1991).

Less than two weeks after the Holloway project review committee report was published in mid-July 1985, an equally significant report was released on the centrepiece of specialist mental health provision in the prison system, Grendon prison (Home Office, 1985). The Advisory Committee of the Therapeutic Regime at Grendon (ACTRAG) had been set up in March 1984 in response to growing criticism from within the Prison Service that it had become too selective in its intake and had moved too far away from traditional discipline-based management (Cullen, 1997; Selby, 1991:97). This first ACTRAG report made some important recommendations which marked a significant development in its role and function. Central recommendations for the future direction of Grendon included:

- A greater focus on the treatment of 'sociopaths';
- More treatment of sex offenders;
- An increase in the number of long-term and life-sentence prisoners;
- The establishment of an Acute Psychiatric Unit for those suffering from a serious breakdown or crisis;
- The head of the prison to be a senior governor grade rather than a Medical Superintendent.

As a whole, the thrust of the report was to encourage a shift towards Grendon serving more of a purpose for the wider Prison Service as a place for managing the most difficult men in the system – 'lifers', sex offenders and so on. This was to have some impact in practice, as Elaine Player, who conducted an evaluation of the regime at Grendon in the late 1980s, observed in interview:

> I know there was an attempt to make Grendon be seen as more useful to the rest of the Prison Service. So that they would take these more difficult cases. And at one point one of the selection criteria was to give other institutions some relief from very difficult and disruptive prisoners. So it wasn't that these men had necessarily been defined as having a personality disorder. These were management problems.

The new emphasis on management was exemplified by the move to have the prison led by an ordinary governor rather than a Medical Superintendent.

This was a significant development, as the medical leadership of Grendon had previously been considered to be one of its most distinctive and important features.

Towards the end of 1985, the House of Commons Social Services Select Committee began taking evidence for their report on the Prison Medical Service. The Committee's report, published in 1986, provided a graphic and highly critical account of the treatment of the mentally vulnerable in prison. Overall, the committee found the quality of medical care provided by the service to be low and made 58 recommendations for improvements. It suggested that the service should seek to:

> Transform into a prisoners' health service, less doctor-dominated, more professional, primarily concerned with the delivery of multi-disciplinary health care and in good working contact with the NHS, universities and the probation service.
>
> (House of Commons Social Services Select Committee, 1986)

The report and the published proceedings of the Committee's hearings contain three central themes: the inadequacies of existing arrangements; the role of the 'failure' of the 'community care' policy; and the restricted scope of mental health interventions.

Running through the Committee's report and the published evidence of witnesses is the clear view that the response of the Prison Medical Service to the problem of mentally disordered prisoners was inadequate. The Committee's reported experience at one prison exemplifies the tone and tenor of much of the report:

> At Bedford prison we were told that a severely disturbed prisoner had recently spent almost eight months naked in a stripped cell. During our visit there, we saw a prisoner lying in a catatonic stupor with only a sheet for covering in an empty cell smeared with filth. This is wholly unacceptable.
>
> (House of Commons Social Services Select Committee, 1986: para 62)

The second theme in the report concerns the view that the problem in the prison system was a consequence of the mental health hospital closure programme and the failure to invest properly in care in the community. Committee members repeatedly put this view forward to witnesses. John Kilgour, for example, then Director of the Prison Medical Service, was pressed several times on this point. Some witnesses themselves made the point. For example, Dr H. Rollin from the Royal College of Psychiatrists argued in his evidence given in December 1985 that:

Until there is some re-thinking of the whole policy of community care, then this problem of the chronic schizophrenic who wanders, like a ping pong ball, between the prison service and the mental hospital service, will increase.

> (House of Commons Social Services Select Committee,
> 1986: para 219)

This view was, of course, a revival of Penrose's law (Penrose, 1939), discussed in the previous chapter, which posited an inverse relationship between the size of the mental hospital and prison populations. Some witnesses directly challenged this idea in their evidence:

There is current argument that emptying the hospitals fills up the prisons and vice-versa and there is no direct evidence that that is actually the case.

> (1986: para 691. Evidence of William Bingley, MIND)

There is not a shred of evidence that there has been a move from the declining mental hospitals to the prisons [. . .] the increase in the chronic inadequate population in the prison has come from the decline in hostels, in large rooming houses in large cities.

> (1986: para 227. Evidence of Dr Paul Bowden,
> Royal College of Psychiatrists)

The third theme in the Committee's report concerned the practical scope of mental health interventions. The Committee, and many of the witnesses, identified that a key problem group was the large number of prisoners who fell outside the ambit of the mental health legislation (and therefore were not eligible for transfer out of prison):

Only a minority of psychiatric cases in prison fall within the scope of the Mental Health Act [. . .] It must be assumed that there will always be a considerable number of significantly disturbed people in prison.

> (1986: para 65)

For these disturbed prisoners, the aims of provision tended to be described in the report in terms of 'care' rather than 'cure'. In other words, the purpose of prison responses was safe management rather than curative treatment. This is a long way from the optimism of the East–Hubert (1939) report in the 1930s and a good example of the broader trend described by Rose (1996c) as the 'death of the social', in which social expertise is downgraded and displaced within 'advanced liberal' forms of government. Lord Glenarthur, then Home Office minister, giving evidence to the Committee, summed up this therapeutic pessimism:

We come back to the difficult area, the core area if you like, of those who are not treatable and are not treatable anywhere, and I am afraid that, realistically, I do not see the end of the day when there is nobody of that type within the Prison Service. Nobody wants them and it is very, very difficult. I do not know how we take it forward.

(1986: para 1323)

Related to this view, there was some discussion in the witness sessions about the idea of 'asylum' as an appropriate goal; this was taken up by the Committee in their final report (1986: para 74). In discursive terms, the use here of the concept of 'asylum' is interesting and significant. On the one hand, it invokes the image of the old Victorian asylums as warehouses for difficult individuals. On the other, there is the idea of a 'safe haven' offering shelter or refuge – the 'best sense of the word', as the Committee report put it (para 74). The notion of 'asylum' thus refers to two kinds of risk: risks posed to others and risks to which they themselves are vulnerable (or 'actuarial risk' and 'clinical risk', as O'Malley (2004:22) terms them). In this sense, the call for some form of asylum is partly an early indication or sighting of the shift in this field from a curative to a risk-management enterprise that would develop considerably in the 1990s.

A further indicator of this shift can be seen in a new focus in some of the research conducted in the 1980s on the impact of imprisonment on the mental state of inmates (Rasch, 1981; Carlen, 1983; Walker, 1983; Coid, 1984), drawing partly on earlier 'classic' North American studies of the 'pains of imprisonment' (Clemmer, 1940; Sykes, 1958). Taylor (1986), for example, building on some earlier studies (Banister et al, 1973; Heather, 1977; Sapsford, 1978), carried out research on psychiatric disorder among life-sentenced prisoners in London prisons and found that two-thirds had a psychiatric diagnosis, with schizophrenia at 9 per cent, depression 13 per cent and personality disorder 33 per cent. More specifically, during this period there was a renewed concern with the risk of suicide or self-injury by prisoners (Dooley, 1990; Lloyd, 1990). Studies by Topp (1979), Phillips (1986) and Backett (1987) all explored the extent to which there was a link between prison suicide and mental disorder and found apparently high rates of previous psychiatric contact in their samples (38, 41 and 61 per cent respectively). Research on self-injury focused in particular on gender issues and the apparent higher prevalence among women prisoners (Cookson, 1977; Cullen, 1985). This interest in prison suicide and self-injury continued into the 1990s, although, as will be discussed in later chapters, the drawing of such a close link with mental disorder came to be questioned.

Whilst the Select Committee's report highlighted the problems posed by the residual group of mentally disordered prisoners ineligible for prison transfer, the government's response to the report focused primarily on improving practical arrangements for transfers to hospitals. As an editorial in *The Lancet* put it:

> Urgent attention [is being given to] the inappropriate presence in prison of mentally disturbed inmates who are detainable under the 1983 Mental Health Act.
>
> (1987:783)

This policy focus on transfers to hospital was matched in practice by increasing numbers of transfers during the decade. As Table 3.1 shows, the increase appears to start in 1984 but accelerates markedly from 1987. Why should this be so when the problem of the residual group of prisoners ineligible for transfer had been so clearly identified as a central issue? The key here was the changing role of the prison, which was increasingly becoming primarily a mechanism of control, containment and exclusion (a trend which accelerated in the 1990s – see Garland, 2001). Prison was seen less and less as a place for treating offenders and more as a place for containing them.

Table 3.1 Transfers to hospital under the Mental Health Act 1983 from Prison Service establishments 1981–1989

Category	1981	1982	1983	1984	1985	1986	1987	1988	1989
Transfers of sentenced prisoners	70	69	70	83	87	84	103	94	120
Transfers of remand prisoners	22	17	24	46	38	53	77	82	98
Total transfers	92	86	94	129	125	137	180	176	218

Following the Select Committee report, an Interdepartmental Home Office and DHSS Working Group was set up in summer 1986 to look at the specific issue of mentally disturbed offenders in prison. An editorial in *The Lancet* suggested that the Working Group was established to tackle problems at local level at the 'interface' of the Prison Medical Service and the NHS (*Lancet*, 1987). The report describes its own genesis in the following terms:

> The subject of mentally disturbed offenders and potential offenders has regularly arisen in the course of discussions between Ministers from the Home Office and the DHSS, and between officials from those Departments. Ministers were concerned to ensure that the mental health services and the prison system together took adequate account of the needs of those who were mentally disturbed and became offenders.
>
> Following consideration by Home Office and DHSS Ministers it was decided that the subject be studied in the wider context of care required for abnormal offenders in the penal system by an inter-departmental

working group of officials from the Home Office and the DHSS. The group was set up at a meeting between Lord Glenarthur and Lady Trumpington on 5 June 1986 and Dr Kilgour, Director of Prison Medical Services, was invited to be its chairman.

(Home Office/DHSS 1987: para 3.1–3.2)

As a construction of the problem this is interesting in one respect at least. There is little or no acknowledgement of the fact that the issue has been considered many times before. Indeed, the Select Committee's report is actually not referred to anywhere in the Working Group's report, nor is the landmark Butler report from the 1970s (Home Office/DHSS, 1975). The impression is given that this has been identified as a problem only relatively recently and that ministers have been reasonably prompt in starting to do something about it. This framing of the issue as a contemporary concern rather than as one that has proved intractable for decades or even centuries renders the administrative and managerial approach set out in the report more intelligible than it might otherwise be. The language of the report is also technical and administrative, in contrast to the Select Committee's colourful descriptions of cells 'smeared with filth' and naked prisoners in 'catatonic stupors'.

Shaw and Sampson (1991:107), at the time both from the Prison Reform Trust, took exception to this feature of the report, describing it as 'a document of stunning complacency in view of the nature and extent of the problem'. In a similar vein, in interview, Ian Bynoe, who in the late 1980s was Legal Director at the mental health charity MIND, argued in relation to the Working Group that:

> It wasn't given the political clout to address the real issues of resources.
> It was more of a paper exercise.

Issues of resources, however, become less important once the emphasis moves away from treatment or 'cure' and towards management and safe containment of the problem. In other words, what Bynoe perceives as the limitations of the Group's report may be less to do with 'political clout' and more to do with its overall approach.

The report made 16 recommendations, half of which related to encouraging and facilitating greater use of existing powers under the mental health legislation to transfer mentally disturbed prisoners into the health system. As Shaw and Sampson (1991:107) suggest, the recommendations were 'all of an administrative nature'. Indeed, this is a hallmark of the whole report, which contains a strong emphasis throughout on procedures, arrangements and systems. For example, section 6, which covers transfers to hospital, focuses almost entirely on the detail of the mechanics of how transfers happen. To give a flavour of this, paragraph 6.9 reads:

Prisons may use either the services of the visiting regional Forensic Psychiatrist or the visiting psychiatrist, or both, in order to secure the necessary co-signature for a section 47 application, except that a direct approach may be made to a local mental hospital consultant where it is known that the patient has had previous hospital in-patient treatment.

This level of detail in a relatively short report (22 pages excluding appendices) on a 'big' issue is of course significant. It defines or 'problematises' the issue as a technical or administrative one. As Foucault (1972) argues, discourse not only enables or allows new ways of thinking about a problem, it also constrains what can be said or thought or done. Thus, in this report, moral and even to some extent psychiatric issues largely lie outside the administrative discourse.

The report defines its focus as 'mentally disturbed offenders in the prison system'. A central issue is how this population is 'made up' in order to be governed. The defining criteria are described in the report in the following way:

> The process of defining and assessing the mentally disturbed offender is complex. It involves the family and social background, physical state, personality strengths and disabilities, and mental state on the one hand; history of criminal tendencies, offences and demonstrated or likely dangerousness on the other; and with the involved and sometimes unpredictable interrelationship between these factors.
>
> (Home Office/DHSS, 1987: para 3.5)

The 'complex' nature of this process and the range of information involved belie any attempt to describe these 'dividing practices' simply in terms of the 'mad or bad' dichotomy. At the level of practice, further considerations are also involved, as Professor Jeremy Coid suggested in interview when describing his own early experiences as a forensic psychiatrist in the 1980s:

> And I was reading these casenotes and it was outrageous [. . .] I was just outraged you know I was fairly young and green reading this stuff saying how *can* they say that this guy, look at what's recorded *here*. He's hearing voices he's been smearing faeces on the wall he's mad as a march hare. How can this person come along do an assessment and say that he's not mentally ill he's a criminal and should be you know deserves what he gets he's a psychopath [. . .] Having had further experience down the track as a regional forensic psychiatrist I then realised that clinical judgement is profoundly influenced at times by the resources that you have. That you start if you don't have any beds then you start prioritising somehow patients and you start making making decisions on the basis of sort of rationalisations. Well maybe they're more you know criminal than

schizophrenia today therefore you know. Certainly here [. . .] in inner London, consultants on ordinary wards are forced to make terrible decisions cos of the shortage of resources.

John Reed made a similar point in interview:

We all know what the policy is, that people who require care who meet the criteria for transfer under the Act should go to hospital. But the Act isn't very explicit and it may well be that if more beds were available more people would be transferred.

The report provides further details about the techniques used in the assessment process:

On reception into prison custody the person will therefore be medically screened by a doctor assisted by a hospital prison officer (or nurse in female establishments). The reception procedures provide for the prisoner to complete a state of health questionnaire, if necessary with the assistance of hospital prison officers, which the doctor is able to use during the conduct of his screening. Where indicated the medical officer will arrange for the prisoner to be located in the prison hospital for further observation or pending a second opinion from a consultant psychiatrist.

There will be some prisoners in respect of whom the requirement for detailed assessment of mental state is clear whether or not that is discernible from the prisoner's presenting behaviour or medical history. Administrative procedures provide for this in all cases where the criminal charge is one of murder (when the prisoner is routinely allocated to the prison hospital) and in certain types of sex offence. Additionally, indications or instructions may stem directly from the prisoner's court appearance.

[. . .] Instances also arise where manifestation of a mental condition becomes apparent only at a later stage, after sentence, and when the prisoner is on ordinary location. These may come to light as a result of abnormal behaviour, or disturbed mental state and be noted by discipline officers or other members of staff or be reported to them by other prisoners. Similarly, cases may be identified during the course of the medical screening a prisoner receives prior to any transfer to another prison establishment.

(Home Office/DHSS, 1987: para 6.4–6.6)

Several techniques are listed here – medical screening, self-completion questionnaire, observation, psychiatric opinion and staff/prisoner opinions about normality of behaviour or mental state. This series of techniques is accompanied by a system of 'documentary accumulation', to use Foucault's phrase (1977:189). The screening report, the questionnaire, the notes of observations and the psychiatrist's report together constitute the documentary techniques by which each individual prisoner is 'described, judged, measured, compared with others' (1977:191). Together these techniques provide a means of 'making up' individuals. The distinction from the disciplinary mode of power that Foucault details in *Discipline and Punish* is that instead of these techniques being used to fix individual differences in order that they can be 'normalised' or 'corrected' (1977:192), rather they are used primarily to determine how individuals can be most appropriately and safely managed in the system. Hence, for example, 'assessment of mental state' is mandatory for those convicted of murder or sex offences who may be a risk to others and, especially for the latter, may also be at risk themselves. There is a sense in which, therefore, the techniques of disciplinary power are adapted for other purposes rather than simply being completely replaced by an entirely new approach. As Garland (2001:23) puts it, there is a 'reconfigured complex of interlocking structures and strategies that are themselves composed of old and new elements, the old revised and reoriented by a new operational context, the newer elements modified by the continuing influence of working practices and modes of thought dating from the earlier period'. There is a further continuity too. As Garland (1990a:177–92) argues, *Discipline and Punish* constitutes to a degree a reworking of some themes in Max Weber's work. He suggests that Foucault's detailed analyses of the operational logic of discipline in prisons can also be described in Weberian terms as the result of the rationalisation of punishment in which technical relations have displaced moral ones. Viewed from this perspective, there is an obvious bridge between disciplinary and administrative or managerial strategies, both being characterised by the transformation of morally charged and emotive practices into a passionless and instrumental process.

This kind of transformation occurs elsewhere in the report in a reference to the importance of public attitudes:

> Consideration of the mentally disturbed offender and the nature and level of care provided takes place in the social climate of the day [. . .] Response to the needs of individual mentally disturbed offenders has to take account of the legitimate expectations of the public that Government agencies will take appropriate measures for its protection.
>
> (Home Office/DHSS, 1987: para 3.6)

Whereas reference to 'social climate' and public expectations might be constructed in terms of emotive responses to the issue – as, for example, in the language of the Social Services Committee report – here it is constructed in terms of public protection. This looks forward to the increasing emphasis on the administration or management of risk, but also at the same time looks backward to the origins of the Prison Medical Service in the late eighteenth century, when its establishment was expressly based on the need to protect the public (at that time from the spread of typhus). As will be further discussed at the end of this chapter, a concern with 'risk' and 'danger' within this field is not entirely novel.

Overall, then, the report is of some significance. Whilst at first sight it is a short and rather inconsequential document compared with the nature of the issue, it marks a substantial strategic shift. A managerial approach to the problem and an increasing emphasis on the administration of risk are major themes within the new governmental strategies associated with the New Right political order. As will be seen below and in subsequent chapters, these themes were to be further developed in the 1990s.

The Working Group report was published in May 1987, appearing amidst, and no doubt also stimulating, a wider discussion of the issues of mental health, crime and punishment. The correspondence pages of *The Lancet* during 1987 contained a running debate about the issue. A letter from a remand prisoner in the hospital block in Brixton prison described the 'shoddy medical attention' and staff interested only in 'impenetrable security and the moral and physical degradation of the inmates' (Rose, 1987). Responses to this letter framed themselves in terms of arguments for and against closer links between the NHS and the Prison Medical Service. Two doctors at Guy's Hospital, commenting on a similar case, suggested that 'this episode supports the case for integration of the Prison Medical Service within the NHS' (Russell and Lipsedge, 1987). The then Director of the Prison Medical Service, Dr John Kilgour, argued against this in his reply (Kilgour, 1987).

An article in *New Society* in May 1987 argued that a two-pronged process was increasing the numbers of mentally ill prisoners (Laurance, 1987). First, overcrowding was creating stress among prisoners which in some cases might lead to mental ill-health. Second, the continuing closure of mental hospitals was leading to former patients ending up in prison. The latter point was also made by the Working Group report (Home Office/DHSS, 1987: para 5.2) and reiterated by Patrick Thompson MP in a House of Commons debate on 13 July 1988:

> The continuing closure of our large mental hospitals is undoubtedly exacerbating this problem.

These two themes were of course familiar ones. As already discussed, concern about the impact of imprisonment on the mental state of offenders was growing during the 1980s, as reflected in the development of research in this area (Topp, 1979; Walker, 1983; Phillips, 1986; Backett, 1987). The second theme was another reference to Penrose's law, as refracted through increasing concerns that the policy of 'community care' was failing. As will be seen in later chapters, the latter was to become a significant issue at the start of the next decade.

The *New Society* article went on to argue:

> The Home Office consistently argues that it should provide less care for mentally ill offenders and the NHS should provide more. It is nervous of improving facilities too much – providing more psychiatric services as at Grendon, for instance – for fear of finding itself saddled permanently with these offenders whom it believes should be treated in hospital. It also believes it is inappropriate for the prison service to become too involved in treatment lest it be seen by the public as having the wrong motives.
>
> (Laurance, 1987:5)

This highlights another dimension of the issue at the level of contingent politics. 'Dividing practices' also have implications for the demarcation of financial responsibilities between Government departments. The balance of these responsibilities between the Department of Health and the Home Office has been a long-standing political issue and, as will be seen in later chapters, is an important influence in shaping events and policy development in this area.

A concern with financial issues is evident in the announcement on 20 December 1989 by David Mellor, then a junior minister at the Home Office, of the setting up of an 'efficiency scrutiny' of the Prison Medical Service. Its general aim, according to the press release, was 'to examine the effectiveness and value for money of the Prison Service's arrangements for providing medical and dental services for inmates of penal establishments'. It was to do this 'having regard to the arrangements and management practices in comparable organisations'. Its recommendations were to include 'performance indicators to enable the Director of Prison Medical Services to monitor efficiency and cost-effectiveness'.

The Scrutiny team was an internal one, consisting of Home Office officials (with one 'medical assessor' from the Department of Health). The team was led by Robert Wootton, a forensic scientist on secondment at the time from the Home Office to the Treasury Staff Inspection Efficiency Department. The press release announcing the establishment of the Scrutiny invited 'interested parties' to send in written submissions. The published report does not provide further information on the nature or source of any submissions received, although several references are made to discussions with Prison Medical Officers.

David Hillier, from the Prison Service Health Care Directorate, suggested in interview that the driving force behind the establishment of the Efficiency Scrutiny was the perceived poor standard of health care in prisons, a view supported by Professor John Gunn:

The much-maligned David Mellor decided that this was absolutely frightful this business of prison doctors. I mean prison doctors have a bad reputation, some of it with justice [. . .] He was pretty unimpressed with the reports he was getting [. . .] He wanted to put a bit of a bomb under it so he said he would look at the efficiency, that was the Thatcher government's kind of benchmark, efficiency, so we had an *efficiency* scrutiny but actually it was about re-organisation. It was a proposal to re-organise.

The report itself has a strong focus on cost concerns. A significant section of it focuses exclusively on financial management issues (paras 6.6–6.12), and elsewhere the emphasis on cost is sometimes taken to almost absurd lengths:

> The overall cost of the scrutiny was £54,000. This includes £2,600 travel and subsistence costs.
>
> (Home Office, 1990a: para 2.5)

John Reed argued in interview that it was not a serious enquiry, limited in scope by being internal:

> The Scrutiny was about the Prison Service looking at itself and deciding somebody else should be responsible for the work.

The real significance of the Scrutiny report, however, lies in its adoption of a new way of thinking about health service provision in prisons, one which had been partly foreshadowed by the Working Group's report in 1987. Garland (2001:188) describes this new rationality as an 'economic' style of reasoning, in contrast to the 'social' style of reasoning that had underpinned most criminal justice and penal policy for the first three-quarters of the twentieth century (see also Rose, 1996c).

The report contained 83 detailed recommendations. The central recommendation was for a closer alignment between the Prison Medical Service (PMS) and the NHS, and specifically that the PMS should move towards becoming a purchaser of health care services from service providers (primarily in the NHS). The six other key recommendations were:

- To widen the role of the PMS to that of a Prison Health Service;
- To appoint a Prison Health Advisory Committee;
- To ensure that all prison establishments undertake medical audit;
- To ensure a closer relation between health service provision and the identified needs of prisoners;
- To improve the medical management of the Prison Health Service;
- To integrate more fully the management of the Prison Health Service into the management of the Prison Service.

The overall thrust of the report was towards improving efficiency, effectiveness and value for money in the provision of health care services to prisoners by introducing some of the 'rigours' of the marketplace and of private-sector management techniques.

The central recommendation concerning the introduction of a purchaser–provider split was highly significant:

> The Prison Service should be a purchaser of clinical services provided through contracts with RHAs, DHAs, FPCs and individuals as appropriate.
>
> (Home Office, 1990a: para 1.13)

The idea of splitting the purchasers of services from providers is to try to create an internal market for services, in the belief that the mechanism of the market produces greater effectiveness, efficiency and value for money. The purchaser–provider split was, more broadly, a key element of the government's reforms of the National Health Service. In response to this specific proposal, eight former doctors in the Prison Medical Service wrote in the *British Medical Journal* that:

> We have serious doubts regarding the viability of the scrutiny team's proposals; in particular we believe that the purchasers (the prison service) will not be able to find adequate providers (NHS doctors).
>
> (Cooper et al 1991:53)

These kinds of doubt were expressed even more sharply in interview by Professor Jeremy Coid, a forensic psychiatrist:

> TS: One of the things that came out of the Efficiency Scrutiny was about the Prison Medical Service becoming a purchaser not a provider . . .
> JC: . . . purchasing what?

Such doubts suggest that any market for prison medical services was likely to be a rather artificial one, which in turn implies that introducing the purchaser–provider split in this context was in part an 'ideological' or symbolic exercise. Certainly, implementing the internal market in the prison context posed some particular practical problems, as John Reed commented in relation to prison governors being given responsibility for purchasing health care:

> I think governors were sold a pup there. They don't have the expertise to purchase it [health care services] – and nor should they.

As well as this central recommendation about creating an internal market, the Scrutiny report is imbued with economic-style thinking and language. Chapter 14, for example, is entitled 'Management Information System (MIS) and Performance Indicators (PIs)'. The role of Performance Indicators is described in these terms:

> Performance indicators need to be aligned to objectives and to target levels of service, and should be available widely and promptly to managers to enable decisions to be taken and budgets controlled.
>
> (1990a: para 1.24)

There are other references to managerial techniques and tools borrowed from the private sector, such as auditing:

> We recommend that the Health Director should set up a framework within prisons in which medical audit should be undertaken.

As Richard Smith, editor of the *British Medical Journal*, observed:

> The report reads more like a management than a medical document. [It uses the] language of the NHS reforms.
>
> (1990:892)

The economic 'habit of thought' thus runs through the report in a very striking way, marking an important shift in the discursive techniques used in the government of prisoners. Most of the new technologies of neo-liberalism – 'monetarization, marketization, [. . .] financial accountability and audit' (Rose, 1993:294) – appeared at some point in the report. The 'new managerialism' associated with New Right politics and, in Britain, primarily with the Thatcher administrations of the 1980s, appeared by the end of the decade to have penetrated even into one of the most unlikely quarters of governmental activity.

3. CONCLUSIONS

In historical research, the attempt to tame complexity (Garland, 1990a:281) and find some strategic coherence can sometimes lead to a tendency to minimise or gloss over any inconsistencies that may also exist. This chapter has certainly found some coherence in terms of an overall trend or pattern. The types of neo-liberal governmental rationalities and techniques associated with New Right politics clearly constituted the dominant strand in the second half of the 1980s in the field examined in this book. The *Efficiency Scrutiny* report exemplifies this trend with its novel 'managerial' language and approach. An increasing concern with the administration or management of risk is also evident in the last few years of the decade. It might be tempting to conclude, therefore, that in the area of mentally disordered offenders the 1980s saw a New Right or neo-liberal re-configuration of the field. However, some interpretive caution is necessary here.

First of all, it is important to recognise that it would be a significant overstatement to try to argue that the 1980s witnessed a wholesale paradigm shift in this field in which a new neo-liberal form of government entirely replaced penal-welfarism. This would be a misleading and inaccurate way of summarising the developments in this period. 'Dividing practices' aimed at offenders with mental health problems still retained elements of earlier strategies. For example, it was noted above that the documentary techniques of disciplinary power did not disappear in the 1980s, but rather began to be re-oriented to new aims. In other words, a more complex and multi-stranded strategy was in fact emerging. This resonates with Garland's (1990a:280) more general injunction to adopt a 'pluralistic, multidimensional approach' in analysing the historical development of penality.

In analytical terms, there is reason to be cautious too. Stenson (2005) has argued that governmental analysis that draws primarily on policy texts does not provide a full picture. Instead, he argues that this needs to supplemented by a 'grounded, empirical, realist analysis of governing practices' (2005:266; see also Garland, 1997b). The *Efficiency Scrutiny* report provides a good example to support Stenson's argument. Although at a discursive level it marked a significant shift, in another sense it served much more a symbolic or ideological purpose rather than a practical one. Its central objective of establishing the contracting out of health care provision did not appear to be achieved in practice to any significant extent in the years that immediately followed the report's publication. Indeed, apart from the pilot 'Durham cluster' initiative, the number of contracts between prisons and the NHS to provide psychiatric services was minimal. In other words, to some extent, the use of 'new managerial' language is merely political rhetoric (calling a review report an 'Efficiency Scrutiny', for example), although, of course, language is not just about meanings but also about the 'ways in which the world is made intelligible and practicable, and domains are constituted [. . .] which are amenable to interventions by administrators, politicians, authorities and experts' (Rose, 1993:289). Language and rhetoric, in this sense, can have 'real social consequences' (Garland, 2001:22; Newburn and Jones, 2005).

It is also useful at this point to make some comments about the emergence of 'risk' and 'risk thinking' during the 1980s. It is possible to overstate the novelty of these concerns with risk. There has been a long-standing articulation of risk within penal administration and penal policy. For example, the 1966 Mountbatten report on the Inquiry into Prison Security and Escapes – at the high point of the era of rehabilitation – recommended, *inter alia*, the classification of prisoners into four different security categories based on the risks they posed. The report's definition of Category A prisoners illustrates this well:

Prisoners who must in no circumstances be allowed to get out, either because of security considerations affecting spies, or because their violent behaviour is such that members of the public or the police would be in danger of their lives if they were to get out.

(Mountbatten, 1966: para 212)

Going back even further, the infamous James Hadfield case in 1800 described in the previous chapter raised major concerns about the most effective way of dealing with dangerous 'criminal lunatics'. Following Hadfield, as already discussed, the nineteenth century saw an ongoing debate and policy developments related to this issue, culminating in the opening of Broadmoor in 1863. John Pratt (1997, 2000b) has analysed in detail the origins of the idea of 'dangerousness' in the nineteenth century. Pat O'Malley (2000:17) argues more generally that:

[Although] we now live in societies in which risk occupies a prominent and distinctive place [. . .] risk is a core characteristic of all modern liberal and capitalist societies, dating back to about the end of the eighteenth century.

A distinction can be made, however, between these earlier references to risk and those in the 1980s described in this chapter. The Mountbatten report, like the developments that followed the Hadfield case, was triggered by concerns raised about the dangers posed by a small number of high-risk individuals. In contrast, risk in the 1980s was much more a way of thinking about whole populations and then sorting them according to levels of risk. In other words, it was a general tool for the management of populations, rather than primarily a way of managing the risks posed by a small number of very dangerous people. In this sense, it does mark a new and distinctive development and one associated more broadly with the emergence of neo-liberal governmental rationalities. Castel (1991), in a landmark essay, describes the transition as one from dangerousness to risk in which:

The new strategies dissolve the notion of a *subject* or a concrete individual, and put in its place a combinatory of *factors*, the factors of risk.

(1991:281, emphasis in original)

There is a curious feature, though, about the 'new' risk management in the 1980s, putting to one side the fact that it may actually not be all that 'new'. Strictly speaking, it is not about risk at all. For most commentators, an essential element of the idea of 'risk' is the use of actuarial and statistical techniques to assess the likelihood of particular future outcomes. Yet the instances of risk thinking described in this chapter do not fit this mould at all, rarely if ever being numerical. O'Malley (2004) suggests that the concept of uncertainty, in which government is through estimation rather than calculation, is critical here. Moreover, in analysing contemporary modes of government, he argues that, rather than looking at either risk or uncertainty as alternatives, the focus should be on understanding particular configurations or assemblages of risk and uncertainty (2004:21–6). As he makes clear, these assemblages do not only involve uncertainty:

> Almost everywhere that risk appears, it is assembled into complex configurations with other technologies, particularly – if not only – with uncertainty.
>
> (2004:27)

This idea of complex hybrids of technologies will be returned to in later chapters, where it will be argued that it constitutes a key characteristic of late-modern penality. At this point, it should be taken as a reminder and a warning that any search for clearly defined strategic transformations is unlikely to be very fruitful or helpful in explanatory terms (see Young, 2002:238; Zedner, 2002:343). Rather, the analytical task is to attempt to trace the shifting configurations of risk, uncertainty and other technologies. Again, there is a resonance here with Garland's (1990a) arguments about the need for a multi-dimensional analysis of penality.

Perhaps the overriding feature of the 1980s that has been brought out in this chapter is a more negative one, or, to be more precise, one concerning an *absence* within discourse, strategies and practices during this period. It is the diminishing ambition in relation to the care, treatment or rehabilitation of offenders with mental disorders that is arguably the most striking aspect of the decade, especially in the prisons context. The limit of ambition is the safe containment and management of these individuals: the provision of a relatively 'safe haven' for them in which they not only do not pose too great a risk to others but also are protected from harm themselves. The Holloway C1 campaign, for example, played particularly effectively on the latter, using the mass media to communicate quite graphically how some highly vulnerable women were being allowed to be further harmed whilst in the custody of the state. Whilst the focus on safe management is in one sense an exercise in the administration of risk as argued above, in another, it is simply the only course of action left when faith in the rehabilitative 'experts' has gone. The 'death of the social' and the discrediting of the social 'experts' of penal-welfarism were thus clearly evident in the Thatcher years of the 1980s. Another way of looking at this is to view this limited strategic ambition or discursive 'absence' as evidence of a transitional phase. In other words, it may suggest that during the 1980s, although penal-welfarism had largely unravelled, it had yet to be replaced by a fully re-configured new strategy. It is therefore a transitional decade between the old and the new. This point will be returned to in later chapters.

The next chapter picks up the story at the beginning of the 1990s, when there appeared to be an unexpected shift in strategic direction. In November 1990, a month or so after the publication of the *Efficiency Scrutiny* report, the establishment of the Reed Review of services for mentally disordered offenders was announced, and in February 1991 Lord Woolf published his landmark report on prison disturbances. The penal landscape and the field of mentally disordered offenders both appeared to be undergoing a major transformation. 'Progressive' penal approaches that seemed to have disappeared in the 1980s appeared to rise suddenly to prominence again. Understanding these developments is the task now of Chapter 4.

The Woolf report and prison reform, 1990–1993

Imprisonment is an expensive way of making bad people worse.

(Home Office, 1990b)

Prison works. It ensures that we are protected from murderers, muggers and rapists – and it makes many who are tempted to commit crime think twice.

(Michael Howard, Home Secretary, 1993)

This chapter examines the period from 1990 to 1993, a period which is often viewed as seeing a resurgence of humanitarian or reformist penal policy. In broad terms, it can be said that this period was first triggered on 1 April 1990, when the disturbances at Strangeways prison began, it developed in earnest towards the end of that year; and then came to an abrupt public halt on 6 October 1993, when the Home Secretary, Michael Howard, made his infamous 'prison works' speech to the Conservative Party conference. The aim of this chapter is to analyse how this apparent, albeit short-lived, renewal of interest in progressive penal policy affected strategies towards mental health, crime and punishment. Specifically, the analytical focus is on the impact on the 'dividing practices' aimed at offenders with mental health problems, with specific and particular reference to prisoners. In investigating this, the first section of this chapter briefly sets out some of the wider social, political and penal context at this time which made this more 'progressive' turn possible. The main section analyses in detail how this affected the area of mental health in prisons. The third, concluding section draws out some of the key themes and issues presented by the analysis in this chapter.

1. CONTEXT: POLITICAL AND PENAL 'CRISES'

The resignation of Margaret Thatcher as Prime Minister in November 1990 starkly symbolised how the neo-liberal project encapsulated in the term

'Thatcherism' was entering a difficult phase in Britain in the early 1990s. With its totemic leader removed from office, much of the thrust of the Thatcherite 'project' appeared to start to dwindle, as a series of policies were halted, altered or reversed. The political confidence engendered by a third successive general election victory in 1987 had ebbed away. The scrapping of the community charge, known as the 'poll tax', became symbolic of the administration's diminishing governmental authority. Gamble (1988:236), writing in the late 1980s, suggested that the 'project' had actually always been a provisional and transitional one:

> Thatcherism should be seen as an attempt to clear the way for a new hegemony, not as that new hegemony itself.

By the end of 1990, this 11 year attempt appeared to be on its last legs. The reasons for this are complex, but a major driver was the return at the start of the 1990s of the economic problems to which Thatcherism had posed itself as the solution – the failure of the 'economic miracle' (see Sked and Cook, 1993: chapter 5). Inflation and unemployment had not been defeated and the economy was in a severe recession. As Sked and Cook (1993:585) put it, 'after more than a decade of Mrs Thatcher, this seemed a poor reward indeed'.

As Thatcherism appeared not to have delivered on the economic front, it is unsurprising perhaps that at this time it began to be questioned whether some of the pains that had been endured during the 1980s were in fact worth it. As John Major took over the reins as Prime Minister in November 1990, the 'harshness' of some of the domestic policy he inherited started to seem not only out of step with the public mood, but also politically inappropriate. In the course of 1991 and 1992, the Major administration set about tempering some of this harshness. For example, in the early 1990s child benefit was raised in line with inflation and compensation was paid for the first time to haemophiliac HIV victims (Sked and Cook, 1993:553). The collective appetite for 'tough' government appeared to have diminished for the time being.

In this analysis, the political conditions for a more 'progressive' reformist penal policy were thus better than they had been for some years. Arguably, however, this shift had started somewhat earlier than this, in the second half of the 1980s. The so-called 'Hurd vision' (after Douglas Hurd, Home Secretary between 1985 and 1989) involved a pragmatic response to the spiralling costs associated with the projected rise in the prison population. Windlesham (1993:237–9) describes a meeting of Home Office ministers and officials at Leeds Castle in September 1987 at which some 'devastating calculations' about the future prison population hastened a less expansionist approach. Thus, as Stern (1993:268–9) observes, some of the political support for the more progressive penal approach at the start of the 1990s was rooted in more neo-liberal, managerialist concerns:

Even those who did not ally themselves with better treatment of prisoners, and did not see themselves as protectors of human rights, were persuaded by a completely different set of arguments, springing from a completely different set of values – efficiency, value for money, good management [. . .] Looked at this way, the prison service seemed the paradigm of an over-centralized, old fashioned, top-heavy bureaucracy that lived in fear of the pressure from its trade unions and could not deliver what it was paid to deliver.

This is an important point, as it helps explain how some of the themes of the 1980s discussed in the previous chapter did not entirely disappear at the start of the 1990s. Rather, as will be seen in the rest of this chapter, they became re-oriented within the evolving penal strategy.

The slow-burning prisons 'crisis' alluded to by Windlesham (1993) had arguably been developing for some time. Riots and disturbances had occurred throughout the 1970s and 1980s (Sim, 1994a:32) and during the latter decade the problem of over-crowding had become increasingly serious. This 'crisis' exploded into the limelight in April 1990:

> The first 25 days of April 1990 saw the worst series of prison riots in the history of the British penal system.
>
> (Woolf and Tumim, 1991:1)

Whilst the idea of 'crisis' is much over-used in the context of British prisons, the riots of spring 1990, which began in Strangeways prison in Manchester and then spread to several others, certainly represented a problem of particularly acute intensity, scale and public visibility. Sparks et al (1996:15) describe the riots as the 'most drastic' event in modern British prison history. As will be seen below, the resulting report of the Inquiry into the disturbances, universally known as the Woolf report, has been viewed by many commentators as signifying the start of a 'new' progressive and reformist agenda for prisons. Importantly, as Player and Jenkins (1994:2) note, the fact that the disturbances in Strangeways began on 1 April, just one day after a major street riot in London against the 'poll tax', served to heighten the sense that the whole authority and credibility of the government was under some threat. Seven months later, of course, Margaret Thatcher resigned as Prime Minister. As will be discussed later, the political and penal 'crises' at the start of the 1990s were closely intertwined.

2. WOOLF, REED AND PRISONERS WITH MENTAL HEALTH PROBLEMS

The early 1990s saw two major policy documents produced: the Woolf Inquiry report and the Reed Review of services for mentally disordered offenders. Together, they set out what was regarded as a 'new' reformist and humanitarian agenda. In this section, the extent to which this actually constituted a major strategic shift will be examined.

Strangeways and the Woolf agenda

The Woolf report is the foundational document of the 'new' reformist agenda and is worth some extended scrutiny. It contained 12 main recommendations which are summarised below. These are set out in paragraphs 1.167 and 15.5 of the report:

(1)   Closer co-operation between the different parts of the criminal justice system;
(2)   More visible leadership of the Prison Service from the Director General;
(3)   Increased delegation of responsibilities to prison governors;
(4)   An enhanced role for prison officers;
(5)   Individual prisoner 'compacts' setting out the prisoner's expectations and responsibilities in that establishment;
(6)   A national system of Accredited Standards for prisons;
(7)   A new Prison Rule that no prison should hold more prisoners than its certified normal level of accommodation (with Parliament to be informed of material departures from this rule);
(8)   Ministerial commitment to provide access to sanitation for all inmates;
(9)   Improving prospects for prisoners to maintain links with family and community;
(10) Division of establishments into small and more manageable units;
(11) Separate statement of purpose and conditions and a lower security cat-egorisation for remand prisoners;
(12) Improved standards of justice within prisons.

Woolf's report has been considered significant in three major respects. First and fundamentally, in contrast with most 'official' explanations for prison 'riots', Woolf placed the concept of justice at the heart of his analysis, arguing that unjust treatment of prisoners undermined the legitimacy of imprisonment (see Sparks, 1994). Second, he suggested that an over-emphasis on physical security and control issues, to the neglect of justice, played a significant part in triggering the disturbances at Strangeways and other prisons. Third, he argued therefore that a successful prison system required a proper balance to be struck between these three elements of security, control and justice. Cavadino and Dignan (1997:115) summarise the impact of Woolf:

> Woolf was widely credited with skilfully constructing [. . .] a [. . .] broad consensus [. . .] in support of a liberal programme to tackle some of the prison system's most endemic and intractable problems.

Indeed, so positive was the response to the report, and across such a wide spectrum of stakeholders, that its reception has been described as hagiographic (Sim, 1994a:32). However, the extent to which the Woolf report actually signalled a significant new agenda has been challenged by some commentators (Shaw, 1992; Sim, 1994a). Sim (1994a), for example, argues that underneath Woolf's reformist rhetoric, an unaccountable and repressive prison system remained intact, largely unchallenged by the substantive content of his report. The political response was certainly somewhat mixed. Whilst claiming the intention to implement Woolf's recommendations in full, the Home Secretary at the time, Kenneth Baker, also moved to introduce a new offence of prison mutiny carrying a maximum sentence of 10 years and made clear in several speeches during the course of 1991 that coercion and repression remained key elements in strategies for maintaining order in prisons (Sim, 1994a:42–3).

The latter aspect of the responses to the disturbances in Strangeways and other prisons has been understated, but it is, of course, a frequently observed phenomenon that one common response to threats to the legitimacy or authority of the state is to re-assert the 'power to punish' (Garland, 1996; Sparks, 2001b:166). The Woolf agenda, and in particular the ways in which it was mobilised politically, involved a more complex folding together of different strategies, as part of a means of restoring legitimacy in the prison system, than some of the more 'hagiographic' accounts provide. This points towards the need for a better understanding of the relationship between the penal realm and the political order (Sparks, 2000a:141). As Sparks (2001b:172) observes, 'punishment is ineluctably a political matter' and therefore understandable partly in political terms. This question will be returned to below and also in the next chapter, when a rather different 'episodic use of punishment as a political tactic' is considered (2001b:170).

Turning to the substantive implications of the Woolf report for prisoners with mental health problems, the issue actually forms only a very small part of the report: just three and a quarter pages out of the 456 in the main body. It is worth considering briefly why this might be the case, given that the problem of the presence of the mentally vulnerable within prisons has such a long history. It partly reflects, of course, the fact that this group rarely features in prison disturbances (Cavadino and Dignan, 1997:17). It is also related to the scale and nature of the inputs to the Inquiry, about which Woolf was particularly and unusually transparent in the report.

Annex 2I to the Woolf Inquiry report lists 171 individuals and organisations that submitted written evidence to the Inquiry. Of these 171, only six (4 per cent) were from 'special interest' groups with a bearing on the mental health problems of prisoners (although, obviously, submissions from other individuals and organisations may have included commentary or reference to mental health issues):

- Department of Forensic Psychiatry, Institute of Psychiatry
- Mental Health Act Commission
- Mental Health Foundation
- National Schizophrenia Fellowship
- Royal College of Psychiatrists
- Special Hospitals Service Authority.

A further three were from organisations with a broader 'health' remit:

- Association for Psychological Therapies
- British Medical Association
- Department of Health.

Prisoners were also invited by Woolf to submit written comments, and a summary of responses is included in Annex 2E. Responses mostly cover the basic themes of poor prison conditions – overcrowding, poor sanitation, inadequate food, poor staff attitudes, excessive time locked in cells and so on. References to mental health issues are few and far between but include:

- Complaints about poor access to medical care (3 out of 75 responses from Glen Parva inmates)
- Complaints about the quality of prison medical services (67 out of 603 responses from 'non-target' establishments, ie those prisons where there were *not* disturbances)
- Some officers being paranoid, alcoholic or in need of psychiatric help (number not clear, but less than 44 out of 603 'non-target' responses)
- The inappropriateness of sharing cells with the 'mentally sick' or psychopaths (number not clear but less than 20 out of 603 'non-target' responses)
- Feelings of 'helplessness' and 'no-one to talk to' (47 out of 603 'non-target' responses).

Prison staff were also invited to submit written responses, and these are summarised in the same Annex. Key themes of these responses include staff shortages, poor prison conditions and media coverage of the disturbances. There are no specific references to mental health issues.

Within the wider Part II of the Inquiry, a series of public 'themed' seminars were held. In the topic guides reproduced in the Annexes to the report, reference to mental health issues is restricted to Seminar C, which focused on 'Co-operation with the Criminal Justice System'. One of the two principal questions to be discussed at this seminar was whether particular categories of inmates ought not to be in prison, and one of the examples given was of prisoners with a history of mental illness.

It can be seen then that the inputs to the Inquiry did not suggest that the issue of mental health would have a particularly high profile within the final report. In terms of the report's substantive content, within a section on 'Diversion from Prison', there is a short subsection entitled 'The Mentally Disordered Offender' containing 26 paragraphs. The first one states:

> This group of offenders has always been a particular problem for the Prison Service. The majority of these offenders, if facilities were available, would be dealt with more appropriately elsewhere than in prison. All too frequently, however, the Courts find themselves without an alternative to prison.
>
> (Woolf and Tumim, 1991: para 10.115)

This clearly sets a framework based on an emphasis on the diversion and transfer of prisoners with mental health problems away from the prison system. Indeed, the majority of the 26 paragraphs focus on this. In this regard, Woolf merely restated or added weight to an already developing prioritisation of diversion/transfer. Home Office Circular 66/90, issued on 3 September 1990, had given a strong impetus to this drive. The covering letter attached to the Circular stated unequivocally:

> The enclosed Home Office circular, which has Department of Health support, draws the attention of the Courts, Prisons, Police and Probation Services to the statutory powers which enable mentally disordered offenders to be diverted away from the criminal justice system. It urges that these powers should be used to their fullest possible extent.

The Circular was followed up by several letters in 1991 and 1992 from the Home Office and Prison Service seeking to maintain the momentum of increasing numbers of prison transfers. In a similar vein to the Circular, in July 1990, two months before it had been issued, the Directors of five national charities involved in the fields of mental health and prisons (National Schizophrenia Fellowship, Howard League, Prison Reform Trust, NACRO, MIND) wrote a joint open letter to the Home Secretary, David Waddington, in which they urged him 'to take a number of steps to divert the mentally vulnerable from the criminal justice system'.

The White Paper *Custody, Care and Justice*, published in September 1991, which was described as concerned with implementing the Woolf agenda, continued this strong emphasis on diversion/transfer:

> Prison is not a suitable place for people suffering from mental disturbance. Whenever possible, such offenders should be diverted to the health or social services when they first come into contact with the criminal justice system.
>
> (Home Office, 1991:101)

This appears to be a fairly clear re-statement of policy, but the second half of the passage shows an important tension within the strategy:

> Where it is unavoidable that those requiring in-patient treatment are committed to prison, then they should be transferred to suitable health service facilities as soon as possible.

The qualification 'those requiring in-patient treatment' implies that the term 'mental disturbance' encompasses only those whose mental condition is such that they will be deemed as in need of in-patient treatment under the mental health legislation. Research by John Gunn and colleagues published at this time (Gunn et al, 1991:43,52) suggests that for sentenced prisoners this would cover only less than 8 per cent of those with identifiable mental health needs (see Table 4.1 for the main findings from the study). The majority of the mentally vulnerable in prison – those with personality disorders, depression, anxiety, alcohol dependence, drug dependence and so on – are effectively excluded from the policy discourse in the White Paper, as they are not 'mentally disturbed' within that document's definition.

This leads to an apparent paradox. The 'dividing practices' implied by the 'new' reformist Woolf agenda are actually highly restrictive, leaving the vast

Table 4.1 Summary of key findings from Gunn et al (1991)

Sample details	Main findings
1,769 males, several prisons	38% psychiatric diagnosis 19% substance dependence 8% personality disorders 5% neuroses 2% psychoses
301 females, several prisons	56% psychiatric diagnosis 29% substance dependence 13% neuroses 8% personality disorders 1% psychoses

majority of those with identifiable mental health problems in prison. However, the issue of how to respond to the residual problem within prisons is only briefly mentioned within the report's sub-section on 'mentally disordered offenders':

> It is, however, clear that there will remain for the foreseeable future, a significant problem for the Prison Service in accommodating mentally disordered offenders. We propose that the Prison Service should there-fore recognise the special responsibility it has for those in its care who suffer in this way.
>
> (Woolf and Tumim, 1991: para 10.136)

'Special responsibility' falls some way short of active engagement in treat-ment or health care provision. The 'problem' is also conceived in quite a restrictive way as one 'for the Prison Service in *accommodating* mentally disordered offenders' (emphasis added). In this sense, it could be argued that in relation to this particular sub-group of the prison population, Woolf actu-ally adopts what might be broadly termed a managerial approach, certainly in terms of the way the 'problem' is framed. There is some continuity here, then, with strategy in the late 1980s, which, as discussed in the previous chapter, largely limited its aims to the safe containment or accommodation of those mentally disordered offenders who were not diverted or transferred from prison. The general shift within late-modern penality from treatment to containment, or from normalisation to management (see Simon, 1993), clearly persisted in the mental health arena in the early 1990s, despite the apparent revival of progressive and humanitarian penal policy signalled by Woolf. Other 'progressive' voices at this time were framing the issue in similar terms. For example, the charity NACRO described the aim of a study in Winson Green prison conducted in 1992 as:

> To gather a clear and comprehensive understanding of the difficulties which mentally disturbed prisoners present to the prison.
>
> (NACRO, 1993:25)

The problem of 'mentally disturbed prisoners' is articulated here in terms of the management difficulties it poses. Given NACRO's traditional emphasis on prison reform and offender rehabilitation, this is a striking construction, suggesting the pervasiveness of the discourse of management and containment in the early 1990s.

The issue of prison suicides provides some further support for this view. It was noted in the previous chapter that the 1980s saw a renewed research focus on this difficult area (Topp, 1979; Phillips, 1986; Backett, 1987; Dooley, 1990) after a long period in which virtually no British studies had been conducted. Indeed, Liebling (1992:19) suggests that prior to Topp's 1979 study, the next most recent systematic study of prison suicides was Charles Goring's *The English Convict* published in 1913. A key finding of the new research in the 1980s concerned the levels of previous psychiatric contact amongst suicidal prisoners; this was connected with debates about the apparently growing problem of the mentally disordered in prison. It was argued in Chapter 3 that this renewed research interest was linked to the emergence of a newly prominent focus on risk management within penal strategies in the 1980s. In the early 1990s, research continued in this vein, as Liebling (1992:33) notes:

> Most prison suicide studies are still concerned with the identification of a profile of the high-risk prisoner: what are the common features of prison suicides, and what do they tell us about possible factors associated with risk? This profile, once accomplished, is typically aimed at the prediction (and therefore prevention) of future prison suicides.

It began to be questioned, however, whether it was possible in the context of prisons to draw such a direct link between mental health problems and suicide. Harding and Zimmerman (1989) asked whether it was abnormal or unhealthy to feel tense and anxious whilst in prison awaiting trial (see also Walker, 1983:64; Coid, 1984; Gallo and Ruggiero, 1991). In other words, imprisonment could engender neurotic symptoms (such as anxiety or depression) in some inmates as a 'normal' reaction to an unpleasant and stressful environment. This might account for part of the elevated psychiatric morbidity in the prison population. In this way, prison suicides might be seen as the end point of a continuum of 'normal' reactions to the 'pains' of imprisonment. However, even more significantly, the idea that prison suicides had very high levels of previous psychiatric contact started to be questioned. A Home Office literature review concluded that 'none of the studies has conclusively shown previous psychiatric contact to be more common amongst prisoners that commit suicide' (Lloyd, 1990). Going further than this, Liebling (1992:45–6) and others (House, 1990) noted that levels of previous contact were actually substantially *lower* among prisoners who committed suicide compared with the community. Whilst research studies showed that over 90 per cent of suicides in the community had a history of psychiatric illness (Barraclough and Hughes, 1987), equivalent rates for prison suicides were only around 30 per cent (Dooley, 1990; Lloyd, 1990). Liebling (1992) argues that prison suicide is not primarily a psychiatric phenomenon, but rather is the outcome of the conjunction of a concentration of 'vulnerable' individuals in a highly stressful and difficult environment (see Medlicott, 1999). A major report by the Chief Inspector of Prisons (1990) on suicide and self-injury took the similar view that the problem could not be viewed in isolation from the unacceptable nature of many prison regimes (on self-injury, see Livingston, 1997).

This way of viewing the issue of prison suicides in the early 1990s linked it closely with wider managerial problems of how to deliver the efficient, effective and safe custody of prisoners. Within discourses of managerialism and risk management, prisoners at risk of suicide or self-injury primarily posed problems for management or safe containment rather than for psychiatric or welfare provision.

The White Paper *Custody, Care and Justice* (Home Office, 1991) makes even clearer how the managerialism of the late 1980s remained a central element within the 'new' progressive penal policy of the early 1990s. A whole chapter is devoted to internal management and structural issues. To give just one example, one of the key priorities set out in the Paper is:

> To provide a code of standards for conditions and activities in prisons which will be used to set improvement targets in the annual contracts made between prison Governors and their Area Managers.
>
> (Home Office, 1991:15)

One issue on which Woolf is virtually silent is gender. As none of the riots and disturbances in April 1990 occurred in a women's prison, consideration of problems specifically relating to women prisoners was explicitly excluded from the Inquiry (Woolf and Tumim, 1991: para 2.18). Player (1994) argues that this was in some respects an unduly restrictive interpretation of his brief; she specifically raises the issue of mental disorder within the female prison population. Woolf is similarly quiet on race issues too, devoting just over one page of the report to a discussion of 'Race Relations' (Woolf and Tumim, 1991: paras 12.135–12.142). These two areas will be returned to below.

Summarising, the Woolf report and the resulting White Paper were heralded as signalling the arrival of a more progressive and humanitarian penal policy. For mentally disordered offenders, the focus was on diversion from the criminal justice system and transfer out of prison. In practice, this affected only a very small minority of this population, the remainder being processed in the ordinary way through the system, with a substantial number ending up and remaining in prison. In two respects, the Woolf agenda constitutes a form of 'progressive' penal policy strongly inflected by 'advanced liberal' forms of government. First, in terms of a style or a set of techniques of government, managerialism and the New Public Management are prominent strands. Second, in terms of the ends or the *telos* of government (Dean, 1994:161), it is effective management, safe containment and the administration of risk that are dominant, rather than treatment or even rehabilitation. The role of the prison, as Garland (2001) argues, shifts towards becoming primarily a mechanism of control, containment and exclusion. This point will be returned to later.

The Reed Review of services

The establishment of the Review of Health and Social Services for Mentally Disordered Offenders chaired by Dr John Reed (known as the 'Reed Review') was announced in November 1990, shortly before the Woolf report was published in February 1991. A month after this, on 14 December 1990, a highly critical report on Brixton prison by the Chief Inspector of Prisons was published, highlighting (among other things) serious inadequacies in the care of mentally disturbed prisoners. This contributed to the sense of a newly urgent 'crisis' in the prison system. The first meeting of the Reed Steering Committee took place in January 1991 and the review ended in July 1992. Both implicitly and explicitly, the review was seen as part of the 'progressive' penal project exemplified by the Woolf Inquiry. Interestingly, although there was this distinct view that the problem of the mentally disturbed and disordered within prisons had worsened during the 1980s, as discussed in Chapter 3, and reached a new 'crisis' in 1990, the research evidence suggested otherwise. Two studies by John Gunn and colleagues, carried out in the early 1970s (Gunn et al, 1978) and the late 1980s (Gunn et al, 1991) respectively, suggested that in nearly 20 years the proportion of sentenced prisoners with mental disorders had scarcely changed, remaining at around one-third.

The establishment of the Review was announced on 30 November 1990 in a speech by Stephen Dorrell MP, then Parliamentary Under-Secretary for Health, at the Royal Society of Health Conference on 'Crime and Mental Illness'. In his speech, Dorrell set out what he describes as the 'underpinning' principle of government policy:

> You will be familiar with the basic principle underpinning Government policy on mentally disordered offenders. It is that, where possible, they should receive care and treatment in hospital from health and social services rather than in the criminal justice system. Our objective is to ensure that we have a just and humane system, providing the most up-to-date methods of care and treatment for such people.

This principle will be considered in more detail below, but it is useful first of all to summarise the substantive content of the Review. The Review made 276 recommendations across its seven volumes. The core and central policy position, as noted above, was that 'mentally disordered offenders should, wherever appropriate, receive care and treatment from health and personal social services rather than in custodial care'. The Review adopted five underpinning criteria for developing recommendations about service provision. These were that 'patients' should be cared for:

(1) with regard to the quality of care and proper attention to the needs of individuals;

(2) as far as possible, in the community rather than in institutional settings;
(3) under conditions of no greater security than is justified by the degree of danger they present to themselves or others;
(4) in such a way as to maximise rehabilitation and their chances of sustaining an independent life;
(5) as near as possible to their own homes or families if they have them.

The specific recommendations of the Prison Advisory Group cover the following areas:

- Bail and remand issues, with a focus on improving assessments, diversion and transfers to hospital;
- Improvements to the arrangements for assessment and transfer to hospital of sentenced prisoners;
- Development of policy relating to the care and treatment of prisoners with mental health care needs (ie for those who are not diverted or transferred);
- Establishment of standards for mental health care screening on reception into prison;
- Establishment of a 'second Grendon';
- Action on suicide prevention;
- Review of options for the treatment and management of personality disordered offenders;
- Endorsement of the proposals for implementing the recommendations of the Scrutiny report;
- A multi-agency approach to discharge planning.

In terms of scale at least, the Review was a major exercise; for some it was viewed as a landmark report, perhaps the most significant since the Butler Report in 1975. For example, Peay (1997:697) states in her chapter on 'mentally disordered offenders' in the second edition of *The Oxford Handbook of Criminology* that it 'provides a comprehensive review of the state of play in the early 1990s, setting the parameters of policy development for the decade.' In interviews for the present study, opinions varied among respondents as to its impact and significance. Some felt it endorsed, consolidated and built on the existing direction of policy in a useful way:

> Well, I think it *was* important. To some extent the Reed Review endorsed existing government policy. Where it recommended changes, on the whole those changes were accepted and an attempt was made to put them into practice.
>
> (Michael Howard)

I essentially saw my role as supporting and reinforcing the work that

John Reed was doing [. . .] I totally supported the John Reed direction.
Very much took the view that such prisoners should be treated as
patients.

(Virginia Bottomley)

Others were rather more negative:

Apart from keeping it [the subject] on the boil a bit I don't think it
achieved very much, I don't think it achieved much at all.

Well it really was a waste of time. It's very difficult to be diplomatic about
it really. It was cumbersome [. . .] They produced lots of documents
which sit on shelves. I'm not convinced it made a big impact.

John Reed himself stated in 2002 that in hindsight the Review had under-
estimated the scale and severity of the problem in prisons, and hence progress
in that area had been more limited (Revolving Doors Agency, 2002). In
interview in 1998, he observed:

I must say I've always taken my hat off to health department ministers
and to the NHS for the way they responded to that. I mean they accepted
the report, we didn't ask them to accept individual recommendations we
just asked them to say is this the sort of blueprint that you would like to
see the service follow and they said yes. And it was obviously always
going to be a long haul implementing them all because it's not just a
question of money but a question of availability of trained staff to provide the services. So I'd always seen it myself as at least a yeah about a ten
year job to implement.

(John Reed)

Focusing on prisons, the report of the Review's Prison Advisory Group
contained three main strands. First, there is a chapter which focuses on diversion and transfer from prison. However, as the report itself acknowledges,
this applies only to a minority of those with mental health care needs.
Accordingly, there is, secondly, a chapter covering the 'care and treatment of
those in need of mental health care who remain in prison'. Third, there is
a chapter describing the range of facilities and provision for the mentally
vulnerable across the prison estate, such as Grendon and Parkhurst C wing.
    Looking first of all at the area of diversion and transfer from prison, the
principle is clearly set out in the Review: 'mentally disordered offenders need-
ing care and treatment should receive it from the health and personal social
services rather than in custodial care'. This is presented as merely a restate-
ment of existing government policy as contained in the White Paper *Custody,
Care and Justice* and Home Office Circular 66/90 – the White Paper, for

example, asserts that 'prison is not a suitable place for people suffering from mental disturbance' – and, indeed, as stated by Stephen Dorrell in his speech quoted above.

There is, though, a critical and significant ambiguity here that was touched on by several interviewees. John Reed, for example, stated in interview that there was no disagreement that the policy should be that 'people who needed care in hospital should have care in hospital and not in prisons'. Another interviewee, David Hillier from the Prison Health Care Service, noted though that this is rather different from the broader kind of statement that prison is an 'unsuitable' environment, as expressed in the White Paper. The consensus that Reed alludes to is in this sense somewhat illusory, as it is based on eliding the difference between these two quite different positions.

Exploring this a little further, the wider interpretation – that is, the notion that prison is an inappropriate environment for individuals suffering from mental disorder – has a distinctly moral and expressive character. The language of 'suitability' and 'appropriateness' is intrinsically based in values and sensibilities. It serves as a reminder that penal practices and institutions are grounded in cultural values and sensibilities. The idea of the 'sick' or vulnerable being confined in penal institutions, particularly individuals who may to some degree be considered not completely responsible for their behaviour, evokes powerful responses which go to the heart of questions about the exercise of the power to punish in civilised societies (Pratt, 1999). The wider interpretation of policy thus resonates with a very long history of commentaries by prison reformers deprecating the presence of the mentally disordered in prison, from John Howard in the eighteenth century to the five campaigning charities that wrote to the Home Secretary in July 1990:

> As Directors of national organizations in the fields of prisons and mental health, we have become increasingly concerned about the presence in our prisons of large numbers of mentally vulnerable individuals.

The narrower interpretation – that individuals who are eligible for in-patient hospital care under the criteria of the mental health legislation should not be in prison – lies closer to the actual policy position set out in the Review. In three key respects, it links closely with 'advanced liberalism' as a governmental rationality. First, it implies a restricted role for governing authorities: intervention is only in the more serious cases and only for individuals suffering from conditions deemed 'treatable'. As discussed in the previous chapter, 'treatability' is a critical concept in the application of 'dividing practices' in this area – for psychopathic disorder, many of the sections in the Mental Health Act 1983 can be invoked only if treatment is 'likely to alleviate or prevent the deterioration of' the condition (see Peay, 2002:753–4). As also noted in that chapter, the practice of 'diagnostic shift' (Coid, 1988) away from mental illness and to untreatable personality disorder thus provides a means of managing and limiting transfers through this legal criterion of 'treat-ability'. One of the drivers for refusing transfers can be a concern about potential 'difficult' behaviour that might be inappropriate or undesirable in the setting of NHS facilities (Coid, 1988; Dell et al, 1991, 1993). Burney and Pearson (1995:307) make the astute observation that it is the perceived unpredictability of the behaviour of some 'disturbed' individuals that can reduce the likelihood that they will be dealt with in a 'confident way'. This might be seen as an example of the neo-liberal tendency described by Richard Ericson (2005:669) as the 'criminalisation of uncertainty', whereby in the face of limited knowledge about threats the preferred response is often more intensive criminalisation. Hence, those individuals who may perhaps turn out to be behaviourally difficult and hard to manage within NHS facilities are more likely to be diagnosed as 'untreatable' and consequently detained in prison (see also Eastman, 1993:13).

Second, it suggests a related and renewed demand for individuals to be responsible for themselves ('responsibilisation') – governmental authorities intervene only in cases where individual prisoners are quite clearly unable to exercise personal responsibility as a result of severe mental illness (see Garland, 2001:124–7). The concept of responsibility is arguably as central to 'dividing practices' as that of treatability, as Colin Allen noted in interview:

> Always in my understanding contingent on somebody being in prison, whether on remand or sentence, is an inference that they're responsible for their behaviour or at least there's an assumption that they're respon-sible for their behaviour until it's proven that they're not. The truth is that in prison custody there are many people who are observedly not responsible for their behaviour and yet the Prison Service has responsibility for them.

As Longford has observed, this raises considerable difficulties:

> If we say that those responsible for the crime should be punished, but that those who are mentally sick should be treated as patients, where do we draw the line?
>
> (Longford, 1992:88)

Third, the position links also to significant questions about resources. Resources are, of course, critical to the neo-liberal governmental project, in relation to its goal of 'rolling back the state' and cutting back public spend-ing. As Virginia Bottomley noted in interview, from her perspective as a former Health Minister:

> On the Reed side, one problem emerged that the Home Office clearly saw the opportunity of cost-shunting. So as Health said these are patients

with health needs so a huge bill emerged and various judges took it upon themselves to demand that I appear in their court to say why I hadn't found a bed. [. . .] I [. . .] very much took the view that such prisoners should be treated as patients. But I would have felt very grateful if the Home Office had felt able to redistribute resources.

Professor Jeremy Coid made a similar observation in interview about this inter-departmental dimension:

The other thing always to be *totally* aware of is there's a *game* that goes on between the Home Office and the Department of Health about these services. And unless one is fully aware of that [. . .] you know that yes yes [. . .] the severely mentally ill should be managed in hospital and not prison, until it comes to the bill whereupon the Department of Health doesn't want to pay it.

In the same vein, Nigel Shackleford from the Home Office Mental Health Unit stated in interview:

There is a great deal of defending boundaries between the Prison Service and the psychiatric services as to where the responsibility should lie and it's driven by resource considerations ultimately [. . .] That's what the prison transfer issue is really all about.

The 'dividing practices' associated with the 'prison transfer issue' in the early 1990s are thus a complex mix of elements revolving around concepts of treatability and responsibility but also underpinned by questions of resources. To characterise these 'practices' solely or even primarily in terms of being about dividing the 'mad' from the 'bad' is a considerable over-simplification, and arguably a misrepresentation, of their actual nature. The 'mad'–'bad' dichotomy can sometimes be a useful shorthand but risks a significant loss of analytical precision.

The ambiguity or the space between these two interpretations was mobilised in quite a significant way. Placing such a strong emphasis on diversion and transfer acknowledged and drew on the powerful cultural uneasiness about imprisoning offenders who are mentally disturbed. Indeed, in the early 1990s it was possible to point to a dramatic and real increase in the number of transfers out of prison in the context of a stable prison population at this time (see Table 4.2). Hence, the Woolf and Reed Review reports were generally perceived to be (relatively) progressive and humanitarian. Yet, at the same time, diversion and transfer actually affected only a very small proportion of the mentally disordered in prison and, as discussed above, the strategy was entirely compatible with neo-liberal governmental rationalities.

Table 4.2 Transfers to hospital under the Mental Health Act 1983 from Prison Service establishments and annual average prison population in England and Wales 1990–1993

Category	1990	1991	1992	1993
Transfers of sentenced prisoners	145	182	227	284
Transfers of remand prisoners	180	264	378	483
Total transfers	*325*	*446*	*605*	*767*
Annual average prison population in England and Wales	44,975	44,809	44,719	44,552

John Reed in interview nicely illustrated that the actual situation in practice was even messier and more ambiguous:

> There's an argument as to whether all people with psychotic illness shouldn't be in prison. On the other hand all people with psychotic illness aren't in hospital in you know most of them as you know are in the community. So there's a big discussion to be had about whether prison is equivalent to the community. One aspect of that is how good is mental health care in prisons. How good is health care in prisons? Are all [. . .] psychotic patients who appear to be in prison known to the prison health care service? My guess is that quite a number of them aren't, that they're out on the wings being quietly mad. Some of [. . .] the ones who are not quietly mad may well be [. . .] in segregation units or even in the close supervision system.

In other words, it is not just that the large number of mentally disordered prisoners who do not meet the legislative criteria for transfer have to remain in prison, but also that many psychotic prisoners have to stay there too (see Coid, 1988; Dell et al, 1991, 1993). Historically, earlier efforts to clear out the mentally disturbed had foundered too. As described in Chapter 2, attempts at the beginning of the twentieth century to remove from prisons a range of categories of prisoners – including the 'feeble-minded', inebriates and the 'mentally defective' – and place them in specialist institutions had a limited impact in practice on the nature of the prison population. This raises the question of why the 'problem' did not appear to be readily susceptible to this kind of solution, an issue that will be returned to in later chapters.

Related to the issue of transfers, and especially to the effectiveness of strategies to increase them, is the wider question of the appropriate configuration of general and forensic psychiatric services. A detailed review article by Eastman (1993) sets out the debate in the early 1990s about service configurations. Within the Reed Review, the Hospital Advisory Group also considered this issue at some length. It discusses the roles of the Special Hospital system, medium secure provision and other secure provision, making it clear that the crux of the matter for the Review is the relative balance of services at different levels of security. As John Reed noted in interview, the critical 'management' challenge is:

> To resolve the central issue of the maldistribution of the availability of inpatient beds. If there are sort of 1500 high security beds, yet we know that only half that number are needed and that half the patients could be in long-term medium or low-security. We know that of the patients in medium security somewhere around half need long-term low security [. . .] But it's taken I think an awful long time to resolve that which is an absolutely crucial issue of how do you get the available resources properly matching the needs of patients.

The 'problem' is thus conceived as how to get mentally disordered offenders into provision at the appropriate level of security: neither too low (which would be poor risk management) nor too high (which would be poor resource management). The 'needs of patients', as Reed articulates them, might be more accurately described as security requirements. The 'vision' of the problem of the configuration of services is thus clearly strongly shaped by a neo-liberal 'way of thinking'. The prison system, within this framework, becomes the default location for those individuals who cannot be appropriately placed within the available psychiatric provision. In this view, the prison 'problem' cannot be resolved without reference to these wider issues about the configuration of psychiatric services.

The second strand in the Reed Review's Prison Advisory Group report, covering the 'care and treatment of those in need of mental health care who remain in prison' (Reed, 1993:231), recognises in part the limited impact of diversion and transfer. It sets out two underpinning 'principles':

- The right of all prisoners to have access, whilst in prison, to high quality mental health care comparable, as far as is practical, with that available in the community [. . .] and
- The importance of continuity of care and therefore of ensuring strong links with the services and agencies providing care outside of prisons.

(Reed, 1993:232)

The idea of 'comparable' health care would resurface later in the notion of 'equivalence' and this will be discussed further in Chapters 5 and 6. It was also enshrined in the terms of reference for the Health Advisory Committee for the Prison Service, which had been set up in January 1992 following a recommendation in the *Efficiency Scrutiny*. In brief, 'comparable' care implies some degree of equivalence of status between prisoners and non-prisoners in terms of the rights associated with citizenship. There is an affinity here with the neo-liberal notion of the rational choice actor and its connection with what Garland (1996, 2001) has described as a 'criminology of the self'. In turn, there is also a link between ideas of equality and rational choice and the new prominence of risk thinking and risk management at this time (see O'Malley, 2004:135–54).

In substantive terms, this strand of the report covers three principal areas: standards of care; reception health screening; and value for money. The idea of developing minimum standards had been recommended in the Woolf report and was committed to in the *Custody, Care and Justice* White Paper. Health Care Standards were eventually issued in 1994 and will be discussed in more detail in the next chapter. Their significance here is that they were in essence the mechanism or means through which the 'comparable' health care described above was to be achieved. The second area, reception health screening, reflects the pragmatic focus on improving the efficiency and effectiveness of the management of prisoners with mental health care needs. Clearly, the safe containment of vulnerable or disturbed prisoners is much easier to achieve if they are effectively identified at reception into prison. The third area, value for money, picks up the agenda set out by the 1990 *Efficiency Scrutiny* and 1987 Working Group reports discussed in the previous chapter. This is the most obvious and explicit example of the centrality of managerialism within the Reed Review. Another example is Annex B in the report of the Prison Advisory Group, from which the following is extracted:

Output measurement can best be established within the framework of a management plan with the following components:–

(i)   A statement of the responsibilities of the organisation.

(ii)   The 'Mission' – a statement of the cultural values of the organisation.

(iii)   Aims – where are we trying to go from here?

(iv)   Functions – the procedural structure of the organisation.

(v)   Organisation – the relationship between the human resources in the organisation.

(vi)   Legislation – the legal authorities within which the organisation works.

(vii)   SWOT – the organisation's strengths, weaknesses, opportunities and the threats it faces.

(viii) Finances – the financial boundaries within which the organisation works.

(ix)   Performance Measurement – the setting of aims and objectives for individuals and the organisation.

In interview, John Reed also stressed the importance of administrative arrangements:

> What you need in order to improve healthcare in prisons – you may need more money I don't know – you certainly need a system where health has parity of importance with security and other prison issues. Now I don't think you'll ever achieve that with health being the responsibility of the Home Secretary. I mean it's not his thing. So these are the sorts of changes that we've got to look for. I mean you could always use more money but you use more money badly if you don't have the proper administrative structure. And certainly I think that one of the most important things we can do is to move to a system where health ministers are responsible for health and prison ministers are responsible for other issues.

This illustrates how firmly neo-liberalism is embedded in the 'progressive' Reed agenda. Central concerns in the Review relate to questions of efficiency, effective management and value for money. Reed himself, in the quotation above, identifies administrative structures as critical. Strikingly, in the reference to using money 'badly', he shifts the moral ground in this field away from its more usual position and towards the need to prevent the misuse or inefficient use of public funds. Ironically, some have argued that it is on precisely these issues of finances that the Review is weakest. Grounds (1994:186), for example, suggests that it is 'less resolute and convincing in considering the financing of their proposals and the feasibility of achieving their recommendations'. He argues that the funding arrangements recommended in the report of the Finance Advisory Group are inadequate for the full implementation of the Review's recommendations. The concern then in the Review with issues relating to 'value for money' is part of a neo-liberal shift towards an 'economic' style of reasoning, but is not necessarily always that closely connected with actual economic or financial matters. As Garland (2001:190) puts it:

> The economic rationality is, above all, a language for doing and representing. It has been superimposed upon practices that sometimes seem [. . .] quite removed from economic considerations.

This is not to argue that it is purely rhetorical or merely a linguistic turn. As noted in the previous chapter, political rhetoric and official representations can have a 'symbolic significance and a practical efficacy that have real social consequences' (Garland, 2001:22). In other words, an 'economic' style of reasoning is actually of much broader significance than (and indeed is distinct from) a narrow concern with financial matters. Rather, it is a refiguring of the 'ways in which the world is made intelligible and practicable, and domains are constituted [. . .] which are amenable to interventions by administrators, politicians, authorities and experts' (Rose, 1993:289). Thus, Garland (2001:188–92) identifies the shift from a 'social' to an 'economic' style of reasoning as a key dimension of what he terms the new 'culture of control' in late modernity.

The third strand in the Review's Prison Advisory Group report focused on the existing facilities for 'caring for inmates with mental health care needs' (Reed, 1993:235). The report describes these as catering for two principal groups: prisoners requiring supportive care whilst awaiting transfer to hospital; and prisoners who do not meet the legislative criteria for transfer but still have mental health care needs. It observes that there are two kinds of facilities: specialist units and more generic provision. The former include Grendon prison, wards within Glen Parva Youth Offender Centre, the Wormwood Scrubs Hospital Annexe and Parkhurst C Wing. Here, the recommendations are relatively modest. There is support for the commitment to a 'second Grendon' already made in *Custody, Care and Justice* and a recommendation that adequate resources should be provided to staff the Wormwood Scrubs Hospital Annexe. The report recognises, however, that 'examples of special provision are atypical of the services for prisoners with mental health care needs' (Reed, 1993: para 5.25). On this, the report picks up the agenda of the *Efficiency Scrutiny* report and recommends that the 'Prison Service should contract-in a specialist mental health care service' (1993: para 5.30) as a means of enhancing the availability and quality of provision. Again, this is a 'progressive' policy but one that is inflected by a neo-liberal 'way of thinking'. The specific impact in practice of this emphasis on 'contracting in' will be considered in the next chapter.

Another development affecting the general service provided to prisoners with mental health care needs was the renaming of the Prison Medical Service in April 1992 as the Health Care Service for Prisoners. This was a recommendation of the *Efficiency Scrutiny* which, as Sim (2002:301) notes, was intended to signal a new beginning for the much-maligned medical service within the prison system. For some, this change was nothing more than a superficial re-labelling, as the late Chris Tchaikovsky said with some passion in interview:

> The Prison Medical Service, you know, whatever it's called now. I can't bring myself to call it a health care service because there isn't any.

The stated policy intention was that the name change indicated a new focus on the needs of prisoners, on contracting-in health care services and on health promotion (Sim, 2002:301). In the years that immediately followed, it appeared not to have much of an impact on the flow of criticism, notably in a series of reports by the Chief Inspector of Prisons throughout the first half of the 1990s. In this sense, events seemed to bear out Tchaikovsky's view that the change was almost entirely cosmetic. Yet the change was of some significance, as it was indicative of a change in the construction of the penal subject. As Sparks (2001b:171) argues, drawing on the work of Mary Douglas, penal practice is underpinned by specific classifications and representations of offenders, and an understanding of these underlying 'ways of seeing' subjects is of great explanatory importance. This mirrors the abiding Foucauldian concern with exploring the different ways in which individuals are constituted as 'subjects' and how these relate to different forms of knowledge and power. Here, in the idea of a 'health care service for prisoners' and the emphasis on health promotion, is a conception of prisoners as 'adaptive, rational, self-disciplined' (Sim, 2002:315). There is clearly an affinity between this notion of the penal subject and the rational actor associated with neo-liberalism and New Right politics. The Eve Saville Memorial Lecture given by Joe Pilling, then Director General of the Prison Service, a couple of months later on 11 June 1992 has been identified as containing the first reference to 'Back to Basics', which, as will be seen in the next chapter, was to become an ill-fated political venture in the unravelling Major administration. The lecture also provides an explicit statement of this changing constitution of the penal subject:

> With the introduction of the Citizen's Charter, very significant changes are taking place to the whole notion of public services and how they should be managed. The central idea behind the Charter is that of quality of service to the customer [. . .] I believe we have two main customers – the prisoner and members of the public at large.
>
> (Pilling, 1992)

It was noted earlier that the Woolf report largely ignored issues of gender and ethnicity. In contrast, the Reed Review explicitly examined both areas. Looking firstly at gender, although the title of Volume 6 of the Review report – *Race, Gender and Equal Opportunities* – suggests a detailed consideration of the issue, in fact only just over seven pages in this volume are specifically devoted to the needs of women. The analysis is fairly thin and some of the content verges on the banal. For example, one of the recommendations is for 'more opportunities for women to meet and share their common experiences'.

An interesting point is the recognition in the report that female offenders may be more likely to be 'perceived' to be 'mad' rather than 'bad', an idea discussed in previous chapters. The study by John Gunn and colleagues (1991) referred to above provides directly comparative data on gender (see Table 4.1). At first sight, the study appears to support this long-standing idea that there is a particularly strong connection for women between offending and mental state, as it found that 56 per cent of sentenced females had a psychiatric diagnosis, compared with 39 per cent of males. Maden (1996:71–7) argues, however, that the broad pattern of diagnoses is actually very similar for sentenced males and females: low levels of psychosis but high levels of personality disorder, neurosis and substance dependence. In fact, he notes, the difference in the 'headline' figures (56 per cent and 39 per cent) is largely accounted for by higher levels of personality disorder, drug dependence and neurosis amongst female prisoners. He goes on to argue further that some of this difference may also be methodological. He reports, for example, that the interviewers felt that the men they interviewed were more likely to deny all symptoms of neurosis (anxiety, depression), particularly as both interviewers were male (1996:115–6). Similar points have been made in relation to victimisation surveys and measures of fear of crime, where it has been suggested that apparent gender differences in fear of crime may be partly explained by many men's reluctance to admit to fear to survey interviewers (Stanko and Hobdell, 1993). Notably, in relation to the most severe mental health problems, the Gunn study found that rates of psychosis were actually slightly *lower* for female prisoners than for males (1.6 per cent compared with 1.9 per cent).

Of even more significance is the extent to which there are differences in the 'dividing practices' aimed at female offenders with mental health problems. The Reed Review notes that in 1989, whilst women accounted for around 4 per cent of the prison population, they made up 20 per cent of the population of the Special Hospitals. A study by Dell and colleagues (1991) of remand prisoners found significantly different outcomes for men and women of psychiatric interventions in the remand process, with psychotic women much more likely to be hospitalised than psychotic men. An earlier study by Hilary Allen (1987) suggested that although women offenders are more likely to receive psychiatric disposals than their male counterparts, the reasons for this are more varied and complex than simple accounts of the over-psychiatrisation of women suggest (see also: Allen, 1986; Frigon, 1995).

The Reed Review's consideration of issues of ethnicity and culture is more substantial. A discussion paper was issued in 1992 and subsequently Volume 6 of the report contained a set of policy recommendations. The core of the problem is diagnosed in the discussion paper:

> The additional problems arising from racism and cultural differences faced by people from ethnic minorities results in many instances in the provision of inappropriate and unacceptable services. Stereotyping often militates against the provision of a service to meet individual need.
>
> (Reed, 1992: para 6.1)

The issue of race and mental health has a controversial history in Western countries, with long-standing attempts made 'to link concepts of madness and race, and to link irrationality with blackness' (Browne, 1996:202; Fernando, 1988). As the discussion paper notes (Reed, 1992: para 6.2), some of the most hotly contested debates have concerned the apparently high rates of schizophrenia amongst African-Caribbean people (Mercer, 1986), a population also disproportionately present in the prison system (Phillips and Bowling, 2002:602–5). Further, 'stereotypes of dangerousness and criminality exacerbate the situation' (Reed, 1992: para 6.7).

Again, comparable data are available from Gunn et al's (1991:43–6) study. This found few clear trends in terms of mental health and race. The prevalence of psychosis among black sentenced males was higher than for their white counterparts, but the difference was not statistically significant. On the other hand, black male inmates were less likely to have substance abuse problems or personality disorders.

In terms of 'dividing practices', in the early 1990s, there was some emerging research evidence. Browne (1991), for example, found that black defendants deemed to be mentally disordered were more likely to receive custodial remands than white defendants and that they were also more likely to be detained for longer periods in prison whilst on remand. Other studies have suggested that there are differential patterns of processing through the penal and psychiatric systems (for example: Cope and Ndegwa, 1990). Browne (1996:203) suggests that these 'dividing practices' are connected with constructions of black people, and especially young men, as having an 'increased propensity to dangerousness'. This, he suggests, opens up a 'series of possibilities [. . .] most of which are disadvantageous to black people – (over)medication, increased surveillance, greater restraint, increased security and so forth'. In the context of an increasing strategic focus on the management of risk at this time, there is a potential for an expansion of the surveillance and control of black people. There is ample evidence that this will often be to their detriment, whether it occurs in the prison system (Genders and Player, 1989; Clements, 2000) or the secure psychiatric system (Prins et al, 1993). In this sense, the emphasis during the early 1990s on diversion and transfer, typically viewed as a humane and progressive development, has a rather different and less positive look for black people, who may suffer similarly repressive and discriminatory treatment in both the psychiatric and prison systems (Browne, 1996; Burney and Pearson, 1995).

To summarise, the Reed Review was a major undertaking, clearly based on a set of explicitly 'progressive' principles – a 'commendable set of aspirations' (Grounds, 1994:185) – and which produced a large number of recommendations. It was seen by many as setting out a blueprint for a new and more 'humanitarian' approach to mentally disordered offenders. However, like the Woolf report, it did not represent a wholesale paradigm shift. The neo-liberalism of the 1980s remained a core strand within the Review, in terms not only of its style and language but also of its deployment of particular governmental technologies and indeed its vision of the 'problem' to be solved.

3. CONCLUSIONS

The conventional narrative for penal affairs in the early 1990s is that in response to the 'drastic' disturbances in Strangeways and other prisons in April 1990, the report of the Woolf Inquiry ushered in a period of 'progressive' penal reform. In the field of 'mentally disordered offenders', the Reed Review followed the reformist Woolf agenda, as did a range of other policy documents and initiatives, including Home Office Circular 66/90 and the Chief Inspector of Prisons report on suicide and self-injury. In support of this narrative, as outlined in this chapter, there is considerable evidence to suggest that there was indeed a major strategic shift during this period. The dramatic increase in transfers to hospital from prison – from 325 in 1990 to 767 in 1993 (see Table 4.2) – was perhaps the clearest example of a real impact of this shift in practice. On the face of it, then, it appears to be the case that in the early 1990s, what went for penal policy in general also applied to mentally disordered offenders.

However, the analysis in this chapter suggests that a more nuanced interpretation is necessary. First, the Woolf report itself and its political mobilisation involved a more mixed amalgamation of elements. It was certainly progressive in its emphasis on justice, overcrowding and the quality of regimes, but at the same time strongly neo-liberal in its managerialist language and orientation towards safe containment as the fundamental task of the prison system. Equally, a more punitive side was also observable in some of the political articulation of the 'new' agenda. The general trend in penal policy was therefore not as coherent or singular as the conventional account suggests. Second, and partly related to this, strategies for mentally disordered offenders, as outlined in the Reed Review reports and associated documents, were also more diverse than might be supposed: progressive in their underlying concern with the quality of care and the importance of community-based interventions, but also deeply neo-liberal in vocabulary and 'ways of thinking'. Notably, the central focus within the Woolf/Reed agenda on diversion and transfer of mentally disordered offenders from prison constituted a set of 'dividing practices' with a very restricted and narrow target group.

This more complex picture raises some significant questions. It was suggested at the beginning of this chapter that in the early 1990s the penal 'crisis' was closely connected with a broader political 'crisis'. In one sense, there is nothing new in this, as penal politics are always englobed by larger movements in the political arena (Sparks, 2001a:196). Yet usually when reference is made to the 'politicisation' of penal issues, this is in the context of appeals to 'penal populism': that is, to the harsher and more punitive side of penal politics. So what exactly was the relationship between the Woolf/Reed agenda and the political order at the start of the 1990s? Some useful theoretical pointers can be found in an article by Richard Sparks in which he explores the 'question of *how* the penal realm intersects with the cultural and the political' (2001b:162, emphasis in original). Drawing on Mary Douglas' work, especially *Risk and Blame* (Douglas, 1992), he argues that 'moments of intense controversy or recrimination [. . .] crystallize societal anxieties and expose lines of division about the competence, trustworthiness and legitimacy of authorities' (Sparks, 2001b:168). It was suggested earlier in this chapter that the 'anxieties' and 'lines of division' at the start of the 1990s were related partly to the perceived failures (economic and political) and excessive 'harshness' of the Thatcher administration of the 1980s. The analysis in this chapter can therefore be framed and understood within this context. In other words, the responses to the disturbances at Strangeways and other prisons took the particular forms they did because of the specific societal anxieties in the early 1990s.

Developing this line of argument, the 'progressive' components of the Woolf/Reed agenda clearly helped to address the anxieties about the harshness of Thatcherite social policy. The first years of the Major government sought to some extent to offer a more consensual and less divisive approach. Serious but humanitarian action to tackle the prison 'crisis' and the problem of mentally disordered prisoners obviously resonated well against this political backdrop. At the same time, the events at Strangeways (and not least their nightly presence on television screens across the country), coupled with dramatic episodes like the 'poll tax' riots, posed a high-profile and core challenge to the authority, legitimacy and sovereignty of government. Its ability to maintain basic order, perhaps the most fundamental governmental power claim, was in question. This drew out some more archaic and purely punitive responses, notably in the speeches made by the Home Secretary, Kenneth Baker, in the months following the publication of the Woolf Report (see Sim, 1994a). Alongside this, the broader and deeper social, economic and political transformations – the coming of 'late modernity' – that had driven the rise to prominence in the 1980s of neo-liberalism and the New Right were also still unfolding. Hence, the Woolf report and particularly the Reed Review report were shot through with neo-liberal rationalities, managerial language and concerns with the administration of risk. Indeed, here there was considerable continuity with penal strategies during the 1980s which, as discussed in the previous chapter, had a distinctly neo-liberal character. Arguments about the most efficient use of government resources were also central, notably in the Reed Review. This not only reflected the neo-liberal concern with value for money and 'rolling back the state' but also, at a more political level, resonated with attempts at the time to address a perceived lack of competence in running the national economy and public finances.

Thus the particular formation of penality and of 'dividing practices' aimed at mentally disordered offenders in the early 1990s is a hybrid one, 'instrumental *and* rhetorical, archaic sometimes *and* advanced, culturally embedded *and* politically tactical, political speech acts *and* institutional logics' (Sparks, 2001b:169). The specific make-up of this hybrid formation reflects and responds to the social conflicts and anxieties about government that existed at this time.

Such a focus on particularities and specificities may be taken as a privileging of the contingent and the 'political' within the explanatory account. Indeed, it might be viewed as mistaking the merely political and short-term events for longer-term and more structural trends. Yet it is of course both dimensions that need to be explained and especially the relationship between the two. Penal policy and practice cannot simply be read off from abstract political rationalities. Whilst they are shaped and framed by these more structural developments, they are the result of specific contingent circumstances as they unfold in particular political and cultural contexts (see also: Downes, 1988:56; Garland, 1990a:128). As Sparks (2001b:170) puts it, particular penal developments can be best understood as a hybridisation 'between the calculative and the representational [. . .] [and] it is this mingling that links the longer-term development of an infrastructure of penal technique and the episodic uses of punishment as a political tactic'. This view of the matter is similar to Pat O'Malley's (1999) when he argues that the apparently contradictory forces of neo-liberalism and neo-conservatism are both aspects of New Right politics. Hence attempts to prise apart or bracket off the 'political' from the 'technical' are misconceived. In more recent work, he has adopted the idea of the *assemblage* or *configuration* to describe these kinds of hybrid forms of governmental technologies (O'Malley, 2004:24).

In the next chapter, which covers the middle of the decade (from mid-1993 to mid-1997), general penal policy appeared to take a dramatic punitive turn under a new Home Secretary, Michael Howard. His 'Prison Works' campaign and call for prisons to be 'decent but austere' were accompanied by a rapid expansion of the prison population. The 'progressive' penal moment described in the present chapter seemed to be quickly and almost entirely eclipsed by a revival of a pre-modern penal strategy. Chapter 5 attempts to understand why this major change occurred and explores whether and how this affected the 'dividing practices' aimed at mentally disordered offenders and especially prisoners.

Chapter 5

Penal populism and austere institutions, 1993–1997

This chapter examines the period from 1993 to 1997, a period which is often viewed as witnessing a resurgence of a punitive pre-modern penal policy. The aim of this chapter is to analyse how this apparent revival of pre-modern penal policy affected strategies in the field of mental health, crime and punishment. Specifically, the analytical focus is on the impact on the 'dividing practices' applied to mentally disordered offenders, with a particular emphasis on the prison situation. In investigating this, the first section of this chapter briefly sets out some of the wider social, political and penal context at this time which made this punitive turn possible. The second and main section analyses in detail the contours of penal strategies in this area. The final section pulls out some of the central themes raised by the analysis.

1. CONTEXT: 'BACK TO BASICS'

As noted at the beginning of Chapter 4, in the early 1990s the 'Thatcher' project, designed in part to respond to the new landscape of late modern society, appeared to have lost direction and momentum. In the first few years of the decade, there was a self-conscious political attempt by the Major administration to re-configure and re-present the project. The Woolf/Reed 'humanitarian' penal agenda discussed in the previous chapter can be partly understood in that political context. By the mid-1990s, however, this political move seemed to be unravelling. Despite winning the 1992 general election, John Major's government was deeply unpopular. Britain was struggling to pull itself out of a long and deep recession and the high unemployment of the early 1980s had returned (Sked and Cook, 1993:553–6). 'Black Wednesday', 16 September 1992, when Britain was humiliatingly forced out of the European Exchange Rate Mechanism, came to symbolise the administration's reputation for economic mismanagement and political incompetence. The murder of two year old Jamie Bulger by two ten year old boys in Liverpool in February 1993 prompted further public and media angst about the apparent breakdown of morality and authority in British society. Against this backdrop,

John Major launched his ill-fated 'back to basics' campaign in 1993 with the idea of restoring some basic conservative 'common sense' to government policy, a campaign foreshadowed, as has already been noted, by Joe Pilling's speech about the Prison Service in 1992. This rapidly collapsed amidst a catalogue of 'moral misdemeanours' by Conservative politicians and ministers, further damaging the administration and leaving an impression of a 'sleazy', undisciplined and inept government. The year 1993 was clearly a pivotal one in political terms, and John Gray (1997) has identified it as marking the beginning of the 'endgame' for the New Right in Britain.

Central to the idea of getting 'back to basics' was a renewed emphasis on the moralising themes within neo-conservatism (Downes and Morgan, 1997:111–12) and this became a key influence on penal policy. It is well documented that 1993 saw the start of a striking reversal of the apparently 'progressive' moment in the first couple of years of the decade discussed in the previous chapter. In an infamous speech to the Conservative Party conference in October 1993, the Home Secretary, Michael Howard, announced that 'prison works' and that, if required to protect the public, he did not 'flinch' from increasing the prison population. True to his word, the latter was to rise with astonishing rapidity over the next few years (see Table 5.1). A 'leaked' memo from Howard two months before his 'prison works' speech revealed that he believed that some prison regimes were insufficiently 'austere' (*Observer*, 22 August). Penal rhetoric and strategy over the next three or four years came to be characterised and driven by what Bottoms (1995) has called 'populist punitiveness'.

Clearly, the political conditions for a populist and moralistic punitive turn in criminal justice policy were firmly in place in the mid-1990s. This will be explored further in this chapter, but, in brief, there are two broad arguments here. First, there is a long tradition within social and political theory which has argued that 'harsh' penal rhetoric and policy is particularly common during periods of economic recession and when governments 'confront crises of popular support and legitimacy' (Sparks, 1996:74; Habermas, 1976; Box, 1987; Melossi, 1993; Sparks, 1994, 2003). Downes and Morgan (2002:297) argue further that at a political level the Labour opposition in the mid-1990s

Table 5.1 Annual average prison population in England and Wales 1993–1997

Year	Average prison population	Percentage rise over previous year	Percentage rise over 1993 baseline
1993	44,552	0%	–
1994	48,621	9%	9%
1995	50,962	5%	14%
1996	55,281	8%	24%
1997	61,114	11%	37%

helped to lock the 'law and order' debate in this period within a populist and punitive framework. The second argument, set out in an influential article by David Garland (1996), is that late modern nation states face a major challenge to their legitimacy as high crime rates have become endemic. One of the responses to this challenge, he suggests, and which he characterises as a form of 'denial', is to reassert sovereign power through a display of 'punitive force'. Both of these arguments will be revisited later in this chapter.

2. HOWARD'S WAY: PENAL POPULISM?

In the wake of the voluminous Reed Review, most of which was published in 1992 and 1993, policy activity directly in this field was more limited in the mid-1990s. On the wider penal plane, however, this period saw some major and highly significant developments. A key issue for examination in this chapter, therefore, is the extent to which the field of 'mentally disordered offenders' 'followed' these wider penal shifts. What follows is divided into three main subsections: first, the rise or revival of 'penal populism' encapsulated in the 'prison works' slogan; second, developments in the status and management of the Prison Service and prison health care provision; and third, initiatives apparently based on more 'welfarist' approaches.

'Prison works'

As has already been alluded to at the beginning of this chapter, Michael Howard's 'prison works' speech in October 1993 abruptly and completely shattered any illusion that the 'progressive' penal policy agenda set in train by Woolf would be sustained. This ushered in a period in which there was a strong emphasis on 'penal populism', as evidenced by the steeply rising prison population (see Table 5.1) and the 'toughening' of penal rhetoric.

A series of prison escapes and security breaches in 1994 and 1995 proved particularly politically embarrassing, given this self-consciously 'tough' penal approach. In September 1994, six prisoners managed to escape from the 'escape-proof' Special Security Unit in Whitemoor prison. Scarcely had the inevitable inquiry reported back in December (Woodcock, 1994) than further embarrassments occurred. There were disturbances in Everthorpe prison on 2 and 3 January 1995. On the second day of the Everthorpe events, three prisoners escaped from Parkhurst prison and went on the run for six days before being recaptured. A broader investigation into prison security, led by General Sir John Learmont, had already been announced in December in response to the Woodcock report on Whitemoor; this was then extended to cover the Parkhurst escapes. The report was published in October 1995 (Learmont, 1995) and prompted Howard to sack the Director General of the Prison Service, Derek Lewis. Taken together, the Learmont and Woodcock reports served to alter the priorities of the Prison Service significantly, with security moved to the top of the agenda (Resodihardjo, 2004:16).

How did this wider political and penal context shape the government of prisoners with mental health problems? This is a complex question to answer. The conventional argument is reasonably straightforward and was pithily summarised by Professor John Gunn in interview:

> So you've got rising numbers of prisoners, decreasing budgets and therefore decreasing services and it had a profound effect on it [. . .] It struck me at the time as totally incredible.

Interestingly, the causal logic of this argument was broadly accepted by Michael Howard in interview, although he was unsurprisingly much more circumspect in his assessment of the magnitude of this impact:

> Now um for the most part I think the Prison Service was able to cope with that increase pretty well. In most prisons there wasn't overcrowding. In most prisons it didn't make any significant difference to the extent to which they were able to provide both education and health care [. . .] I don't think I could put my hand on my heart and say it didn't lead to *any* problems. Um there were places um where the numbers really were up against their limits and no doubt it was more difficult for the staff to do the things which in an ideal world should have been done whether in the mental health field or other fields. I mean I would have to accept that but we built more prisons we opened more prisons so we did increase capacity as the population was going up. But there were some prisons where there were strains and stresses as a result of the increase in the population. I would accept that.

In interview, David Hillier from the Prison Health Care Directorate provided a concrete example of this kind of impact on the system. He noted that a Task Force chaired by Rosemary Wool (then Director of the Prison Health Care Service) was set up in early 1994 to consider the need for a 'second Grendon' (although this had, in fact, been publicly committed to by a previous Home Secretary, Kenneth Baker, in 1991, following a recommendation in the Woolf report). The Task Force report, completed in August 1994, confirmed the need for a new establishment of this kind but was not published, and this recommendation was not implemented. (As will be seen in the next chapter, the 'second Grendon' eventually opened in 2001.) According to Hillier, the required planning was effectively derailed by the rise in the prison population at this time.

Derek Lewis, Director General of the Prison Service between 1993 and 1995, gave a more striking and graphic example in his book about his time with the Prison Service:

One evening late in 1994, the telephone rang at home and I was told about a murder in my local prison at Chelmsford. Two prisoners, both mentally disturbed, had been locked in the same cell as a result of overcrowding and one had brutally murdered the other.

(Lewis, 1997:58)

Yet this kind of impact is clearly more of an unintended by-product of policy rather than evidence of a real shift in ways of thinking or acting on the mentally disturbed in prison. Indeed, in interview Professor Jeremy Coid directly questioned the significance of prison expansion:

I'm not sure whether it's [the rising prison population] been a real impact. I actually think what was more important was in about 93 94 [. . .] the hospital system was full [. . .] I actually think what happened was that [. . .] diversion did take place very successfully in about 92 93. The Home Office was involved um and the Prison Medical Service had a concerted move to divert patients.

Nigel Shackleford from the Home Office Mental Health Unit gave a similar account in interview:

I think what is interesting is that there was a dramatic rise [in prison transfers] between 88 and 94, the total reached 750 and there it has stayed ever since [because of a] lack of beds [. . .] There's no doubt at all from our perspective that the level of transfers has stopped where it is because there are not more beds [. . .] It's not apparent from our perspective that the increase in prison population has affected our work at all. You would expect I think a commensurate increase in prison transfers but that hasn't happened.

Table 5.2 illustrates this stability in the number of transfers during this period

Table 5.2 Transfers to hospital under the Mental Health Act 1983 from Prison Service establishments and annual average prison population in England and Wales 1993–1997

	1993	*1994*	*1995*	*1996*	*1997*
Transfers of sentenced prisoners	284	249	250	265	251
Transfers of remand prisoners	483	536	473	481	495
Total transfers	767	785	723	746	746
Annual average prison population in England and Wales	44,552	48,621	50,962	55,281	61,114

and the absence of a direct relationship with changes in the size of the prison population.

In the accounts offered by Shackleford and Coid, it is actually the levels of investment in health care in the community that are of greater significance than the increase in the prison population. As Wall et al (1999) note, there were 43,000 fewer psychiatric hospital beds in 1992 compared with the number in 1982, so inevitably capacity to increase prison transfers was finite and limited. This might be read as an example of the neo-liberal tendency towards 'hollowing out the state'. Yet there is a paradox here, as Hudson (1998) notes, in that the 'hollowing out of the state' does not inhibit the massive expansion of the prison estate during this period. In this sense, it could be argued that at this time it is more accurate to talk in terms of a redistribution of resources rather than a 'hollowing out' of the state.

As well as the quantitative impact on the prison population, the strategy of 'penal populism' was, of course, a rhetorical one. As has already been argued in the previous two chapters, this does not meant that it was just 'talk' (Garland, 2001:22). Sim has argued, for example, that Michael Howard's references to the need for more 'austere' regimes fundamentally undermined health care within prisons:

> Prisons cannot by definition be healthy places because of the continuing emphasis on making life difficult and uncomfortable for prisoners [. . .] A culture of power still based on the principles of less eligibility [. . .] undermines any move towards a more humane or benevolent delivery of health provision.
>
> (Sim, 1994b:33)

In a related vein, Andrew Coyle, Governor at Brixton prison in the early 1990s, suggested in interview that the rhetoric of 'austerity' gave a 'green light' to those prison staff who wanted to treat prisoners badly.

The prioritisation of security that followed the Woodcock and Learmont reports also placed an additional pressure on health and welfare provision within prisons. As Rosemary Wool, Director of Prison Health Care, observed in a conference speech in September 1995:

> Security has assumed the highest priority. Security is expensive. It costs a lot to strengthen walls and put in geophones and X-rays, and for more dogs. It's also very time consuming. Increasing the amount of searches on inmates and visitors, property and cells, takes a lot of officer time. It thereby threatens the rehabilitative approach.
>
> (Wool, 1996:32)

These three features of the Howard 'regime' – rising prison population, 'tough' penal rhetoric and prioritisation of security – thus had uneven impacts on the mentally disordered. Sparks (1996) has characterised the shift under Howard as a re-emergence of the Victorian doctrine of less eligibility (although, of course, the idea was never entirely displaced within penal-welfarism: Mannheim, 1939; Garland, 1985:258–60). This highlights some further important points about this uneven impact. The concept of less eligibility was built on the liberal notion of individuals as responsible subjects with free will. Correspondingly, the neo-liberal penal subject of the mid-1990s was centred on the attribution of individual responsibility for behaviour. For those with mental health problems, this obviously raises considerable complexities. As discussed in previous chapters, the idea of 'responsibility' is an important element within the 'dividing practices' applied to offenders with mental health problems.

So what was the effect of this repositioning of individual responsibility associated with the revival of less eligibility? The case of offenders with personality disorders is usefully illustrative here. Using figures for 1996 by way of example, Table 5.3 shows how the vast majority of prison transfers are accounted for by those suffering from mental illness rather than personality disorders. Nor does this just apply for 1996. As Wool (1996:32) notes, 'the majority of personality disordered inmates have always remained in the prison system'. There are of course legal impediments to their transfer, as the treatability criterion in the Mental Health Act 1983 applies to psychopathic disorder but not mental illness (see Peay, 2002:753–4). However, this phenomenon, and the way in which the treatability criterion is utilised, is considerably sharpened by the conception of the 'responsible' neo-liberal penal subject. Whilst those diagnosed as mentally ill cannot be readily labelled as 'fully responsible', the position for those with personality disorders is less clear. Consequently, given the need to 'gatekeep' limited psychiatric resources, the treatability criterion in the mental health legislation becomes an important mechanism within 'dividing practices' for channelling some of those diagnosed with personality disorders down a different route. In this regard, it is therefore noteworthy that at a time of expansion of the prison estate, the development of the 'second Grendon' – a facility that would primarily cater for prisoners with personality disorders – was sidelined.

Table 5.3 Transfers to hospital under the Mental Health Act 1983 from Prison Service establishments by type of mental disorder 1996

Category	Mental illness	Psychopathic disorder	Other	Total
Transfers of sentenced prisoners	237	20	8	265
Transfers of remand prisoners	479	0	2	481
Total	716	20	10	746

There are significant gender and race dimensions here too. There is considerable evidence that there are very high levels of personality disorder among women prisoners (Bolger, 1992; Dolan and Mitchell, 1994), although there is debate about whether this situation is different from that for male prisoners (Maden, 1996). Gorsuch's (1998) research on C1, the psychiatric wing of Holloway's health care unit, carried out in late 1994 and early 1995, focused on the process of transfers of the mentally disordered to the NHS. Among the 'difficult to place' women, who struggled to obtain transfer even after referral by prison medical staff, there was a disproportionate number of women diagnosed with personality disorders. Gorsuch argues that the lack of specialist secure provision for women with personality disorders by default shifts the primary location for their containment from the psychiatric to the prison system (see also Wilkins and Coid, 1991). The picture in relation to race and culture is different again. As Coid (1996:11) notes, African Caribbean people are less likely to be detained under the category 'psychopathic disorder' than white people, whilst the reverse is the case for the category of 'mental illness'. He observes that the 'explanation for these contrasts is unclear'.

Agency status and contracting out health care

On 1 April 1993, the Prison Service acquired executive agency status. The Next Steps programme of introducing executive agencies was intended to provide a means for sharpening and improving the management and accountability of a range of operations previously run, in name at least, by government ministers and civil servants (for example, the Benefits Agency and the Passport Office). The appointment of Derek Lewis as the first Director General of the new Prison Service agency, someone from the private sector with no prior prisons experience, underlined the managerialist intent of the change. Lewis himself set out his view of some of the potential benefits of agency status:

> Agency status also brought with it many other management tools that were commonplace in the private sector. The essentials were clarity of roles, operational autonomy, the delegation of decision-making and holding agencies and their chief executives responsible for results.
>
> (Lewis, 1997:64–5)

In slightly more trenchant style, Lewis suggested in a newspaper article in 1996 that:

> Executive agencies [. . .] were not the great leap forward in management thinking that some people imagined. They were a face-saving label to enable the public sector to introduce basic management tools that any private-sector business would have been bankrupt without.
>
> (Lewis, 1996:9)

Foster and Plowden (1996) link Next Steps with the neo-liberal strategy of 'hollowing out of the state', with its focus on achieving better value for money and reductions in public spending in order to avert national 'fiscal crisis'. At a discursive level, Garland (2001) identifies the shift from a 'social' to an 'economic' style of reasoning, of which executive agencies are a good example, as a central characteristic of the new culture of control associated with the strategies for governing crime and social order in late modernity. As he notes (2001:189), the 'chief virtue of new policies [. . .] is their claim to be economically rational alternatives to previous arrangements'. This was precisely the claim of the Next Steps programme.

For the Prison Service Agency, a Director General was to be responsible for directing the operation of the service within a framework of policy and resources set by the Home Secretary (Talbot, 1996). Commentators within the politics and government fields have observed that the way in which agency status worked in practice for the Prison Service between 1993 and 1995 illustrated some key points of tension; these will now be explored (Barker, 1998; Polidano, 1999; Talbot, 1996).

Central to these tensions was the relationship between policy and operations and the implications for the doctrine of ministerial responsibility, which proved particularly problematic and controversial for the Prison Service during its first three years as an executive agency. The spectacular fall out from this was, of course, the sacking of the Director General by the Home Secretary in the autumn of 1995 following the publication of the Learmont report into prison security. Lewis subsequently claimed that he had been wrongfully dismissed; the furore led to an emergency debate in Parliament on 19 October. Detailed accounts of this episode have been given by some of the protagonists (Lewis, 1997) as well as by commentators (Barker, 1998; Polidano, 1999). The House of Commons statement on 19 May 1997 by Ann Widdecombe, Prisons Minister during some of this period, was particularly interesting from a political perspective (see reports of her statement in the *Guardian*, the *Independent*, *The Times* and the *Daily Telegraph* on 20 May 1997). Her central accusation, and the most devastating for Howard, was that he had misled the House of Commons in the debate on 19 October 1995. The crux of the matter concerned the division of responsibilities between Howard and Lewis. The former claimed that his ministerial responsibility was for policy only. As he put it in interview:

> The point about Agency status was to try and get some defined objectives and to try and make the Director-General and his staff responsible for achieving those objectives. But in terms of policy and so on the policy was always still set by the Home Secretary and I think the extent to which Agency status made a difference probably has been exaggerated [. . .] It was Ministers who set policy [. . .] Agency was meant to improve the delivery of that policy.

Lewis (1997:156), on the other hand, describes in his book a very high level of day to day involvement by the Home Secretary in 'operational' matters:

> The flurry of paper between Queen Anne's Gate [location of the Home Office] and the Prison Service had become a blizzard [. . .] Within eighty-three working days, over 1,000 documents went to ministers, including 137 major submissions. The degree of detailed ministerial involvement was greater than most long-serving civil servants could remember in pre-agency days. It was a far cry from the 'much greater autonomy from ministers and the rest of the Home Office' that Ken Clarke [the previous Home Secretary] had publicly promised.

There was particular controversy over whether Howard had threatened to over-rule Lewis's decision not to immediately suspend the governor of Parkhurst prison after the escapes in January 1995. In a famous media interview, Howard refused to answer this question directly despite being asked 12 times (for Lewis's own recollection, see Lewis, 1997:169–70). Talbot (1996) argues that the Framework Document for the Prison Service Executive Agency actually provides for a considerable overlap between policy and operational responsibility for both the Home Secretary and the Director General. Indeed, he describes the idea of operational independence as a 'farce and myth' serving only 'Ministers who wish to take credit for success and have handy scapegoats to blame for failures' (1996:7). Barker (1998:18–19) argues that the importing of a Director General from the private sector, as with Derek Lewis, sharpens further still these debates around ministerial responsibility and the utility of new techniques of public management.

Another way of looking at these tensions as they play out in the penal sphere is in terms of the inherent conflict between the neo-liberal and neo-conservative elements of New Right politics (O'Malley, 1999; Garland, 2001). In an influential article, Pat O'Malley (1999) has argued that the political accommodation of these two contrasting tendencies under the umbrella of the New Right is one of the reasons for the apparently 'volatile and contradictory' character of penal politics and policy in this period. Executive Agencies are intended to be a mechanism for achieving more effective, efficient and transparent management of public services. The imperatives from this perspective may well at times be in conflict with the requirements of an intensely politicised penality drawing on moralistic neo-conservative ideas. Lewis's (1997) account of his time as Director General and his clashes with Michael Howard can be read as an extended illustration of this conflict. To give one example, Lewis (1997:197–8) observed of Howard's 1995 Conservative Party conference speech:

> It was a barn-storming performance, full of populist rhetoric that had the Tory faithful roaring in the aisles. Here was a Home Secretary promising

to do even more to stem the rise in crime [. . .] Howard's political imperative was so overriding that the Prison Service had not been consulted on the implications of these far-reaching penal proposals.

Another even clearer example was the response to the Woodcock report on the events at Whitemoor prison. Lewis (1997:159) recalls that the political exigencies of shoring up a political reputation for 'toughness' on law and order immediately and completely overshadowed any managerialist concerns about cost-effectiveness:

> Howard was keen to accept all sixty-four recommendations in the Woodcock report at once, before anyone had a chance to assess whether they were affordable, let alone good value for money.

There was fairly consistent agreement amongst many of the interviewees that Agency status actually had little direct impact on responses to mentally vulnerable prisoners. However, David Hillier from the Prison Health Care Directorate suggested in interview that Agency status had hindered the coordination of the contracting out of prison psychiatric services, as this was considered an 'operational' rather than a 'policy' issue. In this regard, Bullard (1994:23), writing in 1994, noted that:

> Four years after the publication of the scrutiny of the Prison Medical Service, there are virtually no contracts between the Health Care Service and the NHS to provide psychiatric services.

One of the few examples of contracting-out was the 'Durham cluster' pilot initiated in 1993 and subject to an independent evaluation between 1994 and 1996. The 'cluster' consisted of the three prisons in and around Durham, which contracted two local NHS Trusts to provide a specialist psychiatric service within their establishments. The experience of the pilot was largely positive, although the evaluation found that there were some difficulties in properly establishing multi-disciplinary working and in setting up training for prison staff (Barnes and Robinson, 1996, 1998). In interview, Professor Jeremy Coid, a forensic psychiatrist, suggested that the 'Durham cluster' had been located in one of the more favourable parts of the prison estate, where the prevalence of severe mental illness was likely to have been lower than in busy urban prisons like Pentonville in London.

The broader significance of Agency status was perhaps that it helped to re-open the debate about the most efficient way of organising prison health care. The stated rationale for the Prison Service becoming an Agency was to focus on ensuring that administrative and management systems, structures and processes were improved by injecting some private-sector rigour and 'know-how'. Extending this to prison health care eventually led to careful scrutiny of the case for continuing to manage a prison provision in parallel with the NHS.

This issue had, of course, been considered by the *Efficiency Scrutiny* in 1990 (see Chapter 3), but, as noted above, contracting-out had made little impact. In 1996, the Chief Inspector of Prisons published a discussion document, *Patient or Prisoner?*, which recommended unequivocally that the NHS ought to take on responsibility for health care in prisons:

> It is no longer sensible to maintain a health care service for prisoners separate from the National Health Service. There is an immediate need for the Home Office and the Department of Health, together with the Prison Service and the National Health Service to agree a timetable for the NHS to assume responsibility for the commissioning and provision of health care and health promotion in prisons.
>
> (HM Chief Inspector of Prisons, 1996)

One of the arguments for this recommendation was clearly based on the perceived inefficiencies of the existing state of affairs:

> The National Health Service is a high-quality, cost-effective service [. . .] It is fundamentally unsound for the Prison Service to attempt to replicate [its] functions by operating independently of the NHS. There is no need for two parallel systems and, indeed, serious potential disadvantages from having two systems.
>
> (HM Chief Inspector of Prisons, 1996)

The other arguments made in the document are significant too, as they highlight some important features of the ways in which prisoners with health care needs are 'made up' as subjects in order to be governed:

> Prisoners were members of the wider community before their reception into prison and their health care then was the responsibility of the NHS; the vast majority will return to that community and to the NHS on their release. It is illogical that, during the time that they are prisoners, their health care is provided through separate channels. It is also necessary to recognize the interdependence of health care in prisons and wider health care.
>
> A prisoner's health and health care before offending has impact on what happens in prison, both to the individual prisoner and more widely. A prisoner's health care in prison can, for example, for those with mental disorder or substance abuse, be a major factor in their well-being and chances of reoffending on release. However obvious these statements, they emphasize the interdependence of health care in prisons and in the wider community. Only by the NHS accepting responsibility for health

care in prisons can two essentials – equality and continuity of care – be ensured. (HM Chief Inspector of Prisons, 1996)

These two paragraphs are important in three senses. First, prisoners are conceived, to some degree at least, as 'citizens'. Hence the reference in the second paragraph to ensuring 'equality of care'. Bottoms (1995) has argued that there are connections between late modernity, managerialism and the construction of people as individual citizens rather than as members of intermediate-level social groups (relating to class, family and so on). There is also a connection with the construction of penal subjects as 'rational actors' no different from others (see Garland, 2001). Second, in acknowledging that how prisoners are responded to and treated within prison has an impact on communities and society after their release, the document alludes to the 'public protection' aspect of prison health care. As argued in Chapter 2, this notion of public protection is embedded in the origins of the Prison Medical Service in the late eighteenth century, when the need to prevent the spread of typhus from prison to the community was the principal driver for the 1774 Act which led to the establishment of the Service. Third, the other side of the notion of 'public protection' is that it also constitutes a concern with the administration or management of the risks posed by prison-leavers to the community. The discourse in this report thus looks both forward (prisoners as 'citizens' and/or as sources of 'risk' that need to be managed) and backward (prisoners as a source of 'contagion' for the community). According to O'Malley, this simultaneous 'nostalgia' and 'innovation' within the penal sphere is another symptom of the inherent contradictions within New Right politics (O'Malley, 1999).

It is worth noting here that the *Patient or Prisoner?* report at this stage simply represents the re-opening of the debate. It would be another three years (and under a different government) before any real proposals for change would appear. Indeed, in 1996, the prospects for closer integration of prison health care with the NHS did not seem that great, as a news report at the time in the *British Medical Journal* on the report's publication indicates:

Neither the home secretary, Michael Howard, nor the health secretary, Stephen Dorrell, however, have any political ambition to merge the prison medical service with the NHS [. . .] Labour's spokesman, Chris Smith, also has serious reservations about the NHS providing a prison medical service [. . .] From these initial reactions of the government and its possible successor, the omens for the Ramsbotham report are not promising.

(Wise, 1996)

The response from the Acting Director of Prison Health Care, Dr Mike Longfield, reproduced at the back of the document, was similarly ambivalent:

> The Chief Inspector's discussion paper is a timely and helpful rehearsal of one of the options for change that may be available to the Government in this area [. . .] However, we do not underestimate the difficulties that would arise from attempting to implement the Chief Inspector's suggestion.
>
> (HM Chief Inspector of Prisons, 1996)

The contracting-out of health service provision to the NHS, of course, still involved 'state' or government provision of the service. A more radical neo-liberal development was the contracting-out of certain prison functions to the private sector, a development which gathered pace in the mid-1990s. The aim was to introduce some market competition into the prison system in order to improve efficiency and effectiveness. In 1994, the number of con-tracted-out prisons doubled as Doncaster and Buckley Hall opened in June and December respectively. The impact on health care was initially felt to be negative, with Derek Lewis (1997:92) reporting that Rosemary Wool was expressing concerns about provision in Doncaster as early as August 1994, just two months after the prison had opened. After these initial problems, however, performance appeared to improve. Indeed, in interview, Professor John Gunn described the achievements at Doncaster as 'astounding' and Michael Howard made the following assessment of health care provision:

> I think it was better in the private prisons just as I think to be perfectly honest most things were better [. . .] There was a much greater tendency to think things through from scratch and to come up with the best solu-tion. Whereas in the public sector prison service you get inevitably people tending to do things in a particular way because they've always done them that way. I mean that's a natural feature of an organisation of that kind. Now most of the people in private sector prisons hadn't always done the job in any particular way so they had to think it through from scratch. And in doing so they very often came up with a more efficient and effective way of doing things. And that applied to health care as much as it did to anything else.

Howard nicely captures here the idea of the introduction of 'quasi-markets' being a technique for freeing up organisations to innovate and thereby improve efficiency. As Pat O'Malley (2004:57–76) argues, the idea of entre-preneurialism and the figure of the entrepreneur are central themes within liberalism, in both its classical and its neo-liberal guises. In this view, private-sector managers are 'pioneers of uncertainty' rather than just managers of risk. Hence, O'Malley (2004) argues more broadly that the analysis of neo-liberal forms of government needs to proceed by identifying and examin-ing how configurations or assemblages of risk and uncertainty operate as governmental techniques.

Continuing welfarism

In August 1994, Health Care Standards for prisons were issued. These had 'progressive' roots, having been recommended by Woolf and Reed as a mechanism not only for improving health and welfare provision within prisons but also for levering up the quality of regimes more broadly. Standard 1.2 states that all new receptions should receive a doctor's examination within 24 hours of reception (following an initial screening by a Health Care Worker on the day of reception). In relation to the mental health component of the doctor's examination, it stipulates that:

f)   Examination of the patient's mental health should take account of any known psychiatric history, with particular regards to in-patient admissions, alcohol and substance abuse, and any attempt at self-harm. A present mental state examination should be performed, including assessment of the patient's general appearance and behaviour, thought processes, affect, memory, concentration, orientation, cognitive function, insight and, where applicable, an assessment of the level of dangerousness.

g)   In cases of florid mental illness, particularly of psychotic intensity, the doctor should strive to obtain the patient's transfer to an appropriate hospital setting, under the relevant section of the Mental Health Act 1983.

There is clearly a mixture here of diagnostic examination and risk assessment. Health Care Standard 2 goes on to set out the required level of mental health service provision. It describes the overall objective as to provide 'services for the observation, assessment, treatment and care of prisoners with mental health care needs'. These are split into six areas of activity: accommodation and equipment; integrated care regime; prevention of suicide and self-harm; care of patients exhibiting challenging behaviour; application of the Mental Health Act 1983; out-patient care. Again, these represent a mix of therapeutic and risk management activities. There is a strong emphasis on processes, documentary procedures and record keeping.

The covering letter sent out with the Health Care Standards from Rosemary Wool, Director of the Prison Health Care Service, makes it clear that the Standards are infused with managerialist thinking:

It is hoped that the Standards will assist you discharge your responsibility for the delivery of health care within the establishment by providing a process-oriented basis for delivering the outputs identified in the Operating Standards.

This is evident throughout the document itself. There are many references to 'audit', 'inspection', 'needs analysis' and even ' "customer satisfaction" surveys', with prisoners cast as the 'customers'. Curiously, however, despite this managerialist language, no performance management regime was put in place to monitor compliance with the Health Care Standards. Governors were given three years to implement them (that is, until 1997), but they started to be properly audited only in 1999. As David Hillier from the Prison Service Health Care Directorate put it in interview, the Standards were in effect only 'aspirational' and therefore 'as a method of driving change they weren't the best'. Thus, John Reed described in interview the negligible operational impact of the standards:

> Patients in inpatient care in prisons spend a very large proportion of the day locked away. Therapeutic programmes almost don't exist. Health care standards says that people patients should be unlocked for 12 hours a day and have 6 hours a day of 'purposeful activity'. They don't. Nothing like it. I've never been to a prison which came anywhere within sight of that yet these are these healthcare standards were approved by the Prison Board and they were all meant to have been implemented by the middle of 1997. They haven't.

The section in Standard 2 that sets out the requirements for providing an 'integrated care regime' is interesting. It describes the regime as 'multi-disciplinary, involving health care staff, other prison staff (including psycho-logists, probation officers, chaplains and teachers), visiting specialists, and voluntary agencies'. It states that regular multi-disciplinary case conferences will be held to review selected individual cases. As Nikolas Rose (1996a:16–17) argues, following Castel (1991), this type of approach signals a very different form of governing the conduct of psychiatric patients in which the goal of case management is the administration of risk. In furtherance of this new goal, the primacy of psychiatric diagnosis is displaced in favour of multi-disciplinary expert assessments of risk. Hence the need to draw in a wide range of professionals. Alongside this, other sections of the Standards are even more explicitly oriented towards the management of risk: Standard 2.3 focuses on the prevention of suicide and self-harm and Standard 2.4 on the management of patients exhibiting 'challenging' behaviour.

The further rise of risk concerns at this time can be seen in broader arenas too. For the Prison Service, Derek Lewis, the Director General, spelt this out unequivocally and bluntly in his speech to its annual conference in November 1993: 'Our business is the management of risk'. In the mental health field, as Peay (2002:749) notes, another example of this trend was the 'introduction in 1994 of mandatory inquiries into homicides committed by those who had had contact with the specialist mental health services'.

The issuing of Health Care Standards was timely in a further sense, as there was a resurgence in the mid-1990s of the 'moral' condemnation of the poor treatment of mentally vulnerable prisoners. The case of *Knight v Home Office* ([1990] 3 All ER 237) at the beginning of the decade had controversially ruled that prisoners were not entitled to the same standard of care as NHS patients; this was seized upon by campaigning organisations like NACRO (Jones, 1992), MIND (Bynoe, 1992) and others. A prisoner writing in the *British Medical Journal* stated bluntly:

> Standards of medical care in some prisons are so low they border on the negligent.
>
> (Leech, 1993)

This kind of critique of prison health care is strikingly reminiscent of the tenor of the House of Commons Social Services Select Committee report on the Prison Medical Service from 1986 (see Chapter 3). References to poor standards of prison health care also appear in 'official' prison discourse in this period and are often linked to negative comparisons with NHS provision in the community. For example, Sir David Ramsbotham, the Chief Inspector of Prisons, noted in his annual report for 1995–1996:

> We are concerned in particular about the number of prisoners with mental health problems, whose condition in prison is more likely to worsen than improve [. . .] It has to be said that, although many health care staff in prisons can demonstrate an ever wider range of qualifications and flexibility in their work and working practices, the overall service provided across all establishments does not match up to National Health Service standards [. . .] Unless proper care is provided, prison can exacerbate mental health problems, which has a long term impact on the individual concerned and the community into which he or she may be released.

In December 1995, Ramsbotham caused some controversy by walking out in the middle of an inspection at Holloway prison for women because of the exceptionally poor conditions found there by the Inspectorate team. Among the catalogue of complaints was the lack of care for the mentally disordered and mentally ill. This had echoes of the Holloway C1 campaign in the 1980s described in Chapter 3.

On the same theme of standards of health care, Derek Lewis, Director General of the Prison Service, in a speech to the Board of Visitors conference in 1995, stressed the importance of:

> Improving the quality of healthcare. We want to provide a service which matches the standards of the NHS in the community.

Reed and Lyne (1997), writing as members of the Prison Inspectorate, reveal the centrality of standards to the health care elements of prison inspections and also indicate the Inspectorate's role in the mid-1990s in arguing for greater NHS involvement in prison health care provision:

> The current policy for improving health care in prisons is not likely to achieve its objectives and is potentially wasteful. The prison service needs to recognize that expertise in the commissioning and delivery of health care is overwhelmingly based in the NHS.
>
> (Reed and Lyne, 1997:1420)

Ironically, at the same time as these unfavourable comparisons were being drawn between NHS and prison mental health provision, provision in the community was also being severely criticised. The cases of Christopher Clunis – a mentally ill man who killed Jonathan Zito in an unprovoked attack outside a London tube station – and of a patient who was seriously injured after climbing into the lion enclosure at London Zoo became symbolic of a perception that the policy of 'care in the community' was failing. This, of course, was not a new view. As Chapter 3 showed, it was a strong theme during the late 1980s. However, in the mid-1990s there appeared to be a stronger political motivation to attempt to address the issue, or at least to be seen to be doing so, for reasons that are discussed below. The Secretary of State for Health at this time, Virginia Bottomley, was extremely active in response to criticisms, introducing in Autumn 1993 a 'Ten Point Plan' to bolster community care. In interview she summarised her concern in this regard:

> I believe that care in the community is the right way forward but it can only work with a more determined and rigorous approach. Incarceration is never a first option for me.

The Ritchie Inquiry into the Clunis case was also taken up and became influential on policy (Ritchie et al, 1994). In explaining this response, a parallel might be drawn here with the earlier discussion of the rise of 'penal populism' in the context of the 'Tory endgame' (Gray, 1997). A politically weak government, faced with high-profile cases suggesting that its community care policy was failing to provide adequate security for the public, reacted to try to restore its governmental authority. Hence the strong emphasis within policy on the introduction of safeguards to ensure the security of the general public, the guarantee of security being, as Garland (1996) suggests, the most basic promise made by a sovereign state to its citizens. In this sense, it can be argued that the increasing focus on risk in the mid-1990s in this area is a more mixed phenomenon that some accounts allow (see Sparks, 2000a). Risk discourse is not just an aspect of neo-liberal 'ways of thinking', it also takes on at the same time a more politicised form which is inextricably linked with responses to wider 'problems of state sovereignty and legitimation' (Sparks, 2000a:141). Furthermore, as noted in Chapter 2, in the field of mentally disordered offenders concerns about dangerousness have long been at the forefront of policy debate. Even thirty years ago, Bottoms' (1977) discussion of the Butler Report was framed in terms of a 'renaissance' of the idea of dangerousness. Indeed, the Butler Committee itself was set up following the case of Graham Young, a man released from Broadmoor Hospital who subsequently committed several murders and violent offences in the community. Taking an even longer view, the very establishment of Broadmoor can be traced back to the James Hadfield case in 1800. Clunis thus had a long lineage.

As was noted above, the development of prison Health Care Standards was in part rooted in the progressive Woolf/Reed agenda. In the mid-1990s there were some other progressive developments. 'Welfarist' responses to 'mentally disordered offenders' in general continued to flourish during the mid-1990s, stimulated by the earlier Reed review, Home Office Circular 66/90 and Home Office funding. As Burney and Pearson (1995:291) noted in a paper written in 1994, 'practical initiatives are proliferating, particularly with the aim of diversion from custody and/or from prosecution'. Indeed, a new voluntary organisation, Revolving Doors Agency, came into existence in September 1993 following an important research report (Jones, 1992) with the aim of conducting research and development work in the field. These new initiatives also generated an associated body of new research knowledge about the operation of the various new schemes and the nature of their client groups (Joseph, 1992; Burney and Pearson, 1995; Laing, 1995; Robertson et al, 1995; Keyes et al, 1996). Much of the impetus for those schemes focusing particularly on diversion from custody was on addressing the problem of custodial remands being used as a means of accessing a psychiatric assessment. As Grounds (1991a) observes, and as has been noted in previous chapters, this practice had long been deprecated, even as far back as the late nineteenth century. Dell et al (1991) described it as an inhumane and ineffective way of securing help for mentally disordered offenders. In the mid-1990s, alongside the proliferation of diversionary schemes, a number of studies were carried out to measure the prevalence of mental disorder in the remand population. The main findings from these studies are summarised in Table 5.4. In brief, the pattern, as with the sentenced population, is of high levels of mental disorder and low levels of psychoses, but both are higher than for sentenced prisoners.

Elaine Player, an academic criminologist, referring to the establishment during this period of programmes for sex offenders, drug users and others, observed in interview that:

> Whilst there was this very punitive trend, it was also matched by to some extent the beginning of 'we've got to do something with these men' [. . .]

so we were beginning to see the need for treatment in usually quite highly specific forms [. . .] Treatment was beginning to creep back in to the vocabulary.

Michael Howard himself agreed with this point:

TS: Often you read in analyses of policy that come the 1980s rehabilitation was dead.
MH: That's completely untrue, that is completely untrue [. . .] I think you're right to say that sort of descriptively people began to talk about it more in terms of drugs or anger management or whatever rather than rehabilitation as a whole.

Table 5.4 British studies of mental disorder in remand prisoners

Main author	Sample details	Main findings
Watt 1993	31, male, Bristol	26% psychiatric disorder 13% personality disorder 3% psychosis
Brooke 1996	750, male, several prisons	63% psychiatric disorder 38% substance misuse 26% neurotic illness 11% personality disorder 5% psychosis
Birmingham 1996	569, male, Durham	26% mental disorder 4% psychosis
Swyer 1996	male, Winchester	33% history of mental health problems 4% psychosis
Brown 1996	male, local prison	41% neurotic problems 52% substance abuse 22% psychotic symptoms

Rehabilitative or treatment initiatives are thus recast in the mid-1990s in more instrumental terms. The case of Grendon prison is a good example. When it was originally set up in 1962, it was described as a facility for the mentally disordered with a particular emphasis on the personality disordered (Snell, 1962). By the mid-1990s it had not only narrowed down to an almost exclusive focus on personality disorders but, at the same time, its aims shifted away from purely therapeutic goals towards more instrumental ones. As Elaine Player described in interview:

I know there was an attempt to make Grendon be seen as more useful to the rest of the Prison Service. So that they would take these more difficult cases. And at one point one of the selection criteria was to give other institutions some relief from very difficult and disruptive prisoners. So it wasn't that these men had necessarily been defined as having a personality disorder. These were management problems [. . .] [Some prisoners] didn't really have any other symptoms apart from their behaviour. They were just difficult men. Sometimes they were violent.

Thus it came to be argued increasingly in the 1990s that one of the main benefits of Grendon was that it was a good model of how to manage a prison. In Player's words:

Arguably it's a very good way to run a prison [. . .] it's a very effective way of running a community of 250 men with minimum conflict where you've got a concentration of difficult prisoners, a mix of very very vulnerable people and extremely aggressive you know what they used to call plastic gangsters who in other institutions one would have simply killed the other [. . .] it is a good way to run a prison.

3. CONCLUSIONS

Although the mid-1990s is usually presented as a period in which Michael Howard's 'penal populism' is the overriding policy driver (see, for example, the account in Cavadino and Dignan, 1997), the empirical material analysed here suggests a rather different picture, at least as far as mentally disordered offenders are concerned. First, the actual impact of the punitive turn is uneven and cannot be simply or directly read off from the headline rhetoric of 'austerity' and 'prison works'. Second, neo-liberal forms of government, notably managerialism and risk management, remain a major influence. Indeed, it is arguable that this rather than 'penal populism' is actually the dominant strand in this period. Third, progressive and welfarist approaches, building on the Woolf/Reed agenda discussed in the previous chapter, continue to be important, although they remain to some extent inflected through a neo-liberal political rationality. The most striking overall feature then, echoing the conclusions to the previous two chapters, is that there is no single logic or rationality operating in the mid-1990s. The government of offenders and prisoners with mental health problems is multi-faceted and multi-stranded. This causes some difficulties for attempts to encapsulate the overarching direction of policy in this period, as this observation by Rosemary Wool, then Director of the Prison Health Care Service, about prisoners with personality disorders nicely illustrates:

Should they be repeatedly punished? Or does this threaten their mental health still further? Or should they be treated? And is this treatment 'primary care', and therefore solely the responsibility of the Prison Service? Or is it 'secondary care', and therefore at least partially the responsibility of the NHS? Or is it just management?

(Wool, 1996:32)

It is perhaps partly for this reason, a sense maybe of the deep complexity and unfathomability of the penal field in this 'volatile and contradictory' time (O'Malley, 1999), that some of the leading sociological commentators have resorted to psychoanalytical or psychological metaphors. Garland (1996; 2001:131–5), for example, as noted above (see also Zedner, 2002:348–52), writes about governmental responses to the 'crisis of penal modernism' in terms of 'denial' and 'acting out', terms which he acknowledges in a footnote are derived from Freudian psychoanalysis (2001:131, footnote 71; on 'denial', see also Cohen, 2001). Jock Young (1999), on the other hand, uses the vivid image of bulimia as a metaphor for the tensions in a late-modern society which is based simultaneously on cultural inclusion and structural exclusion.

What explanatory lessons can be drawn from the account presented in this chapter? Accepting that the picture is multi-faceted, the analytical challenge is to understand on what terms these different elements cohabit (Sparks, 2000a:130). This will also help to further understanding of why these developments occurred in this way at this time.

Taking up this challenge, there appears, first, to be good evidence assembled in this chapter to support an argument that the development of neo-liberal forms of government as a response to the shift to late modernity is a longer-term structural trend rather than a temporary or short-term one. In other words, it is starting to look like a transformation operating in Sparks' (1996:81) words 'on a long wave of historical development' (see also Melossi, 1985). Hence it persists even when the 'headline' trend appears to be quite different, as, for example, during the reformism described in the previous chapter and during the 'penal populism' described here. Managerialism, risk thinking and risk management have thus been central themes not only in this chapter but also in the previous two. For this level of analysis, the concepts and ideas that have come under the banner of 'governmentality' (see Foucault, 1991b; Garland, 1997b; Rose, 1999a; O'Malley, 2001) are invaluable tools, enabling the diagnosis of the rationalities and technologies associated with the government of conduct in neo-liberal or 'advanced liberal' societies.

However, whilst the 'governmentality' approach may help analyse and explain this longer-term development, it cannot account for the sudden emergence of 'penal populism' in the mid-1990s. As a short-run episode, and one apparently driven to some extent by 'low' politics, it might be argued that 'penal populism' is 'mere' politics or surface noise and that explanation is neither useful nor necessary. Yet, as the analysis in this chapter has shown, and indeed as argued in an important series of papers by Richard Sparks (1996, 2000a, 2000b, 2001a, 2001b, 2003; Leacock and Sparks, 2002), the episode is highly significant and reveals a great deal about the nature of penal policy and politics in late modernity.

In the introduction to this chapter, two explanations were very briefly sketched out; these will now be revisited in the light of the analysis presented above. First, there is the essentially political explanation revolving around the idea of legitimacy and the argument that at times of political or economic crisis, states attempt to re-assert their authority and legitimacy by self-consciously communicating through penal rhetoric their prowess at maintaining order (Habermas, 1976; Box, 1987; Melossi, 1993; Sparks, 1996, 2003). This certainly provides a plausible account of the mid-1990s punitive turn, with Michael Howard's approach as Home Secretary constituting a response to the dissipating authority of the Major administration during the 'Tory endgame'.

In terms of empirical historical explanation, it is worth considering here exactly how the processes implied by political explanations might actually happen. In other words, how exactly does this 'vulnerability' to toughness in penal rhetoric and policy manifest itself, and how does this tendency come to 'fruition' in particular contexts or circumstances (and not in others)? Michael Howard in interview gave the following account:

> Well the truth is that I pursued policies that were very significantly different from my predecessors [. . .] I did lay more emphasis on the importance of imprisonment and the part that could play in bringing crime down and I went to considerable lengths to change the criminal justice system in order to make it more effective and stop the extent to which it was becoming impossible to convict anyone of anything [. . .] So my approach to those areas of responsibility was different I think to that of most of my predecessors [. . .] I was the author of the policies. I had pretty good support throughout from the Prime Minister. The views of the rest of the cabinet varied. It wasn't a collegiate decision a cabinet decision that we needed to be tough on crime so go away Home Secretary and come up with a number of policies. It wasn't like that. I was the author of the policies, I put the policies to the cabinet but I did have pretty consistent support from the Prime Minister.

This individualistic explanation ('I was the author of the policies') would tend to contradict structural accounts, suggesting that with a different Home Secretary the policy outcomes might have been different. However, as Professor Paul Rock observed in interview, this view arguably draws a false and unhelpful distinction between the levels of structure and of individual actors:

> What a person represents is not simply psychological, a person is himself
> or herself a synthesis a distillation of experiences which have been earned
> in other organizations so that [. . .] in the identity of individuals there will
> be [. . .] an ongoing blend of other social influences what used to be called
> social forces which come to bear on a policy [. . .] Ultimately all influences
> are mediated through individuals.

This insight suggests how macro and micro explanations can potentially be linked and also indicates a particular conception of the relationship between structure and agency in policy making. In the case being discussed here, the account might go something like this. First, the political and economic problems facing the Major government in the mid-1990s placed the administration in a crisis of political legitimacy. Second, most policy decision makers were to some degree influenced by the need to address this crisis. In the Home Office, an ambitious and politically right-wing Home Secretary 'had decided that he was going to make his name in the Home Office' (Lewis, 1997:108) in order 'to establish his credentials [. . . as a] credible candidate for No 10' (Lewis, 1997:103). In such circumstances, talking 'tough' on 'law and order' satisfied Howard's need to position himself for higher office, made wider political good sense as a response to the political crisis and also resonated with his own right-wing beliefs. For a beleaguered Prime Minister, it represented a possible 'life boat' out of treacherous political waters, hence Major's 'pretty consistent support' for Howard's policies. For others in the Cabinet, who as the quote above indicates were more mixed and lukewarm in their response, some may have been anxious about a potential future rival for the party leadership gaining too much strength, whilst others with more centrist political views may simply have found the 'tough' policy direction misguided or distasteful. Hence the absence of collegiate cabinet support. In this way, the circumstances that make such a policy turn more likely are structurally related, but whether, when and how it actually happens can be understood only in terms of the specific micro-level contingencies and context. In this type of explanatory account, there is space for both structure and agency, and the relationship between the two is articulated reasonably clearly and coherently.

The second explanation for the 'penal populism' of the mid-1990s is based on Garland's (1996; 2001:131–5) argument that it represents a form of 'denial' in which the evident inability of the state to control crime in the face of high crime rates is simultaneously denied and symbolically re-asserted via a display of punitive power. This is clearly a related line of argument to the first explanation, since, as Garland (1996:462) observes, 'punitive outbursts and demonizing rhetorics have featured much more prominently in weak political regimes than in strong ones'. The distinction between the two explanations is that Garland foregrounds the issue of crime – specifically, the 'normalisation' of high crime rates – within his account alongside the political dimension. As discussed earlier, in the context of mental health policy, the response to some high-profile 'failures' of community care at this time – such as Virginia Bottomley's Ten Point Plan – could be explained in a similar way as a symbolic re-assertion of the sovereign state's ability to ensure the security of its citizens.

More illuminating perhaps is the insight offered by the analysis in this chapter on the complex question of the relationship between neo-liberal strategies and 'penal populism' in the mid-1990s. The analytical issue is to explain how these sharply contrasting approaches and perspectives co-exist. Garland has described them variously as 'contrasting' (1990a:180), 'contradictory' (1996:446) and 'antithetical' (1997b:203) and suggests that this conflict within contemporary penal policy accounts for its volatile and contradictory nature. Sparks (2000a, 2003), on the other hand, argues that the relationship is not so much one of pure conflict but rather a more nuanced and complex liaison, in which punitiveness and risk management co-exist and interrelate. In a similar vein, O'Malley (1999) argues that the two seemingly opposing tendencies find a home under the broad umbrella of New Right politics, although the resulting 'package' is 'volatile and contra-dictory' rather than stable. In support of these types of argument, a critical feature of the analysis in this chapter is the suggestion it contains that issues of risk and punitiveness are closely bound up together. In interview, when asked to summarise the purposes of imprisonment, Michael Howard stated:

> Threefold. Punishment, deterrence and prevention. If you don't provide a proper means of punishment people lose confidence in the criminal justice system. They start taking things into their own hands. We've seen a lot of examples of vigilante activity which I don't think any civilised society can tolerate. Deterrence because I think it is clear people don't welcome being sent to prison and the prospect of being sent to prison has an influence on their behaviour. Indeed there are studies that show that the greater the likelihood of being sent to prison for serious crimes the fewer crimes are committed. So there is a relationship between the two. Thirdly, prevention in the sense that while someone is in prison he can't commit a crime other than against fellow prisoners or prison officers. That's not to minimise the significance of those crimes but clearly burglars can't burgle if they're inside.

In other words, 'penal populism' is not purely about retributive punish-ment, but also makes a claim to increase public safety through a mixture of deterrence and incapacitation (Sparks, 2000a:136). It is about punishment as an end in itself, but also about imprisonment as a means of managing crime risks. Other examples of these kinds of liaison have also been presented here. The responses to the Clunis report, for example, which centred on a 'tighten-ing up' of the safeguards for the care of patients in the community, involved a politicised appeal to risk management which, far from being dispassionate or purely instrumental, was highly emotive and impassioned. Here, the multi-vocality of the idea of risk becomes apparent. It is not solely a technical neo-liberal matter, it is also an emotive one, as the quotation from Howard above also suggests. It can be seen in this example, too, how risk management can be just as much a form of 'populism' as the appeal to punitiveness. As Sparks (2001a:197–8) suggests, 'populism' is a style or technique that can be deployed to various purposes and need not be just employed for morally conservative ends.

Summarising then, ideas of 'hybrids' (Sparks, 2000b:138) or 'assemblages' (O'Malley, 2004:21–6) are particularly useful here as they emphasise the need to look at changing configurations within what is a multi-stranded rather than a monolithic penal policy. Penality in the mid-1990s is neither exclusively punitive and populist nor 'all about risk'. Rather, there is a complex hybrid of different elements, in which each part interacts with and influences the others in a dynamic and recursive way. This resonates with Garland's concept of the social realm:

> A multi-layered mosaic, the product of layer upon layer of organisational forms, techniques and regulatory practices, each one partial in its operation, each one dealing with the residues and traces of pervious strategies as well as its contemporary rivals and limitations.
>
> (Garland, 1985:155)

Furthermore, by understanding penal politics in a 'more substantively political light', as O'Malley (1999) and Sparks (2001b, 2003) advise, a better sense of how and why particular events unfold at particular times can be developed. In this way, what Sparks (2001a:196–7) calls the 'explanatory hiatus' between the speculations of social theory and empirically grounded research can start to be bridged. Indeed, the analysis above suggests that it is possible to draw together the insights of high-level social theory with a more politically oriented understanding and, beyond this, even to identify the role of individual agents in the manner of a micro-sociological approach (see Rock, 1988, 1995, 1996).

The next chapter picks up the narrative in May 1997, when a new government came into power following a period of 18 years under Conservative rule. The New Labour administration proceeded to set out and deliver a strategy that was in many respects progressive and innovative but also aroused considerable anxiety, especially in relation to proposals to address the risks believed to be posed by certain individuals with severe personality disorders. The continuities and novelties of policy and strategy during the period from 1997 to 2005 will now be discussed and analysed in Chapter 6.

New Labour and risk management, 1997–2005

This chapter examines the period from 1997 to 2005, a period during which the New Labour administration sought to shape a new penal policy after 18 years of Conservative government. The aim of this chapter is to analyse how the arrival of New Labour and its particular approach to penal policy and crime control affected strategies in the field of mental health, crime and punishment. Specifically, the analytical focus is on the impact on the 'dividing practices' applied to mentally disordered offenders, with a particular emphasis on the prison situation. In investigating this, the first section of this chapter briefly sets out some of the wider social, political and penal context at this time. The second and main section analyses in detail the contours of penal strategies in this area. The final section pulls out some of the central themes raised by the analysis.

I. CONTEXT: THE RISE OF NEW LABOUR

The previous chapter covered the period that has been termed the Tory 'endgame' (Gray, 1997). As described there, through the mid-1990s the Conservative government saw its authority and credibility drain away. The once-famed Tory claim to economic competence had been shattered by the 'Black Wednesday' debacle and the unravelling of the 'back to basics' campaign had left an image of the party as morally questionable, a feature encapsulated by Opposition politicians in the idea of 'sleaze'. In May 1997, after 18 years of Conservative rule, the Labour party, branded as 'New Labour', came to power in a landslide general election victory.

The general approach of the New Labour administration has in some respects been difficult to pin down (Downes and Morgan, 2002:294). On the one hand, there has been a traditional social democratic or socialist concern with tackling disadvantage and inequalities, as in policies to end child poverty and to narrow health inequalities. A dedicated 'Social Exclusion Unit' was set up to address the most pressing problems of exclusion and in its early years produced important reports on homelessness, renewing deprived neighbourhoods and other topics. Yet, on the other hand, some commentators have characterised New Labour as a Centre Right project, pointing to, for example, its policies on taxation and privatisation. The latter highlights a crucial dimension, which is that, even in tackling its more social democratic priorities, New Labour has been willing to deploy neo-liberal ideas, principles and techniques in ways that would not have been countenanced by the party even a decade previously. Hence, public–private partnerships have flourished in the diverse fields of prison management, the building of schools and hospitals and other previous 'no go' areas for Labour. It is perhaps this strong neo-liberal character – even in the pursuit of traditional 'leftist' objectives – that has rendered the New Labour project so ambiguous.

In the criminal justice sphere, as Downes and Morgan (2002:297–8) catalogue, there has been a similar mix of punitive and progressive policies since 1997. Examples of the latter include the establishment of multi-agency Youth Offending Teams; the expansion of drug treatment for offenders; the Human Rights Act; and the development of restorative justice. The most potent symbol of the former has been in the prison system. As Table 6.1 shows, the prison population continued to grow substantially under New Labour, adding, it should be remembered, to the steep rises that occurred in the mid-1990s during the 'Howard years' (see Chapter 5). After rises in 1997 and 1998, there was then a period of relative stability until a substantial rise in 2002, followed by smaller but still significant increases in the following two years. Against the already high point of the 1997 prison population, by 2004 there had been a 22 per cent increase.

By mid-October 2005, the prison population stood at 77,599 and the Home Office raised the possibility that it might need to release some prisoners early to ease the unprecedented pressure on prison places (see reports in national newspapers on 13 October 2005). Penal expansionism seemed to be almost impossible to halt.

Table 6.1 Annual average prison population in England and Wales 1997–2004

Year	Average prison population	Percentage rise over previous year	Percentage rise over 1997 baseline
1997	61,114	11%	–
1998	65,298	7%	7%
1999	64,771	-1%	6%
2000	64,602	0%	6%
2001	66,301	3%	8%
2002	70,861	7%	16%
2003	73,038	3%	20%
2004	74,658	2%	22%

2. REFIGURING HEALTH CARE AND MANAGING 'DANGEROUS' OFFENDERS

There has been considerable and significant policy activity in the field under examination in this book since the election of the New Labour government in May 1997. This falls within two principal areas. First of all, building on the *Patient or Prisoner?* discussion paper issued in 1996, there has been a series of developments in the configuration and organisation of mental health care provision for prisoners, including the establishment of mental health 'in-reach' services and the staggered transfer of responsibility for provision to the NHS. Second, in July 1999 a government Green Paper announced a new initiative, the Dangerous and Severe Personality Disorder (DSPD) programme, designed to address the perceived problem of violent offending by individuals diagnosed with personality disorders who appeared to slip through both the penal and the psychiatric nets.

An important part of the backdrop to responses in this field during this period was the publication of the findings from a psychiatric survey of the prison population conducted by the Office for National Statistics (ONS) between September and December 1997. The ONS survey purported to show that nine out of ten prisoners showed evidence of at least one of the mental disorders considered in the study (Singleton et al, 1998). The survey findings will be analysed in more detail below, but it was this headline figure that provided a particular and additional impetus to policy development from 1998 onwards. Whilst the survey at the start of the decade by John Gunn and colleagues (1991) had indicated a significant problem, and one largely unchanged in scale since his earlier study in the 1970s (Gunn et al, 1978), the ONS survey appeared to show that things had substantially worsened in the intervening years. The implication of course was that the Reed Review, the focus on diversion and transfer and the other developments discussed in Chapters 4 and 5 had all failed to improve the situation in prisons.

Refiguring prison mental health care provision

The *Patient or Prisoner?* discussion paper (HM Chief Inspector of Prisons, 1996) described in the previous chapter was followed in late 1997 by a report entitled *The Provision of Mental Health Care in Prisons* by the Health Advisory Committee for the Prison Service (HAC, 1997). This was then followed in March 1999 by a joint Prison Service and NHS Executive paper which set out a blueprint for *The Future Organisation of Prison Health Care* (Prison Service/NHSE, 1999). In 2001, a further document, *Changing the Outlook*, was issued, focusing on the development of mental health services within prisons (Department of Health/Prison Service/National Assembly for Wales, 2001). Together, these documents set out a blueprint for a major refiguring of prison health care provision; this will now be examined in more detail.

To recap: first, as discussed in the previous chapter, *Patient or Prisoner?* presented the argument for change in two stages. First of all, it noted that standards of health care in prison consistently fell below NHS standards in the community. Second, it argued that in order to remedy this deficiency, the NHS should assume responsibility for provision within prisons. It was proposed that this should be via a purchaser–provider relationship. The case made was both an ethical one (prisoners are citizens entitled to the same standard of health care as individuals in the community) and one rooted in concerns about the efficient use of resources (the Health Care Service for Prisoners was needlessly trying to duplicate operations already delivered more successfully by the NHS).

The report by the Health Advisory Committee for the Prison Service was published in late 1997 and took on the agenda of *Patient or Prisoner?* a stage further. It focused on three substantive issues:

- The arrangements for assessment by and transfer to the NHS and the problems currently encountered in these areas.
- The arrangements for the throughcare/after care/care programme approach to the management of prisoners with mental disorder when they are released.
- What constitutes 'equivalence to the NHS' in terms of the mental health care of prisoners.

(HAC, 1997:3)

Looking at these in turn, the report's analysis of the issues around transfer to the NHS centres on four related points: first, that there was a substantial increase in the number of transfers over the previous ten years; second, that nevertheless there remained unmet need; third, that the transfer system did not always operate effectively, with considerable delays sometimes occurring; and fourth, that the principal reason for these delays and the unmet need was the pattern of distribution of secure bed spaces. The central recommendation was for the provision of more medium secure beds.

The construction of the argument in this way is interesting. It frames the primary purpose of transfer as the allocation of individuals to the correct level of security within the psychiatric system. In other words, it is an exercise in population management in which the end goal is the administration of risk. Rose (1996a, 1998) suggests that this new focus on risk management within psychiatry is linked to neo-liberal (or 'advanced liberal' as he prefers to term it – on this, see O'Malley, 2004:75–6) forms of government. Calls for the expansion of medium secure bed spaces were not, of course, new. For example, it was a key recommendation of the Butler report in 1975 (Home Office/DHSS, 1975). It might be more accurate, then, to describe the Health Advisory Committee's argument here as a renewed emphasis rather than a novel departure.

The second of the three substantive issues covered in the Committee's report concerns the 'management' of individuals with mental health problems leaving prison. In this section of the report, the focus is on the mechanisms, procedures and systems for 'bridging the gap' between services within prison and those in the community. Much of the discussion recalls the managerialism of the Working Group report on mentally disturbed prisoners from 1987 (see Chapter 3) with its detailed attention to structures and systems and concern for efficiency and effectiveness. The idea of a 'worker employed to work in prison but with links to outside statutory agencies' (HAC, 1997:30) would be picked up later in the proposals for mental health 'in-reach' teams.

The third substantive issue, defining the meaning of 'equivalence of care', picks up the discussion on this in *Patient or Prisoner?* (see Chapter 5). It is underpinned by two points: first, that 'the need for the concept of equivalence arises from the fact that the system for the delivery of health care to prisoners is separate from the system of delivery of health care for the general population' (1997:6). This clearly positions the discussion in terms of the proposals for the NHS to provide services within prison. Second, the idea is that prisoners are citizens with the right to equal access to health care 'delivered to the same standard as to the [general] population' (1997:6). Indeed, the covering letter from Dr John O'Grady, Acting Chairman of the Committee, that accompanied the report asserted that the 'theme running through this report is that prisoners are citizens'. As argued in Chapter 5, this construction of penal subjects as individuals essentially no different from other members of society links to Garland's (2001) analysis of crime control in late modernity and specifically to the emergence of what he calls the 'new criminologies of everyday life'. The penal subject becomes the *homo economicus* of neo-liberalism along with the rest of the population. The idea of 'citizenship' as the fundamental basis of self-identity for individual subjects has, as Burchell (1991:121) observes, been an 'enduring theme in Western political thought', but he suggests that citizenship takes on a particular form within (neo-)liberal government: that of the 'rational interest-motivated economic' agent (1991:144). Critical to the argument here is the idea that this conception of citizens is a means of rendering individuals as governable subjects (1991:144). In these terms, the Committee's reference to prisoners' 'rights' to equivalent health care is a misrecognition of the nature of the relationship of the individual to the exercise of governmental power. To talk of citizens having 'rights' to 'state' provision is to avoid the 'problem of power at the level of government' (1991:145). In an interesting essay, Colin Gordon (1986) argues, drawing partly on Foucault's (1967) thesis in *Madness and Civilization*, that psychiatry itself can be understood as a technology aimed at satisfying a 'problem of citizenship' (1986:278). By this he means that it is tasked both with protecting social order and with restoring the status and faculties of the 'insane' as citizens (1986:278). It is partly for this reason that the Committee's argument about psychiatric provision within prisons ends up being conducted in the language of citizenship (see also Garland, 1985:249–50). A Council of Europe (1998) recommendation adopted in April 1998 also shared the Health Advisory Committee's language of 'rights' and made similar arguments about 'equivalence of care'.

Overall, then, it can be seen that the Health Advisory Committee report, although ostensibly very much in the 'progressive' mould of earlier reports by Reed and Woolf (see Chapter 4), is also clearly aligned with neo-liberal government. This raises the interesting question of how and why neo-liberalism appeared to outlast the New Right Conservative government in Britain and find a new place within the New Labour administration. This will be discussed in the conclusion, below.

In 1998, the ONS survey alluded to above was published. The findings are summarised in Table 6.2. Several points are noteworthy. First, there is the overall high prevalence of psychiatric morbidity in the sample. The survey purported to show that 9 out of 10 prisoners suffered from one or more of the five main mental disorders covered by the research. On the face of it, this was an exceptionally high figure, exceeding by some margin the levels found by the previous surveys conducted by John Gunn and colleagues (Gunn et al, 1978, 1991) and by smaller-scale studies from the 1950s onwards (see Chapter 2).

Table 6.2 Summary of findings from Singleton et al (1998)

Sample details	Main findings
1,254, male (sentenced), several prisons	64% personality disorders 63% alcohol misuse 51% drug dependence 40% neurotic disorders 7% psychosis
676, female (sentenced), several prisons	63% neurotic disorder 50% personality disorders 41% drug dependence 39% alcohol misuse 10% psychosis
1,415, male (remand), several prisons	78% personality disorders 59% neurotic disorder 58% hazardous drinking 51% drug dependence 10% functional psychosis
218, female (remand), several prisons	76% neurotic disorder 54% drug dependence 50% personality disorders 36% hazardous drinking 21% functional psychosis

Second, however, several caveats about the findings need to be made. Two of the five 'mental disorders' investigated were drug and alcohol dependency; these formed a substantial section of the detected morbidity. Whether these are properly 'psychiatric' issues is a matter of debate. The category of 'personality disorder' is also conceptually difficult, as it is partly defined by violent, criminal or anti-social behaviour and hence unsurprisingly is common within the prison population. Again, personality disorder constitutes a large proportion of the detected morbidity. It could be argued, then, that the '9 in 10' headline figure may be misleading. Thirdly, the ONS survey was able to address questions of gender and ethnicity, as it produced directly comparable data generated by the same methods. On gender, female prisoners had higher levels of neurotic disorder and functional psychosis, whilst males had higher rates of personality disorder and alcohol misuse. These findings are not particularly consistent with those of Gunn and colleagues (1991), who found the opposite pattern on personality disorder and psychosis, although there is agreement between the two on neurotic disorder (see Chapter 4). In terms of ethnicity, the ONS survey found that black and minority ethnic prisoners were more likely to suffer from a personality disorder but less likely to have a functional psychosis than white prisoners. Again, this reversed the findings from the Gunn survey (see Chapter 4). Overall, notwithstanding the caveats about the findings expressed above, the ONS survey appeared to point to a very much worsened problem within prisons. Half a decade after the Reed Review, the situation in prisons appeared to have deteriorated. If any additional impetus for change were needed, the publication of the ONS survey at this juncture certainly provided it.

The joint Prison Service and NHS Executive paper published in March 1999, *The Future Organisation of Prison Health Care*, was highly significant, setting out a blueprint for developments for the next five years (Prison Service/NHSE, 1999). It proposed moves towards increased NHS provision of mental health care within prisons via a formal partnership between the NHS and the Prison Service. This constituted another big step towards abolition of the Prison Health Care Service and the integration of prison health care within the NHS, although it still fell short of the full transfer of responsibility.

Like the Health Advisory Committee Report, it adopted the idea of 'equivalence of care' as a guiding principle, defining it in the following way:

> Prisons should not, either by acts of omission or commission, make it more likely that people [. . .] have access to substandard health care services in comparison to those available in the community.
>
> (Prison Service/NHSE, 1999: para 10)

In a review of the *Future Organisation* report, Paul Bowden (2000:474), a forensic psychiatrist, strongly countered this 'guiding principle', arguing that it is 'unachievable and perverse' on the basis that:

> Prison itself is an environment prejudicial to health, for is not the definition of crime both transgression of the law and an invitation to impose a sanction in the form of punishment, and how can punishment be imposed without compromising health.
>
> (2000:474–5)

A similar argument was made by John Gunn in interview:

> Imprisonment is meant to be a punishment. It's meant to be a place where to put it very crudely you damage people's health. Punishment almost by definition is damaging people and it's thought to be the price they have to pay for what they've done wrong [. . .] So there's a fundamental conflict between using prisons as therapeutic institutions to make people better and this kind of underlying punitiveness. Now it's very difficult to say that because when you actually get in to a prison and you see prison officers prison governors working hard to improve the lot of their charges being really concerned about them and working for them and so on, you think well that's all nonsense. But I think at a policy level it's much harder for governments and politicians to be saying 'our prisons are going to be centres for treatment' [. . .] So there is this conflict all the time and it's one of the reasons that I have always argued – in spite of my admiration for some of the work that's done in prisons – I've always argued that really if you want proper treatment you have to do it somewhere else. Therefore I'm one of the people that argue that people should be transferred out of prisons and that we desperately need secure hospitals and that 'security' and 'hospital' can go together but 'imprisonment' and 'punishment' are not compatible with treatment.

Catrin Smith (2000) too suggests that the whole idea of 'healthy prisons' is contradictory. Sim (1994b, 2002) has argued that the continuing construction of prisoners as 'less eligible' subjects, a construction he suggests is ingrained in prison officer culture, not only undermines the very concept of equivalence (which is founded on a notional equality of status) but also militates against its achievement in practice. What is the significance then of this debate? The key here, it is suggested, lies in referring back to the discussion above about 'citizenship'. It was argued there that to frame the issue of 'equivalence' in terms of prisoners' 'rights' to a certain standard of health care evaded the problem of the exercise of governmental power. The point of tension is that prisoners are at one and the same time 'made up' as citizen-subjects and as punishable subjects. In this light, Smith's (2000) argument about the prioritisation of particular health issues within prison – mental illness, drugs and

HIV rather than, for example, asthma – is interesting. She suggests that 'these issues tend to be problematised and hence targeted because of their association with deviancy and with issues of security and the maintenance of order in prisons' (2000:346–57). In other words, rather than simply a tension or conflict, there is actually a liaison of some kind between health care provision and punishment in which the duality of the penal subject – citizen and object of punishment – is resolved. Hence many commentators over a long period of time have described, and usually deprecated, the blurring of the boundaries between prison medicine and the practice of punishment (Sim, 1990). Reed and Lyne (1997), for example, observed from their experiences in the Prison Inspectorate:

> In some prisons healthcare staff adopted over-punitive attitudes. One NHS general practitioner doing sessional work in prison said of mentally disturbed prisoners: 'One or two nights in the special [unfurnished] rooms tends to bring them to their senses.' A nurse in charge of a ward said: 'What they [young prisoners] respond to best is a good shouting at.' One doctor sanctioned the 'nursing' of a suicidal patient naked in an unfurnished room in early spring.

The argument made here is that it is misleading to view these examples of 'bad' practice simply as aberrations. Rather, they are indicative of the multifaceted way in which prisoners with mental health problems are 'made up' as subjects in order to be governed. This links to the broader argument running through this book: that the very presence of the mentally disturbed within prisons is an intrinsic feature of the use of institutional confinement as a method of punishment.

In terms of objectives, the report identifies its core purpose as to address issues of efficiency, effectiveness, quality, funding and accountability in the provision of prison health care. In doing so, it defines its task as to set out a 'new organizational and accountability framework' (1999: para 31). This is based on its diagnosis of the operational problems of health care delivery having their origin principally in difficulties in the 'interface' or relationship between the NHS and the Prison Service. In common with many previous reports on the issue dating back to the 1980s, as discussed in the previous three chapters, it adopts a managerial approach to a problem conceived essentially as one rooted in systems, processes and structures.

Within the process, reception screening is identified as the 'key to the care that a prisoner will subsequently receive' (1999: para 55). From the late 1990s, research on the effectiveness of reception screening developed rapidly (Birmingham et al, 1997, 1998, 1999, 2000; Birmingham, 2001; Parsons et al, 2001), indicating in broad terms that in practice health screening on entry into prison was largely 'cursory and ineffective' (Birmingham, 2001:463; Mitchison et al, 1994). As Birmingham (2001) notes, the reception medical examination dates back to the 1865 Prison Act, passed at a time when concerns about the ability of some prisoners to withstand the rigours of prison discipline were starting to emerge (see Chapter 2). In the context of the last years of the twentieth century, reception screening takes on a particular importance as a tool to aid the administration of risk. In principle, it enables the prison authorities to identify the suicidal, self-harmers, the mentally ill, the dangerous, the violent, the vulnerable and so on. Screening is a means of *monitoring* the prison population as they enter the system and, as Richard Ericson (1994:161, capitals in original) argues, monitoring is a key element of risk management:

> Surveillance is the production of knowledge about (monitoring), and supervision of (compliance), subject populations. Knowledge production and supervision are mutually reinforcing, and together they create surveillance as a system of rule [. . .] Surveillance is THE vehicle of risk management.

Following the report, in April 2000 the Directorate of Prison Health Care in the Home Office was abolished and a new Health Care Policy Unit and Task Force, based in the Department of Health, was set up. This was a major shift, as John Reed argued in interview, anticipating the change:

> One of the most important things we can do is to move to a system where health ministers are responsible for health and prison ministers are responsible for other issues.

At the same time as these transformations were taking place, an older tradition – criticising prison medical practice – was being revived. In April 2001, a highly critical report by the British Medical Association (BMA, 2001) claimed that prison health care was reaching crisis point. Whilst the BMA's report was scathing and uncompromising (see also Prison Reform Trust, 2005), a series of more sober research articles painted a similar picture. On the issue of prison transfers, for example, several studies indicated that the process remained slow and difficult (Isherwood and Parrott, 2002; Earthrowl et al, 2003; Reed, 2002:123, 2003:287). Indeed, Reed (2002:123), based on his experience as Chief Medical Inspector in the Prison Inspectorate between 1996 and 2002, describes a quite dismal situation:

> Uncertainty on area of residence/area of offending rules causes endless problems and delays. Even when the responsible service is clear, identifying the appropriate consultant can be difficult [. . .] Patients often wait weeks or even months before a psychiatrist arrives to do a first assessment [. . .] After assessment and agreement that transfer to the NHS is appropriate, a common problem is that differences of opinion arise about

the level of security a patient needs. It is common for patients to wait in prison while they are passed back and forth from local service to medium secure service to special hospitals and back again. I have found prisoners with serious mental illness waiting in prison where treatment is entirely inadequate for over a year while this debate goes on [. . .] Even when accepted for transfer, patients can wait for months in prison, again largely untreated, until a suitable bed is available. The longest wait I have found from acceptance to transfer was 20 months pending admission to Broadmoor. A recent visit to a young offenders institution showed that at least 10 young people were awaiting transfer to the NHS and that the average waiting time was 82 days.

Despite Home Office Circular 66/90 and the drive in the early 1990s to increase transfers from prison (see Chapter 4), 10 years later the systems and processes appeared not to be working effectively. As Table 6.3 shows, against a backdrop of a rising prison population, the number of transfers did not rise above the 750 mark that had already been attained in the early to mid-1990s (see Table 5.2 in Chapter 5). Indeed, in the three years from 2000 to 2002 the number actually dropped to well under 700, before recovering in 2003. The warning about policy failures presented by the ONS survey (see above) appeared to be borne out by these figures. A study by Sim (2002) went further than this, arguing that not only were there failures in the delivery of policy – he presents a dismaying picture of the poor quality of prison health care – but that the policy itself was too narrowly drawn and fundamentally flawed. He suggests that the anticipated improvements from the partnership between the NHS and Prison Service were proving slow to materialise (2002:319).

A further policy document, *Changing the Outlook*, was issued in December 2001, this time produced with the Department of Health in the lead

Table 6.3 Transfers to hospital under the Mental Health Act 1983 from Prison Service establishments and annual average prison population in England and Wales 1997–2003

	1997	1998	1999	2000	2001	2002	2003
Transfers of sentenced prisoners	251	258	267	270	222	223	296
Transfers of remand prisoners	495	481	464	392	413	421	425
Total transfers	*746*	*739*	*731*	*662*	*635*	*644*	*721*
Annual average prison population in England and Wales	61,114	65,298	64,771	64,602	66,301	70,861	73,038

(Department of Health/Prison Service/Welsh Assembly, 2001). It builds further on the policy direction of the earlier reports already discussed above, but locates developments in the wider context of the 'modernisation' of health care provision. The idea of 'modernising' public services was becoming an increasingly strong theme within New Labour. Its meaning varied in different contexts, but it was characterised by a willingness to refigure structures, organisations and delivery mechanisms in novel ways, including the introduction of private-sector provision into areas that had hitherto been exclusively public-sector. It was notable, for example, that the 'second Grendon', that had been committed to ten years earlier, finally opened in 2001 as a privately managed prison.

The language of *Changing the Outlook* makes it clear that 'modernisation' is to some degree a synonym of managerialism. References to 'whole systems' thinking, 'innovation', 'effectiveness', 'change' and 'flexibility' appear throughout the report. This is partly a consequence of the overall aim of bringing prison health care into the mainstream of the NHS, the latter of course having already been through a number of years of 'marketisation' and managerialism.

One of the key substantive developments was the introduction of mental health 'in-reach', in which NHS mental health teams were to come into prisons to deliver a multi-disciplinary service to prisoners. The idea of 'in-reach' was in a sense a corollary of the concept of equivalence of care. As John Reed put it in interview:

> There's an argument as to whether all people with psychotic illness shouldn't be in prison. On the other hand all people with psychotic illness aren't in hospital in you know most of them as you know are in the community. So there's a big discussion to be had about whether prison is equivalent to the community. One aspect of that is how good is mental health care in prisons.

In other words, given that in the community not all mentally disordered people are treated in hospital, it should not be expected that all mentally disordered prisoners will be transferred to hospital. Some will need to receive a service within the prison. The concept of 'equivalence' implies that the provision for these prisoners should be comparable with that provided by community mental health teams. The 'in-reach' teams were intended to do exactly that (Wilson, 2004). The first teams became operational in July 2001 in 12 prisons across England and Wales. The programme was rolled out to further prisons later that year and during the following three years. By 2004, around 70 prisons (nearly half the total prison estate in England and Wales) were served by mental health 'in-reach' teams.

In April 2003, funding responsibility for prison health care moved for the first time to the Department of Health, as the first step in a five year process leading ultimately to the complete integration of prison health care within the NHS by 2008. This marked a further step, as the delivery partnership envisaged by the 1999 *Future Organisation* report evolved into full NHS responsibility for the delivery of health care in prisons.

Summarising, under the New Labour administration a substantial refiguring of prison mental health care provision occurred in the period from 1997 to 2005. It is anticipated that by 2008 the NHS will have full responsibility for all prison health care; the aspiration is that this provision will be delivered to the same standard as outside the prison system. This is a major change and one that many had been campaigning for over a long period of time. The Prison Reform Trust, for example, published an edited collection on the subject in 1985. Its achievement was seen as a 'progressive' goal which would lead to improvements in the care provided to vulnerable prisoners (Royal College of Psychiatrists, 1979; Shaw, 1985; Candy, 1985). This has almost certainly been an important driver for this policy development, but, as the discussion above should make clear, it has also been strongly shaped by more neo-liberal concerns under the New Labour label of 'modernisation'. This recalls Stern's (1993:268) analysis of the drivers for the Woolf/Reed agenda of the early 1990s (see Chapter 4):

> Even those who did not ally themselves with better treatment of prisoners, and did not see themselves as protectors of human rights, were persuaded by a completely different set of arguments, springing from a completely different set of values – efficiency, value for money, good management.

The hope is clearly that the refigured structures for delivering prison mental health care will not only lead to more humane treatment of vulnerable prisoners but also result in increases in the efficiency and effectiveness of this provision.

'Managing the monstrous': the Dangerous and Severe Personality Disorder Programme

One of the most controversial 'new' initiatives in New Labour policy in this field was first announced by a Green Paper consultation document published in July 1999, *Managing Dangerous People with Severe Personality Disorders* (Home Office/Department of Health, 1999). This proposed the development of new services and legislation to deal with the 'problem' of those people who pose a serious danger to others as a result of a personality disorder. Its development was strongly influenced by the case of Michael Stone, who was convicted in 1998 of the murders of Lin Russell and her daughter Megan.

The overarching purpose of the programme was summarised in a Government factsheet issued in 2002:

> A programme of work to develop better ways of managing the very small number of people with a severe personality disorder who, because of their disorder, also pose a significant risk of serious harm to others.

This makes it clear that the key criterion for inclusion in the programme is the assessment of 'risk of serious harm to others' associated with the disorder, rather than the diagnosis of the disorder itself. The Green Paper states in this regard:

> At present individuals in this group may, broadly speaking, be detained in prison as *punishment* following conviction for an act they have committed, or in hospital to receive *treatment* designed to bring about an improvement in diagnosed mental disorder. The approach the Government has developed to managing dangerous severely personality-disordered people involves the idea of detention based on the *serious risk* such people present to the public.
>
> (Home Office/Department of Health, 1999:9, emphasis in original)

Some commentators have taken this as evidence that 'risk management' has now assumed overriding priority as the goal in this area:

> There can no longer be much pretence. Current policy in mental health and crime in England and Wales, as in many other western countries, is not dominated by humanitarian concerns; rather, it is permeated by perceptions and attributions of risk.
>
> (Peay, 2002:747)

Eastman (1999:549) argues in relation to the proposals that:

> In pursuing, above all, public protection, it [the government] intends services that essentially hybridise punishment and health care, with law that allows preventive detention of even the unconvicted.

Institutionally and organisationally, the proposals straddled the health and penal fields: the proposals were produced by a joint Home Office and Department of Health Working Group; and the new services were to be located within both prisons and Special Hospitals. Their basic purpose and rationale was described in the following terms in the White Paper *Reforming the Mental Health Act* that followed in 2000:

> Tackling the challenge to public safety presented by the very small minority of people with severe personality disorder, who because of their disorder, pose a high risk of serious offending. There are two key elements to these proposals:

- to ensure that dangerous people with severe personality disorder are kept in detention for as long as they pose a high risk to others; and,
- to provide high quality services to enable them to deal with the consequences of their disorder, reduce their risk to others and so work towards successful reintegration into the community.

> (Department of Health/Home Office, 2000: para 2.1)

The 'problem' with existing arrangements was also very specifically identified:

> Successive Governments have grappled with the problems posed by people who are DSPD. At present neither mental health nor criminal justice legislation deals adequately with the risks this group pose to the public. In many cases, an individual who is DSPD has to be released from prison at the end of a determinate sentence even though they are assessed as presenting a continuing risk of harm to others. Individuals who present a risk to others because of their severe personality disorder are rarely detained under the Mental Health Act 1983 because they are assessed as being unlikely to benefit from the sorts of treatment currently available in hospital.
>
> (Department of Health/Home Office, 2000: para 2.2)

The two main difficulties were thus seen as the release from prison of dangerous individuals at the end of fixed-term sentences and the inability to compel the admission of individuals to secure psychiatric facilities where their personality disorders are deemed 'untreatable'. The White Paper also notes that 'the deficiencies in the law are accompanied by a lack of specialist provision for the assessment and treatment of this group' (2000: para 2.3).

Accordingly, there were three substantive components of the proposals: powers to enable the indeterminate detention of DSPD individuals; removing or altering the 'treatability' requirement in the mental health legislation; and the development of new services for DSPD individuals. Most controversially, the proposed new powers for indeterminate detention were to apply in both civil and criminal proceedings. In other words, it would be possible for an individual to be detained indefinitely on the basis of their predicted future dangerousness even where they had not committed an offence.

In the Green Paper, it is suggested that there may be between 2,100 and 2,400 individuals who fall within the definition of DSPD, 98 per cent of whom are men. It is estimated that 1,400 of this group are in prison, 400 detained in hospital and between 300 and 600 in the community. These estimates have been criticised as 'inadequate' (Gledhill, 2000:444) and as a 'hopeless underestimate' (Peay, 2003a:19). This raises the question of whether it is 'proper to build a power of indeterminate detention when the information on the number of people who are likely to be affected is so inadequate' (Gledhill, 2000:444).

Principal responses to the initial proposals centred on concerns about the potential for human rights breaches, especially in relation to the proposals for preventive detention through civil proceedings. Organisations as diverse as Liberty (a civil liberties and human rights pressure group) and the Royal College of Psychiatrists voiced disquiet on this issue. The letters pages and editorial columns of all the main professional journals – for example, the *British Medical Journal* and *Psychiatric Bulletin* – saw debates about the professional ethics and practicability of the proposals as they unfolded. (For a sample of contributions to the debate, see: Mullen, 1999; Gunn and Felthous, 2000; Haddock et al, 2001; Birmingham, 2002; Coid and Maden, 2003; Outen, 2003.) In terms of practicalities, a key area of debate concerned doubts about the ability of practitioners to define, identify, assess and predict 'risk' and 'dangerousness' with any degree of accuracy and consistency (Peay, 2003a; Smith, 2003). As the work programme developed, such anxieties continued to be expressed (Hudson, 2003). The idea of detention being potentially indefinite also aroused concerns. Virginia Bottomley, a health minister in the Major administration during the mid-1990s, stated in interview:

> It makes me very uneasy about the [government's proposals] which are essentially these are totally hopeless people who can't be treated and nobody wants in society [. . .] my anxiety is that this will be 'lock em up and throw away the key'.

How can some sense be made of these highly controversial proposals? Why did they emerge at this point? How do they fit within the wider context of penal strategies during this period? It will be argued here that proposals for the DSPD programme can be most fruitfully considered in terms of constituting a revised set of 'dividing practices' targeted at a particular sub-population.

First of all, then, a reminder of Rabinow's (1984:8) helpful definition of 'dividing practices':

> Essentially 'dividing practices' are modes of manipulation that combine the mediation of a science (or pseudo-science) and the practice of exclusion – usually in a spatial sense, but always in a social one.

There are two elements here: the 'mediation of a science' and the 'practice of exclusion'. Looking at the first, questions about the nature of the science that might be used to identify individuals suitable for the DSPD programme have been a major part of the debate. As noted above, the ability to define the group and to predict 'dangerousness' have been doubted (Peay, 2003a; Smith, 2003). This was a strong theme in a report on the proposals by the Home Affairs Committee in 2000 (Home Affairs Committee, 2000). Both in the report itself and in the published written and oral evidence to the Committee, many people expressed the view that the science was unable to provide predictions of adequate accuracy. Farnham and James (2001) writing in *The Lancet* suggested acerbically that there was little 'scientific' about the process:

> Would-be clairvoyants engaged in this form of assessment exercise will make use of 'tools' in the form of actuarially-based checklists, which give spurious scientific value to estimations that perform less well than chance.

Buchanan and Leese (2001) attempted to quantify this lack of precision in assessments of future dangerousness, concluding that:

> Six people with DSPD would have to be detained for a year to prevent one person from acting violently during that year [. . .] For every ten people with DSPD who would be violent, five would be identified and detained and five would be missed [. . .] For every ten people with DSPD who would not be violent, seven would be identified and released and three would be detained.
>
> (2001:1958)

They note further that in practice assessments may be even less accurate than this, for a variety of reasons (2001:1958).

All this suggests that the 'mode of manipulation' involved here seems to be mediated by what can best be characterised as a 'pseudo-science'. Part of the difficulty with assessments and some of the wider anxiety surrounding the proposals are concerned with the fact that the category of 'Dangerous and Severe Personality Disorder' is a 'neologism that has no legal or medical status' (Farnham and James, 2001). In other words, it is in a real sense a 'moral invention' (O'Malley, 1992). The Green Paper offered the following definition of the term, which nicely illustrates how it is a category defined largely in terms of the problems posed by those who fall within it:

> The phrase dangerous severely personality disordered (DSPD) is used in this paper to describe people who have an identifiable personality disorder to a severe degree, who pose a high risk to other people because of serious anti-social behaviour resulting from their disorder [. . .] The overwhelming majority are people who have committed serious offences such as murder, manslaughter, arson, serious sex offences, or grievous bodily harm.
>
> (Home Office/Department of Health, 1999:12)

This lack of 'scientific' status explains a good part of the ire of psychiatrists directed at the DSPD programme, namely that it is based on a politically invented category rather than an existing psychiatric one: hence, for example, the complaint of Farnham and James (2001) that it lacks 'status' (see also Gunn and Felthous, 2000). It could be argued more broadly, of course, that the notions of psychopathic disorder and personality disorders were themselves earlier 'inventions'. The late Aubrey Lewis (1974) famously described psychopathic personality as a 'most elusive category' and, more recently, Forrester (2002:339) has observed that:

> The term 'psychopathic disorder' has survived more than 40 years despite clear evidence that it lacks meaning, precision and reliability [. . .] (as, incidentally, does the clinical diagnosis of personality disorder).

McCallum (2001) argues even further that the very concept of 'personality' was itself invented in response to concerns about the government of certain categories of dangerous conduct. This suggests that the critical point to understand about DSPD is not that it is a neologism – the same could be said of many other now well established legal and psychiatric categories – but rather that it is an invention designed to address a particular 'problem'. Or, more precisely, it is a discursive resource that 'makes up' a category of people in order that their dangerous conduct can be better governed (O'Malley, 2001:134).

Before considering the specifics of the government of the conduct of this group – that is, Rabinow's (1984) 'practice of exclusion' – some further points can usefully be made about the 'invention' of the category of DSPD. In evidence given in 2000 to the Home Affairs Committee examining the DSPD proposals, the forensic psychiatrist Nigel Eastman made the following illuminating point about the crucial distinction between mental illness and personality disorders:

> An illness is something that arises in somebody who is, if you like, essentially classified as normal before they get ill, so the illness amounts to a change away from their normal functioning [. . .] A personality disorder is very different from that because it is essentially a developmental disorder, it *is* the person and it is not, so to speak, treatable in the same way as an illness.
>
> (Home Affairs Committee, 2000: para 176, emphasis in original)

In other words, a key feature of DSPD is that it is more or less an unchanging characteristic of individuals rather than a temporary aberration created by illness. In a perceptive paper on new sex-offender laws in North America, Jonathan Simon (1998) notes that this legislation constructs these offenders as examples of the 'intransigence of evil'. In this sense, he describes the laws as concerned with 'managing the monstrous'. Clearly, the presumed longevity of personality traits, in contrast to the notion of mental illness, similarly implies a degree of 'intransigence' to the dangerous behaviour of those individuals categorised under the DSPD label. The perceived causal association between their personality traits (which, as Eastman puts it, *are* the person) and their potential for serious violent behaviour marks them out as 'monsters' requiring an exclusionary response. In this way, whilst the DSPD programme is certainly concerned with risk management, it is a form of risk-based government which is transformed in to a highly emotive hybrid centred on 'vengeance' against those marked out as the 'other' (Simon, 1998:464; O'Malley, 2004:147). Perhaps more precisely, though, rather than simply an appeal to 'vengeance' or retribution as an end in itself, the promise, as Sparks (2000a:136) suggests, is more about increased protection through the use of confinement. Hence, as described above, the DSPD programme was presented in part as a response to the 'problem' of dangerous individuals being released from prisons at the end of determinate sentences. This resonates with Nikolas Rose's (2000) analysis of 'advanced liberal' forms of government. He argues that whilst some individuals can be managed within 'circuits of inclusion', others are controlled through 'circuits of exclusion'. Exclusionary strategies are targeted at those individuals for whom affiliation or inclusion is deemed impossible. The focus becomes on managing these 'anti-citizens [. . .] through measures which seek to neutralize the dangers they pose' (Rose, 2000:195). Garland (1996:461) too has identified this kind of dualistic strategy, on one side of which lies the 'alien other' whose dangerousness can be countered only by removing them from circulation in order to protect the public.

This analysis to some extent runs counter to that set out by Castel (1991) in his landmark essay on the shift from 'dangerousness to risk' (see also Corbett and Westwood, 2005:129–30). He argues that the deployment of the preventive technology of confinement against dangerous subjects has come to be replaced by interventions targeted at combinations of those abstract factors which are known to increase the probability of undesirable behaviour. The DSPD programme arguably brings together both 'dangerousness' and 'risk'. In making the diagnosis risk factors are invoked but, at the same time, given that the relevant 'dangers' are related to *personality*, there is a sense in which the focus then turns to the diagnosed individual as a dangerous subject – hence the emphasis on confinement as the response. The idea discussed above, of the DSPD proposals being concerned with 'managing the monstrous', highlights the coupling together of a novel focus on risk with a more archaic concern about dangerous subjects. It is thus another example of the co-presence of innovation and conservatism within recent penal politics (O'Malley, 1999).

Turning now to the second element of Rabinow's definition of 'dividing practices', the principal mode of the 'practice of exclusion' associated with the DSPD programme is confinement or incarceration. This practice melds together risk management, punishment and public protection into a hybrid technique of spatial and social exclusion. As discussed in Chapter 2, there is a long history of the use of institutional confinement as a response to offenders with mental health problems. The distinctive feature of the DSPD programme, as already noted, is the primacy it places on confinement as a means of protecting communities from the potential future dangers (essentially violence and sex offences) posed by the targeted group (Corbett and Westwood, 2005:128). For Foucault (1967), the 'Great Confinement' of the seventeenth and eighteenth centuries was more concerned with controlling unproductive elements of the labour force, whilst even the establishment of specialist institutions like Broadmoor in the nineteenth century was aimed as much at easing the management problems of prisons as with protecting the public.

Notwithstanding these points of difference, it is possible to overstate the novelty of the DSPD programme. A much-cited paper by Bottoms (1977), written nearly 30 years ago, discusses the 'renaissance' of dangerousness in the context of the then recent Butler Committee on Mentally Abnormal Offenders (Home Office/DHSS, 1975), arguing that Butler's proposals constituted in many respects 'simply revivals of an earlier mode of thought and practice' (1977:71) (see also Forrester, 2002). One of Butler's recommendations was for the introduction of a new form of reviewable indeterminate sentence for offenders 'who are dangerous, who present a history of mental disorder which cannot be dealt with under the Mental Health Act, and for whom the life sentence is not appropriate' (1975:76). The strong resemblance to some of the DSPD proposals is evident. Indeed, the issue of offenders suffering from psychopathic disorder has been revisited a number of times in the 1980s and 1990s. An ill-starred consultation document in 1986 set out proposals to amend the Mental Health Act 1983 to make special provisions for psychopaths (DHSS/Home Office, 1986; Peay, 1988), and in the early 1990s a Working Group chaired by John Reed had recommended the introduction of a new 'hybrid order' in cases where treatability was uncertain (Reed, 1994). The hospital and limitation direction order introduced by the Crime (Sentences) Act 1997 was a significantly altered version of Reed's 'hybrid order'; it aroused considerable controversy, as it appeared to have subverted the original Reed recommendation with a new emphasis on public protection and punishment (Eastman, 1996; Chiswick, 1996; Eastman and Peay, 1998).

The DSPD proposals might be best characterised, then, as a recasting within the context of late modernity of some long-standing themes. Following Leacock and Sparks (2002), it could be added that this recasting is strongly inflected and modulated by the particular and specific complexities of New Labour's approach to the penal field, an approach in which the centrality of public protection is perhaps the only constant in an otherwise highly mobile field.

As already noted, an interesting feature of these 'dividing practices' is that the proposed new high secure places were to be located in both prisons and

Special Hospitals. This raises the question of whether there are differences between units in the health sector and those in the penal system. Planning and delivery guidance issued in 2005 stated the following in a sub-section entitled 'Hospital or Prison?':

> Each of the units will broadly be taking similar groups of people based on the admission criteria. There may be instances however when a hospital rather than a prison setting is more appropriate. This will be decided on a case by case basis and will be influenced by the following considerations:
>
> * The individual has mental health needs that can be best met in a hospital environment;
> * An individual is near the end of their sentence and is likely to require continued detention under mental health legislation in order to complete treatment.
>
> (Department of Health/Home Office/Prison Service, 2005)

The statement in the initial paragraph suggests differences are minimal. The second bullet point implies a rather blurred dividing line. Whilst it refers to the need to transfer to hospital 'in order to complete treatment', it might presumably also be required on grounds of dangerousness (given that new legislation has still to be enacted – see below). Some might categorise this blurred division as indicative of a blurring of the boundary between the 'mad' and the 'bad'. It has been suggested in previous chapters that this dichotomy is an unhelpful simplification of a more complex process. The analysis above of the DSPD programme certainly supports this view. The 'dividing practices' associated with the programme are multi-faceted and are clearly not reducible to the 'mad'–'bad' dichotomy.

Finally, it is noteworthy that at the time of writing in late 2005, the DSPD proposals first set out in the 1999 Green Paper have still not been implemented in their entirety. The development of new services has unfolded at a relatively slow pace. Prisoners began to be admitted to the DSPD unit at Whitemoor prison in autumn 2000 and in 2001 there was a commitment to provide 300 new high secure DSPD places. However, there was then no further expansion of places until the opening of a temporary 10-bed ward at Broadmoor in spring 2003. This was followed a year later with the opening of the Westgate Unit at Frankland prison and the Peaks Unit at Rampton Hospital. The 70-bed Paddock Centre at Broadmoor began taking admissions only in October 2005 and is not due to reach capacity until spring 2007. Overall, the target of 300 places is still some way from being met – a Home Office update on the Programme issued in October 2005 stated that only 160 places were occupied at that point (Home Office, 2005). The new legislation has developed even more slowly. The White Paper on reforming the Mental Health Act appeared in December 2000 and a draft Mental

Health Bill was then published in 2002. This Bill was strongly criticised by campaigners and others, and a revised version was produced in September 2004. The second version of the Bill was itself then criticised strongly in a pre-legislative scrutiny report by a parliamentary committee published in March 2005. A third version of the Bill was due to be presented to Parliament before the end of 2006, but this commitment was shelved in March 2006.

Indeed, it is not clear now how much of the original proposed legislative change will end up being implemented. There are some indications that the removal or alteration of the 'treatability' requirement is now seen as the only required legislative change, rather than new civil powers of detention. Whilst the Green Paper back in 1999 had declared that 'to meet our objective of improving public safety there will need to be changes in legislation to provide authority for the detention of dangerous severely personality disordered people on the basis of the risk they present, and if necessary, for detention to be indefinite' (Home Office/Department of Health, 1999:19) and had made specific reference to the introduction of new civil powers, by 2005 the position seemed to be rather different. The Home Office update on the Programme in October 2005 stated that there is 'no specific DSPD legislation' (Home Office, 2005). It noted the proposed change to the treatability requirement in the Mental Health Bill, but suggested that by itself this was likely to have only a 'marginal impact'. The introduction of indeterminate sentencing for 'dangerous offenders' under the Criminal Justice Act 2003 is referred to as much more significant for the Programme, although this of course involves criminal and not civil proceedings.

This very slow unfolding of the programme, and the backtracking on some of the original proposals about legislation, can be contrasted with the urgent tone of the initial documents. It could be concluded from this that in political terms the *announcement* of the policy was as important as its actualisation in practice. In other words, being seen to respond quickly and robustly to the apparent legal anomalies revealed by the Michael Stone case was critical and urgent; implementing the proposals for change was less so, as the perceived problem was actually relatively rare, involving a small number of cases. As always, and as acknowledged several times in previous chapters, political rhetoric is rarely just 'talk' but can also by itself have real consequences. In this regard, some have suggested that the DSPD proposals helped to cement the public perception of a link between mental disorder and violence (Smith, 2003:17). Evidence for this link has been the subject of a long-running and controversial debate (Monahan, 1992; Monahan et al, 2001), and it has been argued that much of the media representation of the issue has taken on the character of a moral panic (Muijen, 1996). A provocative but insightful essay by Pearson (1999) serves as a reminder that the concept of a moral panic, as developed by Cohen (1972), is predicated on there being a kernel of reality to the anxieties played upon and stirred up by the mass media. He argues that ignoring this may be as misleading and unhelpful as some of the media scaremongering.

To summarise, it has been argued that the DSPD programme constitutes a revised set of 'dividing practices' aimed at addressing 'dangerous' offenders with mental health problems. At one level, the programme is evidence of the rise of 'risk' and 'risk thinking' in neo-liberal government. On another, it speaks to a more visceral and emotive desire to confine the 'dangerous monsters' in our midst. Jock Young (1999:96–120), drawing on and extending others' observations about the increasing resort to the figure of the dangerous 'alien other' (Garland, 1996:461; Simon, 1998; Rose, 2000:195; O'Malley, 2004:147), suggests that this strategy of 'essentialising the other' and 'manufacturing monsters' is in fact an integral component of the 'exclusive' society that has emerged with the coming of late modernity in the last third of the twentieth century. He cites several examples of this type of essentialist 'demonisation'. In this way, the DSPD programme can be seen as an instance of the complex and 'finely-tuned dangerousness matrix' of neo-liberal government (Pratt, 1997:178). In its concern with managing future and unknown risks, there is a resonance too with the argument developed recently by Richard Ericson (2005:669) that increasingly the neo-liberal governmental response to uncertainty and limited knowledge about risks of future harms is to resort to more intensive criminalisation. He suggests that the greater the uncertainty, the more intensive the criminalisation is likely to be. This idea draws on O'Malley's (2004) thesis that neo-liberal government needs to be understood in terms of assemblages or configurations of risk and uncertainty, rather than simply focusing on 'risk'.

3. CONCLUSIONS

The late 1990s and early twenty-first century under the New Labour administration have been viewed by some commentators in the criminal justice and mental health fields (for example, Peay, 2002) as a period characterised above all by an overriding concern with risk and risk management. The analysis in this chapter certainly reveals the centrality of risk to developments in this area. However, it should also be clear that risk is far from the sole or even the predominant feature during this period. Other aspects of neo-liberalism, notably managerialism, remain a strong element. There is also evidence for 'progressive' developments harking back to the Woolf/Reed agenda of the early 1990s. In the DSPD programme, there is a complex melding together of aspects of neo-liberalism with more punitive elements. Overall, then, it seems that, as was argued in the previous three chapters, there is no single paradigm or logic guiding strategy in this area. The government of offenders and prisoners with mental health problems is multi-faceted and multi-stranded. However, perhaps for the first time since the demise of penal-welfarism in the 1970s, there does appear to be emerging a clearer single rationality, namely neo-liberalism. This has been an ever-present strand within governmental strategies since the 1980s, as described in the previous three chapters. Whereas, though, in the 1980s and 1990s it was simply one element among several, by the early twenty-first century it appears to be becoming not the only but certainly the leading or dominant component in strategies in this field. Whether this is merely a short-run dominance or a more enduring trend or 'master pattern' remains to be seen in the coming years.

The apparent dominance of neo-liberalism in this recent period is in certain respects a curiosity. Whilst there was an obvious affinity with this approach for the New Right Thatcher and Major administrations, it might have been expected that the arrival of New Labour in 1997 would downgrade the importance of neo-liberalism. In fact, the opposite appears to have happened. As Leacock and Sparks (2002:209–17) argue, however, the New Labour approach is a complex and 'ever mobile' one. It cannot be crudely characterised as purely neo-liberal, or at least it cannot if the concern is to develop a more nuanced and sophisticated account of the criminal justice and penal realms during this period. There are then two analytical challenges: first, how to account for the persistence of neo-liberalism under New Labour; and second, how to trace the complex 'braiding' together of 'conceptual threads' that characterises New Labour's penal strategy (Leacock and Sparks, 2002:216).

Taking these in turn, the answer to the first challenge is perhaps relatively straightforward. It involves arguing, first of all, that the 'sweeping social, economic and cultural changes that signalled the coming of late modernity also prompted major political realignments' (Zedner, 2002:347) and, furthermore, that these realignments were of a fundamental rather than merely party political character. In other words, in late modernity, the politics of welfare and punishment have been transformed. O'Malley (1999) argues that within New Right politics, penal strategy needs to be understood as a political alliance between neo-liberalism and neo-conservatism. It could be argued by analogy that within New Labour politics, it needs to be understood as a different alliance, namely one between neo-liberalism and what might be termed neo-progressivism. In this view, the constant is neo-liberalism, which might be seen as the core of late-modern government, its correlative governmental strategy. What changes, and is the source of the 'volatile and contradictory' (O'Malley, 1999) character of penal politics, is the nature of the political alliance made by particular administrations. To understand developments at any one time therefore requires an engagement with the 'substantively political' logic of penal policy and politics (Sparks, 2001a:195). Summarising this argument, then, neo-liberalism is the hallmark of late-modern government which would be expected to persist under administrations of whatever political hue. However, different political alliances and hybrids with neo-liberalism are forged under different political umbrellas and banners, such as the New Right or New Labour. This kind of argument could be used to address some aspects of the critiques of Garland's (2001) *Culture of Control* thesis that Zedner (2002) and Young (2002) have made, in which, *inter alia*, they suggest that Garland fails to account for certain penal and criminal justice developments under New Labour. It also implies the need for careful and detailed empirical research rather than abstract theorising.

The second analytical challenge is more difficult to meet. It is hoped that the analysis in Section 2 of this chapter achieved to some extent this kind of tracing of the complex weaving together of diverse strands within New Labour. The question here really is how to conceptualise this. In a sense, this is nothing new. As the previous three chapters have shown, as well as many other studies in this field (for example, Garland, 1985), there is always a multi-faceted picture to try and grasp when analysing penality, hence his description of the social realm as a 'multi-layered mosaic' (1985:155). However, there does seem to be a particular type of complexity and novelty within New Labour's approach to penal affairs. As Leacock and Sparks (2002:216) suggest:

> It is the very juxtaposition between familiar and novel sightings on the penal landscape that designedly disrupts existing political classifications and suggests the need for new thinking. If we wish to trace out a history of the present configuration of risk ideas in criminal justice we will have to acknowledge that they do not all originate in one place, either ideologically or temporally.

This seems to be pointing towards the idea that within New Labour there is a particularly innovative and eclectic mix of different elements, old and new, left and right. This would certainly resonate with perceptions that 'old' ideological barriers (for example, to private sector involvement in public service provision) have been breached by New Labour. What does this imply or require in analytical terms? One particularly fruitful approach is likely to be that of genealogy or the 'history of the present' (to which Leacock and Sparks obliquely refer in the quotation above), as this involves the attempt to understand how present-day practices have come about by tracing their historical lineage. The originator of the idea of 'histories of the present' is of course Foucault (1977:31; see also Dean, 1994), but others have utilised broadly similar approaches to great explanatory effect, notably, for example, David Garland (1985, 2001). Thus, in the analysis above of the DSPD programme, the weaving together of strategies for risk management and 'managing the monstrous' was traced, as was the recasting of older ideas about dangerousness. Pratt's (1997) study is a good example of a more extended analysis of the genealogy of the contemporary government of dangerousness (see also McCallum, 2001).

The analysis in Section 2 of this chapter has raised some interesting points about risk that are worth considering here. First, Jill Peay's (2002:747) claim quoted earlier that 'current policy in mental health and crime [. . .] is not dominated by humanitarian concerns; rather, it is permeated by perceptions and attributions of risk' may perhaps be an overstatement. She may be guilty to a degree of what Leacock and Sparks (2002:199) term the error of 'totalisation (as if risk were the only issue)'. As has been shown, under New Labour risk is but one strand (albeit an important one) among several within the complex multi-faceted strategies at play in the field of mental health and crime. What might be termed 'humanitarian' concerns are undoubtedly one of the other strands. It is worth remembering too that the DSPD programme, which is where New Labour's 'risk thinking' has been at its most evident, was intended to affect only around 2,000 individuals. The initially proposed civil powers of detention, which were the most controversial, were likely to have 'caught' a considerably smaller sub-group of people (perhaps a few hundred or even less). To take this as evidence of risk 'taking over' is arguably to get things out of proportion. Certainly the concept of risk has a distinctive place within the New Labour approach, and it shapes the thinking and behaviour of contemporary practitioners in equally distinctive ways (Peay, 2003b), but the strategic picture at the beginning of the twenty-first century is more mixed than bald claims for the pre-eminence of risk allow.

The second interesting point to be made about risk during this period is that it is hardly describable as truly actuarial or probabilistic in nature. Risk assessments in the DSPD programme, for example, revolved much more around 'technologies of uncertainty' than probabilistic assessments of actuarial risk (see O'Malley, 2004:1–28). Whilst the various government documents listed 'risk factors' that might be used to assess individuals for DSPD, these were not really numerical or probabilistic in form (see Rose, 1998). The line between risk and uncertainty was blurred. The critical analytical implication is, as O'Malley (2004) argues, the need to examine forms of government as hybrid configurations of risk and uncertainty (see also Ericson, 2005).

The next and final chapter in this book attempts to draw together the central arguments that have been made in the preceding chapters. It begins by summarising the narrative account of strategies towards mentally disordered offenders and prisoners during the period from the 1980s to the present, as set out in Chapters 3–6. It then goes on to look at some of the central themes, concepts and ideas examined in the book and seeks to pull together the findings from the work. In conclusion, some possible future directions for research and policy are discussed.

Chapter 7

Conclusions

As I write this, two new reports on mental illness and the US prison system are released [. . .] The first report, by Human Rights Watch, is dynamite: it points to between 200,000 and 400,000 mentally ill persons being in the US prison system – that is, between 10 and 20 per cent of the gargantuan prison population. The prison has become the primary mental health facility in the United States, overtaking those institutions which are primarily designated for mentally ill people. They are there as a consequence of the underfunded, disorganized and fragmented community mental health services [. . .] Further, this rise in the incarceration of mentally ill people must have been spurred on by the drop in tolerance of disorderly behaviour which occurred in the 1990s, with the focus upon so-called quality-of-life crimes. Indeed, one suspects that a major incentive for the development of such policies was the control of mentally ill persons wandering the streets without proper facilities or treatment. Thus, the people least capable of controlling their behaviour are caught up in this control sweep. Once in prison, of course, matters get only worse: prisons make sane people mad and mad people madder. And, within prison, people who are unable to control their behaviour are the targets of the disciplinary sweep of the prison. And, as the second report [. . .] points out, [. . .] whilst 11.6 per cent of New York inmates are on the mental health caseload, 23 per cent of those on disciplinary lockdown are mentally ill.

(Young, 2004:550–51)

In characteristically forceful style, and despite the fact that he is commenting on the US situation, Jock Young here captures in a nutshell some of the key contours of the debate explored in this book: the shock felt at the very presence of the mentally disordered in prisons; the sheer numbers of people involved; the apparent link with the emptying out of the mental hospitals and the failure to fund community facilities adequately; the use of incarceration as a tool for controlling the 'troublesome'; and the deleterious impact of imprisonment itself on the mentally vulnerable.

The first main task of this chapter is to pull together some critical observations about these and other important issues, drawing on the analysis in the preceding chapters. The second principal task of this concluding chapter is to try to answer that most difficult of questions, 'What should be done?' What does the account presented in this book imply about the future direction that policy and research in this field should take?

First of all, though, before turning to these two tasks, a brief summary will be presented of the narrative account set out in the heart of this book, in Chapters 3 through to 6. The overarching research question addressed in this book has been whether – and how – the major structural transformations that have accompanied the shift to late modernity have shaped the 'dividing practices' deployed in the government of prisoners with mental health problems. The summary below will now bring together the answer to that question.

I. THE IMPACT OF LATE MODERNITY ON THE GOVERNMENT OF PRISONERS WITH MENTAL HEALTH PROBLEMS

After the 'golden' post-war decades, the 1970s saw the start of some major social, economic and cultural shifts across the industrialised Western world, including in Britain. Significant structural transformations occurred in the economy, the labour market, the family, the mass media, communications and the role of the (welfare) state. Unemployment, increasing job insecurity, economic downturns and major changes in gender roles within families and the workplace all signified the 'rapid unravelling of the social fabric of the industrialized world' (Young, 1999:vi). This was accompanied, at a political level, by the rise of the New Right – the Thatcher government in Britain and the Reagan administration in the United States – and the corresponding demise of social democratic or socialist political parties. This political re-alignment was both an indicator of and a response to the challenges presented by these structural transformations. It was characterised by the coupling of neo-liberal economics with neo-conservative social policy and defined itself as 'anti-welfarist'. This set of transformations during the last three decades of the twentieth century together constituted the shift from modernity to late modernity.

At the same time, recorded crime rates saw a massive and sustained increase across all offence categories right up until the early 1990s. Thus, recorded offences in England and Wales rose from 1 per 100 people in 1950 to 10 per 100 in 1994 (Garland, 2001:90). Garland (2001:90) argues that this steep increase in crime rates was closely linked to the enormous social, economical and cultural transformations described above.

The crime control and penal complexes were also transformed in the last third of the twentieth century, and not just by the immediate consequences of increased crime rates. Most notably, there was an expansion of the use of prison, particularly in the 1990s. Perhaps even more significant than this were some other features of the crime control complex. In the 1980s and 1990s a whole series of innovations were introduced: the rise of the status of victims and the restorative justice movement; the privatisation of some elements of the criminal justice system; and the development of local inter-agency crime prevention partnerships. The correctionalism that had formed the core logic of penal-welfare strategies during the first two-thirds of the twentieth century was now pushed to the margins.

The question this book has sought to address is how this set of transformations, the shift to late modernity, affected the government of prisoners with mental health problems. Chapters 3, 4, 5 and 6 explored this through the detailed analysis of empirical material, and the account presented there is now summarised below.

The 1980s: the 'neo-liberal' decade?

Chapter 3 described how during the 1980s, under three increasingly self-confident Conservative administrations led by Margaret Thatcher, there was clearly a shift towards neo-liberal forms of governing prisoners with mental health problems. The best example of this was the Home Office *Efficiency Scrutiny of the Prison Medical Service* published in 1990 (Home Office, 1990a), but it is also evident in the 1987 Interdepartmental Working Group report on mentally disturbed prisoners (Home Office/DHSS, 1987). In this new neo-liberal 'way of thinking' there was a strong emphasis on managerialism with its deployment of private-sector techniques for improving efficiency, effectiveness, accountability and value for money. This was exemplified by the description of the 1990 Home Office review of the Prison Medical Service as an 'Efficiency Scrutiny'. The previous Home Office review, the Gwynn report published in 1964, had been rather more prosaically titled the 'Report of the working party on the organization of the prison medical service' (Home Office, 1964). The late 1980s also saw the emergence of a distinctive focus on the administration or management of risk and an emphasis on the management or containment of offenders rather than their rehabilitation or treatment. There was thus a shift from a 'social' to an 'economic' style of reasoning or 'way of thinking' (Garland, 2001:188–9). This all supports the argument that under the umbrella of New Right politics, a new neo-liberal form of government emerged in response to the shift to late modernity.

However, the analysis in Chapter 3 also showed that strategies and 'dividing practices' in this field were multi-faceted. For example, concerns about the 'treatment' of mentally ill prisoners did not disappear. Indeed, the number of transfers from prison to hospital increased by nearly 60 per cent between 1986 and 1989; following Home Office Circular 66/90 issued in 1990, this trend was to accelerate in the early 1990s. Thus, rather than a wholesale paradigm shift towards neo-liberalism, it is more accurate to see the 1980s as a period which saw the insertion of some novel neo-liberal 'ways of thinking' about and 'ways of acting' on mentally vulnerable offenders into existing strategies.

The early 1990s: the revival of a humanitarian approach?

Chapter 4 described the apparent revival of 'progressive' penal policy, led by the Woolf report and the ensuing White Paper *Custody, Care and Justice*. The Reed Review adopted a similar direction in the field of mental health and crime. There were also new funding initiatives to stimulate the development of court diversion schemes and a concerted (and successful) drive to increase prison transfers to hospital. This was all evidence of a strong focus on locating and routing mentally vulnerable offenders towards treatment. At this 'headline' level, the early 1990s could therefore be described as seeing a revival of humanitarian approaches and a concern with keeping the mentally unwell out of prisons. It was argued in this chapter that this development was partly related to the unravelling of faith in the 'Thatcherite' economic project and the related political desire to sound a less harsh tone on some social policy issues. A robust but humanitarian approach to mentally disordered offenders resonated quite well with this political imperative.

However, again, the analysis in Chapter 4 suggests that, despite this 'headline' shift, the picture was actually less clear-cut and more multi-faceted. Neo-liberal managerialism remained an underpinning feature. Indeed, the Reed Review is thoroughly imbued and infused with managerialist thinking, with a recurring focus on 'value for money', monitoring, performance measurement and so on. There was also a continuing emphasis on the administration of risk. The evidence therefore does not support the view that there was a wholesale paradigm shift in the early 1990s towards 'humanitarianism' of the Woolf/Reed kind.

The mid-1990s: the return of Victorian penal values?

Chapter 5 described the sudden reversal of the 'progressive' moment of the early 1990s and a shift towards a repressive 'penal populism'. This shift was certainly evident, although its impact on the government of prisoners with mental health problems was more varied and less direct than for penal policy more generally.

However, as with the previous two chapters, it was also apparent that strategies were multi-faceted. For example, the 'progressive' Reed agenda persisted in the drive to improve the quality of prison health care via Health Care Standards. Neo-liberalism also continued to be a major strand within strategies in this field, in terms of both the further extension of managerialism and the ongoing concern with the management of risk.

The late 1990s and early twenty-first century: The 'risk society'?

Chapter 6 presented the most recent developments under the New Labour administration first elected in 1997. It described how risk thinking and a concern with the management of the risks believed to be presented by some offenders with mental health problems became a prominent theme. The DSPD programme exemplified this tendency, as its central purpose was to intervene with individuals solely on the basis of the assessed risks they posed to others.

Yet, as with earlier 'headline' shifts, this focus on risk was not an exclusive or overriding one. Managerialist techniques and approaches were also central elements. Traces of both 'penal populism' and humanitarianism were apparent too, in a complex and multi-faceted strategic picture.

The overall trajectory of strategies

How can we best make sense of the overall strategic trajectory or narrative suggested by the analysis in these four chapters? It is clear, first of all, that the post-welfare politics that emerged in Britain from 1979 saw the demise of the forms of social and penal regulation that had held sway during the first two-thirds of the twentieth century, the penal-welfarism described by Garland (1981, 1985). The shift to late modernity was clearly accompanied by new forms of penality and these did impact on the government of prisoners with mental health problems. The trajectory of research on Grendon prison during the period neatly illustrates this, as evaluations of the regime shifted from measuring 'success' primarily in terms of 'psy' outcomes (Gunn et al, 1978; Robertson and Gunn, 1987) to measuring it through reconviction studies (Marshall, 1997; Taylor, 2000) and its effectiveness in safely managing 'difficult' prisoners (Genders and Player, 1995).

However, it is evident, secondly, that strategies did not appear to settle in any obvious single new direction. There has not been a simple transition from penal-welfarism to a new late-modern form of penality. This is an important point to stress. As Foucault famously warned some 20 years ago, the temptation to see neat and finished patterns in contemporary history is a strong one:

> One of the most harmful habits of contemporary thought is the analysis of the present as being precisely, in history, a present of rupture, of high point, of completion, or of a returning dawn [. . .] the time we live in is not *the* unique or fundamental irruptive point in history where everything is completed and begun again.
>
> (Foucault, 1983)

Indeed, four different 'headline' shifts were identified during the period from the 1980s to 2005, and even within these it was shown how strategies were in fact multi-faceted. There appeared to be a complex, heterogeneous and changing strategic 'mix' during this period. It was not a case of a succession of distinct paradigms. In fact, the field has something of a *kaleidoscopic* character during the period examined in the central chapters of this book, as new patterns were continually created through the rotation and re-orientation of the same constituent parts (punishment, treatment, containment, risk management and so on). The critical analytical question of course is how to interpret this. Can we step back and see any overall pattern?

One interpretation is simply that this period has been a transitional one and, therefore, by definition one characterised by flux and uncertainty. It is only when the 'dust settles' and a new re-configured field emerges that strategy becomes more settled. Garland's (1985:161–202) analysis in *Punishment and Welfare* of a previous period of penal transition at the start of the twentieth century supports to some extent this idea that such periods of strategy formation can be unstable. Another explanation that has been referred to already several times in previous chapters is that offered by O'Malley (1999). He argues that the 'volatile and contradictory' character of recent penal strategies is the result of fundamental tensions within New Right politics between neo-liberalism and neo-conservatism.

Both these explanations have some force and tell part of the story. O'Malley's article is certainly insightful and astutely argued. However, the analysis in preceding chapters points towards a slightly different view of the matter, or at least a different perspective on the issues at stake. Following the line of argument developed in a series of papers by Richard Sparks (2001a, 2001b, 2003), it has been shown in this book how a full understanding of the changing contours of the penal landscape is possible only by paying close, careful and serious attention to the political order and culture. It is only in this way that it becomes possible to understand why particular developments unfold at particular times and in particular ways. It involves attempting:

> To keep both the foreground of the scene (some local and maybe short-run variations in national penal rhetorics and practices, condensed into the familiar political slogans) and the background (the more deeply embedded but less obvious tendencies of contemporary crime-control systems) adequately in focus in the same shot.
>
> (Sparks, 2001b:170)

Taking this view, it can be argued that the government of prisoners with mental health problems since the 1980s has been underpinned by neo-liberal rationalities and techniques, but that these neo-liberal elements have formed part of mobile hybrid formations which have been inflected and shaped by the changing political order during this period (that is, the rise and fall of the

New Right and then the emergence of New Labour). In theoretical terms, as discussed in Chapter 1, this approach involves bringing together three explanatory building blocks: the analysis of governmental discourses (in the manner of the 'governmentality' approach); the consideration of changing representations or mobilisations of 'punishment' within the political culture; and the specific contingent circumstances which shape the unfolding of practical actions and events. Whilst the first two of these elements are clearly conceptually separate, they are 'generally not *found separately in empirical reality*' (Sparks, 2001b:170, emphasis in original). Hence the need to try and bring the instrumental and the representational into a 'single analytic frame' (2001b:169). The third element partly involves the incorporation of the kind of micro-sociological approach developed by Paul Rock (1988, 1995, 1996) and others (Duke, 2003).

An important dimension of neo-liberalism that has formed part of the strategic pattern traced in this book is the distinctive place of risk within governmental rationalities and technologies. Several lines of argument about risk have been developed and can be usefully brought together here. First, it has been clearly shown in the preceding chapters that a concern with risk and its management has indeed permeated the penal realm during the last two decades of the twentieth century and that this has in turn shaped the 'dividing practices' examined in this book. Second, however, it has been argued that the novelty of risk should not be overstated. Risk is not a new concept, nor is risk thinking a new phenomenon. The idea of risk has long been articulated within both penal administration and the mental health field. Indeed, more broadly, it is possible to trace the genealogy of risk back to the origins of political liberalism and modern capitalism in the late eighteenth century (O'Malley, 2000, 2004). Crucially, 'within this genealogy the meaning and place of risk has shifted rather than being a constant' (O'Malley, 2000:29), and so the explanatory focus here has not been simply on the 'rise of risk' but rather on the distinctive place risk has come to assume within neo-liberalism. Third, in this regard, and as noted above, the analysis in preceding chapters has repeatedly substantiated the point that risk is seldom present on its own, but instead forms part of complex and mobile hybrids or assemblages. It is the changing composition of these hybrids that needs to be traced and understood. Specifically, O'Malley's (2004) argument that risk invariably appears alongside the related but distinct concept of uncertainty has been supported by the analysis presented in this book. Fourth, it has been shown that risk has a polysemic or multi-vocal character. It is not always simply a technical or administrative tool of neo-liberalism, it can also form part of highly emotive or politicised hybrids, as for example in the controversial DSPD programme. The use of risk can, in other words, be just as politically 'populist' as the appeal to punitiveness (Sparks, 2001a); indeed, there may be a liaison between the two (Sparks, 2000a). Taking these four points together, the book implicitly makes a case for a particular cultural and political construction of risk as the most compelling version of the concept, at least when used in the penal context. Following Sparks (2000a, 2001b), the analysis presented in Chapters 3 through to 6 shows how risk discourse needs to be understood as a fundamentally mixed discourse – 'moral, emotive and political as well as calculative' (Sparks, 2001b:169) – which straddles the public and professional aspects of the penal realm. Viewed in this light, it thereby provides a way into some familiar but important questions about order, legitimacy and conflict (Sparks, 2001a:208).

2. CRITICAL ISSUES AND THEMES

In investigating the nexus between punishment and madness, and specifically the government of prisoners with mental health problems, a number of important issues and themes have been explored. This section will now try and bring together what has been learnt in the preceding chapters. Specifically, it will cover four key issues: the link between imprisonment and mental health problems; the concept of 'dividing practices'; gender; and culture and ethnicity.

Unravelling the connections between imprisonment and mental health problems

The quotation from Jock Young at the beginning of this chapter refers, *inter alia*, to the common view that the problem of mental disorder in prisons is a consequence of the closing down of the mental hospitals and the underfunding of community care. The argument is that the mentally ill and mentally disordered have been ejected from mental hospitals, have found the levels of care and support in the community to be totally inadequate and, as their mental state has deteriorated, have found themselves swept up by the criminal justice system and incarcerated in prison. The prison system thus becomes a *de facto* replacement for the mental hospitals. The general proposition that there is an inverse relationship between prisoner numbers and mental hospital patient numbers – as one goes up, the other goes down – is so well established that it has even gained a title, Penrose's law, after a paper published nearly 70 years ago by Lionel Penrose (Penrose, 1939; see also Biles and Mulligan, 1973; cf Gunn, 2000).

This is a persuasive line of argument and has been deployed to great effect by campaigners seeking to critique the failings of the community care policy. However, it is also almost entirely false. As Chapter 2 showed, the problem pre-dates the hospital closure programme and the community care policy not just by decades but by centuries. It was one of the issues that most troubled John Howard during his investigations into the state of the prisons in the late eighteenth century (see also Carlen, 1986:263–4). Even in the late nineteenth century, a period that saw the massive expansion of the public asylum system following the Lunacy and County Asylums Acts of 1845, it was a major and continuing problem (see also: Smith, 1981; Long and Midgley, 1992). Neither did it appear to worsen significantly in the decades that followed the 1950s, when the mental hospital closure programme actually began. The two surveys conducted by John Gunn and colleagues in the early 1970s and late 1980s respectively (Gunn et al, 1978, 1991) showed a stable rate of mental disorder in prisons despite the large reduction in psychiatric hospital beds that occurred during this period. There was little evidence either that it was the former long-stay hospital patients who were ending up in prison. Furthermore, there is international research showing that the problem is an intrinsic feature of Western prisons, regardless of the variations in their health, welfare and penal systems. Fazel and Danesh (2002) review 62 surveys from 12 countries (Australia, Canada, Denmark, Finland, Ireland, the Netherlands, New Zealand, Norway, Spain, Sweden, the UK and the USA) and conclude that there is a fairly consistent picture across the board. They also refer to studies in non-Western countries such as Nigeria (Agbahowe et al, 1998), Dubai (Ghubash and El-Rufaie, 1997) and Kuwait (Fido and Al-Labally, 1993), although these were not included in the review. Given, then, that it is clearly a cross-cultural phenomenon, as well as a trans-historical one, it is hard to sustain the argument that the contemporary situation in Britiain is the result of particular health and welfare policies there in recent decades.

So how can the problem be explained? It was suggested in Chapter 2, drawing particularly on Foucault (1967), that it should not be viewed as the result of an aberration or a malfunctioning of systems, but rather as an intrinsic element of the whole project of using institutional confinement as a method of punishment. The essence of confinement used in this way is the exclusion within institutions of the 'deviant', the rule-breakers, the troublesome, the dangerous and the vulnerable. The unity of the category of the confined coheres around the perceived gravity of their transgression of social 'norms', the relative 'difficulty' of their behaviour for families and communities and their lack of productiveness in the legitimate labour market. From this perspective, the confinement of some of the mentally disordered within prisons is unsurprising. It is because of this fundamental nature of the problem that attempts to 'clear out' the prisons of the mentally vulnerable usually make little apparent difference. Hence the various initiatives and legislation at the beginning of the twentieth century described in Chapter 2 failed to solve the problem, as did the drive to increase diversion and transfers in the 1980s and 1990s described in the central chapters of this book.

'Dividing practices': Beyond 'mad or bad'

A critical and recurring question in this field is the distinction between offending related to mental ill-health and simple wrongdoing. The issue is often summarised in the question of whether an individual is 'mad or bad'. It has been argued throughout this book, however, that this 'commonsensical' (even arguably journalistic) dichotomy or division is a misleading simplification which leads to some analytical imprecision.

Nevertheless, the concept of 'dividing practices' has been fruitfully deployed as an analytical tool in this book. As was described in Chapter 1, the notion was initially developed by Foucault in some of his important early works, such as *Madness and Civilization*, *The Birth of the Clinic* and *Discipline and Punish*. In these works, Foucault explores how 'dividing practices' serve as political strategies which categorise, separate, normalise and institutionalise populations. An understanding of these practices thus goes to the heart of any analysis of how human conduct is governed.

If the categories of 'mad' and 'bad' do not adequately capture the relevant divisions in this field, then the obvious question is what other categories are implicated in 'dividing practices'. The preceding chapters have suggested that there are several key dimensions to these practices. First of all, there is indeed the commonsense question of allocating moral responsibility for behaviour. Did the individual knowingly commit a wrongful act, or was their awareness of what they were doing obscured by their mental disturbance? In other words, were they 'bad' or 'mad'? This, of course, has proved to be an exceedingly difficult question to answer.

Second, and relatedly, another set of divisions turns this attribution of responsibility on its head. Chris Tchaikovsky in interview made this telling observation:

> I *did* think it was very interesting that the judge felt – wrongly I suspect – that the public would be happier – this is my view, might be wrong – Peter Sutcliffe being classified sane rather than insane. In other words that it would be better if he went to prison than to a Special Hospital. Now if that is the case, and I think it is just anecdotally, that needs looking at because I've no doubt that every woman in the country – I don't know about men – but every woman in the country would be much happier to have known whatever he was paranoid schizophrenic hearing voices and sent to Broadmoor whatever than putting him in the prison system. And if that was expediency if it was just thought it was in the public interest to send him to prison rather than a Special, again that needs looking at.

The important point Tchaikovsky makes here is that the response to an individual does not necessarily always follow from an official determination of the extent to which they are responsible for their actions. In some cases, it can happen the other way round. In other words, the desired response or disposal comes first and leads to the attribution of responsibility. In the case she cites, of Peter Sutcliffe, she implies that the desired response to his offences was most strongly influenced by the judge's perception of 'public opinion'. This suggests a Durkheimian view of punishment as a means of both expressing and reinforcing social solidarity (see Garland, 1983). It also resonates with arguments about the importance of being attentive to questions of representations of punishment (Sparks, 2001a) and the cultural dimension of penality (Sparks, 2001b; Garland, 1990a, 1990b).

Third, there is the vexed question of 'treatability', which principally surrounds the concept of 'personality disorder'. It has been shown how this category serves an important discursive function within 'dividing practices'. Often, treatability shades into issues of the allocation and availability of resources, between government departments and between different local agencies. It was shown in preceding chapters how, for example, at the level of decisions about treatability taken by psychiatrists, these can sometimes turn on whether or not an appropriate psychiatric bed is available.

Last, as discussed above, and as many commentators have observed, this book has shown how over the last 20 years the field has become increasingly colonised by risk management concerns. Assessments, attributions and judgements about the future risks posed by individuals have strongly shaped 'dividing practices'.

This research has thus shown that the 'dividing practices' investigated in this book go far beyond the simple 'mad'–'bad' dichotomy and actually encompass a series of inter-connected but different questions about responsibility, the social order, cultural sensibilities, treatability, resources and risk management. They are complex and multi-faceted, being resolved in different ways at different times for different individuals. It is for this reason – rather than any intrinsic difficulty in answering the philosophical question about responsibility for behaviour (difficult though this may be sometimes) – that the boundaries and divisions are often perceived to be blurred and unclear.

Perhaps the most significant finding about the 'dividing practices' analysed in this book is that they are historically contingent and vary over time. The categories that underpin these divisions are not fixed or naturally occurring phenomena. Rather, these categories of person are created or 'made up' and 'become known in order to be governed' (McCallum, 2001:36). The categories, and the knowledges and discourses within which they are articulated, are thus tools for the exercise of governmental power over the conduct of individuals. Thus, as Foucault (1977:27) famously put it:

> Power and knowledge directly imply one another [. . .] there is no power relation without the correlative constitution of a field of knowledge, nor any knowledge that does not presuppose and constitute at the same time power relations.

Crucially, it has been shown how transformations in the social, economic and cultural spheres have shaped 'dividing practices' in fundamental ways. In this sense, this book in part picks up the agenda of earlier critiques of psychiatry in the 1960s, by Laing, Cooper, Szasz and others, which sought 'a theoretical understanding which connects madness, and deviant forms of experience, with social and political structure' (Pearson, 1975:18), although it does so from an entirely different theoretical perspective.

Gender

It was noted in Chapter 2 that the idea that there is a particular connection for women between offending and mental health problems has a long history. The ways in which women in general and female offenders in particular have been especially affected by processes of psychiatrisation have been the subject of numerous studies and commentaries over a long period of time (Chesler, 1974; Busfield, 1983; Showalter, 1985; Carlen, 1985b; Dobash et al, 1986; Allen, 1986, 1987; Zedner, 1991; Frigon, 1995; Maden, 1996; Rock, 1996). This body of work indicates that the connections for women between mental health and offending and their processing through the psychiatric and penal systems are complex and are closely related to fundamental issues about the construction of gender in society.

Despite the long-running interest and debate alluded to above, a striking feature of the central chapters in this book is that they reveal the lack of attention paid by policy makers to issues of gender and the specific needs of mentally vulnerable women prisoners. Even in as monumental a piece of work as the Reed Review, only seven and a half pages within the seven main published volumes directly address gender. In the interviews conducted for this research, there was also little mention of gender. Indeed, in only three of the interviews are issues relating to women raised to any great extent, and all three of these interviewees had specific reasons for doing so: Professor Paul Rock had done research on Holloway Prison; Colin Allen was a former governor of Holloway; and Chris Tchaikovsky was the Director of the pressure group Women in Prison. In an era in which research subjects are no longer 'innocent' in relation to feminist perspectives (Heidensohn, 1994), this is interesting and noteworthy in itself (see also Howe, 1994).

One way of explaining this would be to argue that the implicit assumption is that women's needs do not differ significantly from those of men. Indeed, Maden (1996:152) argues exactly this point on the basis of his prison survey research:

> All mentally disordered offenders are disadvantaged by their status as offenders, and as a result of mental disorder. In addition, they are likely to be poor and socially disadvantaged, and a sizable minority suffer discrimination on ethnic grounds. For women, discrimination based on gender is added to this list. However, it has been shown that the influence of gender may be positive or negative, often in an unpredictable way. The additional disadvantage due to gender may be almost insignificant when

set beside the disadvantages of being a mentally disordered offender, and lacking economic and social power. The impression gained during the course of this study was that female mentally disordered offenders had more in common with similar men than they did with other women who were not mentally disordered offenders [. . .] It remains true that mentally ill women in prison have special needs (not least, protection from abusive men), but the main problem may be the overall lack of services for mentally disordered offenders.

Even if this is the case, it is arguable that 'equality' might not always be entirely beneficial for women. A recent and interesting contribution by Snider (2003) suggests that 'equality' in the penal field has in practice constituted a regressive development for women. She argues that feminist perspectives in criminology have unwittingly and ironically led to increased penal repression for women by their success in arguing for 'equality' of treatment for male and female offenders. In other words, gender inequalities in penal treatment have been resolved by levelling up rather than levelling down.

However, when considered through the lens of 'dividing practices' rather than simply service provision, there are strong reasons to doubt this type of equality thesis. A number of research studies have indicated significant disparities in the application of 'dividing practices' to male and female offenders that have persisted since at least the 1960s (Allen, 1987; Grounds, 1990, 1991b; Stafford, 1999; Bland et al, 1999; Mackay and Machin, 2000; Kesteven, 2002). Broadly speaking, this body of research suggests that women offenders are more likely to receive psychiatric disposals than their male counterparts, but that the reasons for this are more varied and complex than simple accounts of the over-psychiatrisation of women suggest (cf Snider, 2003). A pragmatic issue here is the smaller number of specialist facilities available for female offenders.

All this implies a significant point. Although, as this research has shown, women are virtually invisible at the level of national policy for mentally disordered offenders, in terms of 'dividing practices' gender is of immense significance. It can influence sentencing and psychiatric disposals (Allen, 1987), receipt of psychotropic medication in prison (Maden et al, 1994) or in Special Hospitals (Bland et al, 1999) and the application of disciplinary punishment in prison (O'Brien et al, 2001). This indicates not only the explanatory value of the idea of 'dividing practices' but also the continuing need for research in this area to include a serious focus on gender.

Culture and ethnicity

The connections between culture, ethnicity, psychiatry, mental ill-health, crime and punishment are complex and highly controversial (Mercer, 1986; Fernando, 1988, 1991; Browne et al, 1993; Gunn et al, 1991; Browne, 1996;

Phillips and Bowling, 2002). Central to these debates is the idea that Western psychiatry is fundamentally rooted in white Western culture and its colonial history. It is argued that it is this cultural and historical context that under-pins many of the difficulties and discrimination experienced by individuals from black and minority ethnic groups when they are caught up in the penal-psychiatric complex. It is not possible to explore further here this significant body of literature, but two important points can be made which have emerged from the present research study.

First, as with gender, despite the kind of debate referred to above, a defining feature of policy and strategy in this field since the 1980s has been the relative lack of attention paid to issues of culture and ethnicity and the specific needs of mentally vulnerable prisoners from minority ethnic groups. As with gen-der, this is significant in itself. Unlike for women, however, there is no separate provision at all for offenders from different ethnic groups and so inevitably issues of ethnicity are harder to trace at this level.

Nevertheless, second, there is reason to suggest that some of the develop-ments analysed in this book may have particular consequences in relation to ethnicity. One of the elements within debates about ethnicity and mental health concerns how stereotypes about the perceived dangerousness of black people (and especially young black men) impact on their processing through the criminal justice and psychiatric systems (Browne, 1996; Boast and Ches-terman, 1995; Bhui et al, 1998). Browne (1996:203) argues that these stereo-types open up a 'series of possibilities [. . .] most of which are disadvantageous to black people – (over)medication, increased surveillance, greater restraint, increased security and so forth'. As discussed in Chapter 4, given the distinct-ive focus on risk management that preceding chapters have suggested is an emerging feature of contemporary strategies, there is therefore the potential that, as a result of the impact of these stereotypes about dangerousness, the rise of risk may amount in practice to an increasing focus on the surveillance and control of black people. Whether they end up confined in the prison system (Genders and Player, 1989; Clements, 2000) or the secure psychiatric system (Prins et al, 1993), there is evidence that they may suffer discrimi-natory treatment. In this sense, the focus on diversion and transfer in the 1990s, far from being a straightforwardly progressive development, may have a rather more mixed impact on black people (Browne, 1996; Burney and Pearson, 1995). The impact of late modernity on 'dividing practices' in this area is thus not only gendered but also shaped by issues of culture and ethnicity.

3. FUTURE POLICY AND RESEARCH

Policy recommendations can rarely simply be 'read off' from the findings of research without a fair degree of authorial interpretation. The research–policy link is less straightforward than might be imagined. In the final chapter of *Visions of Social Control*, Stan Cohen discusses some of the complexities, problems and tensions inherent in the distinction between the intellectual role of the academic and the role of the critical commentator who wants to change for the better the way things are done. To illustrate the dilemma, he recounts the parable of the fisherman:

> A man is walking by the riverside when he notices a body floating down stream. A fisherman leaps into the river, pulls the body ashore, gives mouth to mouth resuscitation, saving the man's life. A few minutes later the same thing happens, then again and again. Eventually yet another body floats by. This time the fisherman completely ignores the drowning man and starts running upstream along the bank. The observer asks the fisherman what on earth is he doing? Why is he not trying to rescue this drowning body? 'This time,' replies the fisherman, 'I'm going upstream to find out who the hell is pushing these poor folks into the water'.
>
> (Cohen, 1985:236)

This seemed to suggest that the intellectual role of getting to the root of the problem was ultimately the more important activity, rather than the helping of individuals. The twist in the story, and its troubling nature for Cohen, was the question of 'while the fisherman was so busy running along the bank to find the ultimate source of the problem, who was going to help those poor wretches who continued to float down the river?' (Cohen, 1985:237). He goes on to argue that there needs to be some accommodation between the two activities, and that intellectuals cannot properly avoid at least considering some of the implications of their work:

> It is a simple matter of intellectual integrity and honesty to clarify the policy implications of social-problem analysis [. . .] The point is to clarify choices and values.
>
> (Cohen, 1985:238)

Yet the relationship between values, truth and criticism in research which draws on a Foucauldian theoretical framework is not at all straightforward (O'Malley, 2001; Dean, 1994:213–16). It is a tenet of Foucault's thought that conducting criticism does not necessarily need to involve the critic having privileged access to a superior set of values against which the subject of criticism is (unfavourably) compared. Rather, the focus of the critical project is to analyse the assumptions underpinning practices and to challenge their 'self-evident' or 'taken-for-granted' status (Dean, 1994:117–19). O'Malley (2001:135) describes this as the displacement of 'critique' by 'diagnosis'. This is the basis, however, for one of Habermas's (1987) main criticisms of Foucault: that is, that he lacks a normative basis for his analyses and therefore that his approach lacks the emancipatory character intrinsic to critical thought (Dean, 1994:129).

Following on from this point is the argument that if criticism is undertaken without comparison with a set of values, then it is difficult to use it to determine or recommend more progressive ways of acting. On this interpretation, Foucauldian critical analysis becomes a rather nihilistic tool that can denounce practices but never recommend a better alternative.

Foucault himself did not view this as a negative feature of his work:

> The necessity of reform mustn't be allowed to become a form of blackmail serving to limit, reduce or halt the exercise of criticism. Under no circumstances should one pay attention to those who tell one: 'Don't criticize, since you're not capable of carrying out a reform.' That's ministerial cabinet talk. Critique doesn't have to be the premise of a deduction which concludes: this then is what needs to be done. It should be an instrument for those who fight, those who resist and refuse what is. Its use should be in processes of conflict and confrontation, essays in refusal. It doesn't have to lay down the law for the law. It isn't a stage in a programming. It is a challenge directed to what is.
>
> (Foucault, 1991a:84)

Garland's description of the aim of *Punishment and Welfare* makes a similar point to Foucault, although less stridently:

> It is not a political text, in the sense of one which addresses policy questions, formulates new objectives and prescribes methods for their achievement. It is rather a work of critical analysis which aims to provide a framework within which these questions can be better understood and perhaps more adequately addressed. Its hope is that it can aid the formulation of a more progressive and viable politics in this area.
>
> (Garland, 1985:vii)

The final sentence in the quotation above hints at a partial resolution which he states more forcefully in a passage in *Punishment and Modern Society*:

> Theoretical work seeks to change the way we think about an issue and ultimately to change the practical ways we deal with it. It is, in its own way, a form of rhetoric, seeking to move people to action by means of persuasion, that persuasion being achieved by force of analysis, argument and evidence.
>
> (Garland, 1990a:277)

Garland's argument is that incisive, thoroughgoing critical analysis, by deepening and changing our understanding of an issue, can provide the basis for practical proposals for change. Whilst Garland to some degree glosses over the question of the criteria that should be used to adjudicate between the merits of different practices – it is possible to imagine, for example, a genealogical analysis problematising the notion of a 'progressive and viable politics' – he implies an important point. Although Foucault himself rejects a universal normative basis for his analytical approach, that does not mean that it is not possible to make links to specific normative regimes (Dean, 1994:133). To put it another way, the slide into relativism is not inevitable. Genealogical analysis is concerned in essence with analysing different 'regimes of truth' and their consequences for practice. One obvious 'next step' for this kind of analysis is to express preferences for particular consequences (and hence their associated 'regime of truth') over others, perhaps by reference to a set of values or normative regime. Provided that these values are not allowed to prefigure the form and content of the analysis but, instead, follow after it, and that the links with normative regimes are transparently made, then Garland's vision is achievable and legitimate. This, in essence, is the conclusion that Cohen also reaches:

> Alongside an analytical view of current social-control systems can be placed a more pragmatic sense about possibilities for realizing preferred values.
>
> (Cohen, 1985:261)

In this spirit, the discussion here will attempt to set out a general direction for policy – a sense of some of the possibilities – which might help to realise some 'preferred values'. Some fruitful lines of enquiry for future research will also be outlined.

So what might these 'preferred values' be? As Garland (1990a:287) argues, punishment is a 'social institution which helps define the nature of our society, the kinds of relationships which compose it, and the kinds of lives that it is possible and desirable to lead there'. In this sense, the 'preferred values' we might seek to realise should cover a broader canvas than those narrowly viewed as occupying the penal realm. Garland (1990a:292) thus suggests in this regard that the 'pursuit of values such as justice, tolerance, decency, humanity and civility should be part of any penal institution's self-consciousness – an intrinsic and constitutive aspect of its role'. The question then is what kind of new strategies for the government of prisoners with mental health problems might better help to contribute to the realisation of these kinds of values?

Certainly, efforts in recent years to refigure prison health care provision in order to improve its quality and accessibility, to bring it up to the level of services provided in the community, make an important contribution to the pursuit of decency and humanity. Improving the quality of prison regimes more generally will also clearly be significant, and the ability to achieve that will depend to a great extent on whether the problem of prison overcrowding can be successfully alleviated. A series of recent commentaries have explored the key challenges for the implementation of the government's proposals to address the problem of the mentally disordered within prison (Reed, 2002, 2003; Birmingham, 2001, 2003, 2004; Maden, 2003; Wilson, 2004; cf Sim, 2002). The principal themes within these articles are:

- The NHS being responsible for mental health care for prisoners and providing that care to the same standard as in the community;
- Increasing the investment in mental health staff and services in prisons;
- Improving the provision of mental health services within the community, including more effective diversionary initiatives (on the latter, see also: James, 1999; Shaw et al, 2001; Vaughan et al, 2001);
- Reducing delays and inefficiencies in transfers from prison to NHS hospitals;
- Improving the effectiveness of prison reception health screening;
- Improving after-care services for prison-leavers.

No doubt these are all important issues. In essence, they locate the central difficulties in this field at the level of *resources* (both the overall amount and the maldistribution of resources between agencies, together with poor targeting at certain client groups) and *structures* (who provides care, who is responsible for which individuals, interfaces between agencies and across different points of the system and so on). In these terms, the solution ultimately lies in committing adequate resources and radically reorganising the administrative structures, systems and processes. It would be hard to deny that there is considerable room for improvement on both fronts. One might add Sim's (2002) more critical point that these improvements will not be possible without tackling attitudes which cast prisoners as 'less eligible' subjects (see also Gunn, 2000). However, one of the most fundamental arguments of this book has been the idea that the problem of mentally disordered prisoners is intrinsic to the project of using institutional confinement as a form of punishment. This suggests that however radically health provision is re-organised, or other aspects of service delivery improved, initiatives at that level and of that kind will not address the roots of the problem. This is why attempts to 'clear out' the problem from the prisons via diversion and transfer can never be (and have never been) an effective solution on their own. What is needed is no less than a radical re-think of the whole confinement project. We must face up to the difficult questions about whether there can be ways of responding to the problems of 'deviance', rule-breaking and troublesome behaviour different from resorting to imprisonment or to detention in the Special Hospitals or Medium Secure Units. Only if alternatives can be found will the problem diminish. To put it another way: for as long as we use prisons and other institutions of confinement in the penal-psychiatric complex to the extent and in the way that we currently do, the problem of prisoners with mental health problems will remain.

Such an agenda is a radical and challenging one. Perhaps, given the historical intractability of the problem, this is unsurprising. Tinkering at the margins whilst pursuing largely the same course is unlikely to deliver the goods. As David Garland (2001:201–5) suggests, the core problem underlying our contemporary 'culture of control' is its attempt to address social problems and to maintain social order through penal and exclusionary techniques. In a longer historical perspective, it could be argued that the confinement project represents a similar attempt at a penal response to social problems. The challenge is to re-think confinement and develop new and more social approaches which better embody, signify and communicate the 'values of justice, tolerance, decency, humanity and civility' (Garland, 1990a:292). We will have to 'cure' our dependence on incarceration before the problem can be really solved.

Turning to future research, the research base on which this book has been able to draw is certainly large but, in many respects, is also quite narrow. As was shown in Chapter 2, there is plenty of research from within the 'psy' disciplines but much less from within the social sciences in general and criminology in particular. As a complex, multi-faceted social issue, a general need in this area is for more innovative inter-disciplinary social research which is not constrained by existing disciplinary boundaries. More specifically, there are five areas which, it is suggested, may offer significant lines for future research inquiry; these will now be briefly considered.

First, focused empirical research is needed examining the ways in which the distinctive neo-liberal emphasis on the administration of risk impacts on 'dividing practices'. Specifically, what is required is more detailed micro-level research looking at how 'risk thinking' constrains, enables and shapes the decision-making processes at the various stages at which offenders can be filtered into prisons or the hospital system or, indeed, the new DSPD (Dangerous and Severe Personality Disorder) units. This would involve examining a whole series of 'decision points': civil admissions to hospital; hospital orders; restriction orders; remands to hospital (for treatment or reports); after insanity verdicts; after findings of 'unfit to plead'; transfers to hospital of sentenced prisoners; and transfers of prisoners to or from different provision within the prison estate (eg Grendon, Close Supervision Centres, Holloway C1 Unit and so on). Recent research by Peay (2003a, 2003b) makes a good start on this area but significantly more needs to be done, particularly from within the kind of theoretical framework deployed in this book. There have been several recent and important contributions to the development of the latter which could be utilised in this type of research on 'risk thinking' (for example: Sparks, 2001a, 2001b; Garland, 2003; O'Malley, 2004; Ericson, 2005).

Second, and related to this, as noted above, the distinctive neo-liberal focus on the 'administration of risk' has the potential to have a differential and detrimental impact on black people because of racial stereotypes about dangerousness. Empirical research examining this issue should be a priority. Again, this will require primarily micro-level investigations into decision-making processes as above and also into practice within the main institutional sites (prisons, Special Hospitals, secure units and DSPD units). For the examination of practice, detailed ethnographic research, in the tradition of Goffman (1961), looking at how 'risk thinking' within these sites impacts differentially on black prisoners/patients would be valuable, although not without methodological challenges.

Third, the concept of 'equivalence of care', which underpins current developments in the role of NHS provision within prison health care, requires some further exploration and deconstruction. A whole series of questions needs to be addressed here (see Wilson, 2004). Does 'equivalence of care' cover issues of access, quality and treatment modalities alike? Are the goals of 'care' exactly the same for prisoner-patients as they are for patients in the community? What kind of notion of 'citizenship' for prisoners is implied by the policy and practice of 'equivalence of care'? Most fundamentally, is equivalence achievable, given the differences between community, secure and penal environments (Bowden, 2000; Smith, 2000; Sim, 1994b; Wilson, 2004)?

Fourth, research is needed on responses to offenders and prisoners diagnosed with personality disorders. Clearly, the Dangerous and Severe Personality Disorder programme provides an immediate focus for this. However, more broadly, as McCallum (2001) has shown, there are fundamental linkages between the concepts of 'personality' and 'dangerousness'. Given the growing emphasis on the 'administration of risk' within 'advanced liberal' forms of government (Rose, 1996a), this suggests that the area of personality disordered offenders should be of considerable significance for research. More specifically, connections between personality disorder, gender, culture and ethnicity are also not well understood and could be fruitful areas for research.

Fifth, and finally, following Dean (1994:208–12), some of the research questions posed above can be pushed further by connecting them to the broader genealogical project of exploring the relations between forms of government and practices of the self. For example, the notion of 'equivalence of care' could be problematised in terms of the difficult relationship between 'care of the self' and 'care of citizens', a relationship mediated by the discourses and practices of forensic psychiatry and psychology.

Together, these five areas set out an agenda for future research in this field that will build on and develop the advancements in knowledge made by this book. At a more general level, this book has demonstrated that empirical research studies examining specific subject areas can make a significant contribution to advancing knowledge in the field of penality. Indeed, it is suggested that it is only through empirically based work of this kind that resolution of some key questions can be achieved. Although the literature on penality in the last two decades has been of an exceptionally high quality, much of it has operated primarily at an abstract or theoretical level. For research that seeks to explain historical change, this can ultimately lead to sterility, stagnation and dead ends in debate. As David Garland (1985:viii) puts it in the preface to *Punishment and Welfare*, in which he describes his methodological stance in that work:

> [An] empirical approach is adopted, not through any distrust of theoretical abstraction, but rather out of respect for the limits of such theorization, and a belief that theoretical work can only proceed *pari passu* with the development of a detailed and concrete knowledge of the field under study.

Pierre Bourdieu makes a similar point:

> [Theory] is disclosed only in the empirical work which actualizes it. It is a temporary construct which takes shape for and by empirical work [. . .] The summum of the art, in social science, is, in my eyes, to be capable of engaging in very high theoretical stakes by means of very precise and often very mundane empirical objects.
>
> (Bourdieu, 1996:220–21)

4. PUNISHMENT AND MADNESS

The underlying theme of this book has been an attempt to understand the nexus between punishment and madness. On the face of it, the two appear to be quite distinct and separate. However, as was explored in the historical review in Chapter 2, this nexus has been evident ever since Foucault's Great Confinement of the sixteenth and seventeenth centuries and indeed firmly remains so today at the beginning of the twenty-first century. That this is so should tell us that the relationship is neither transient nor trivial. It is in fact profound and goes right to the heart of some of the most important issues of social life, and of the human condition more broadly.

Roy Porter (2003:4) suggests that the greatest insight that can be taken from *Madness and Civilization* (Foucault, 1967) is that the history of madness can be best understood as an ongoing dialectic between 'Reason' and 'Unreason'. Similarly, Garland (1996, 2001) has argued that contemporary strategies of crime control and punishment are founded on a dualistic division between reasoning individuals and the unreasoning 'other'. There is an interesting parallel here. A clue to its importance can be found in Pat O'Malley's (2004) book *Risk, Uncertainty and Government*. O'Malley shows in this work how the construction of the 'rationality' of individuals has been a central technique within neo-liberalism for governing diverse aspects of life, reaching far beyond the government of 'deviance'. In this way, in exploring the nexus between punishment and madness, the true significance of this book may be the light it sheds on the fundamental questions of how we govern ourselves and others and indeed of who we are.

Appendix

Table A1 Average annual prison population in England and Wales 1976–2003

Year	Average prison population	Percentage rise over previous year	Percentage rise over 1976 baseline
1976	41,443	10%	–
1977	41,570	<1%	<1%
1978	41,796	1%	1%
1979	42,220	1%	2%
1980	42,264	<1%	2%
1981	43,311	2%	5%
1982	43,707	1%	5%
1983	43,462	-1%	5%
1984	43,295	<1%	4%
1985	46,233	7%	12%
1986	46,770	1%	13%
1987	48,426	4%	17%
1988	48,872	1%	18%
1989	48,500	-1%	17%
1990	44,975	-7%	9%
1991	44,809	<1%	8%
1992	44,719	<1%	8%
1993	44,552	<1%	8%
1994	48,621	9%	17%
1995	50,962	5%	22%
1996	55,281	8%	33%
1997	61,114	11%	47%
1998	65,298	7%	58%
1999	64,771	-1%	56%
2000	64,602	<1%	56%
2001	66,301	3%	60%
2002	70,861	7%	71%
2003	73,038	3%	76%

Table A2 Transfers to hospital under the Mental Health Act 1983 from Prison Service establishments 1976–2003

Year	Total transfers	Percentage rise over previous year	Percentage rise over 1976 baseline
1976	51	–	–
1977	63	24%	24%
1978	50	-21%	-2%
1979	86	72%	69%
1980	95	10%	86%
1981	92	-3%	80%
1982	86	-7%	69%
1983	94	9%	84%
1984	129	37%	153%
1985	125	-3%	145%
1986	137	10%	169%
1987	180	31%	253%
1988	176	-2%	245%
1989	218	24%	327%
1990	325	49%	537%
1991	446	37%	775%
1992	605	36%	1086%
1993	767	27%	1404%
1994	785	2%	1439%
1995	723	-8%	1318%
1996	746	3%	1363%
1997	746	0%	1363%
1998	739	-1%	1349%
1999	731	-1%	1333%
2000	662	-9%	1198%
2001	635	-4%	1145%
2002	644	1%	1162%
2003	721	17%	1314%

References

Agbahowe, S., Ohaeri, J., Ogunlesi, A. and Osahon, R. (1998) 'Prevalence of psychiatric morbidity among convicted inmates in a Nigerian prison community', *East African Medical Journal* 75: 19–26.

Aikin, J. (1772) *A View of the Character and Public Services of the Late John Howard*, London: J. Johnson.

Allen, H. (1986) 'Psychiatry and the construction of the feminine', in P. Miller and N. Rose (eds), *The Power of Psychiatry*, Cambridge: Polity Press.

Allen, H. (1987) *Justice Unbalanced: Gender, Psychiatry and Judicial Decisions*, Milton Keynes: Open University Press.

Anthony, H. Sylvia (1973) *Depression, Psychopathic Personality and Attempted Suicide in a Borstal Sample*, Home Office Research Study No 19, London: HMSO.

Backett, S.A. (1987) 'Suicide in Scottish prisons', *British Journal of Psychiatry* 151: 218–21.

Banister, P.A., Smith, F.V., Heskin, K.J. and Bolton, N. (1973) 'Psychological correlates of long-term imprisonment: II Personality variables' *British Journal of Criminology* 13(4) 323–30.

Barham, P. (1992) *Closing the Asylum: The Mental Patient in Modern Society*, Harmondsworth: Penguin.

Barker, A. (1998) 'Political responsibility for UK prison security – Ministers escape again' *Public Administration* 76: 1–23.

Barnes, D. and Robinson, F. (1996) *The Durham Pilot Project: Contracting for Mental Health Care Services in the 'Durham Cluster' of Prisons*, Durham: Department of Sociology and Social Policy, University of Durham.

Barnes, D. and Robinson, F. (1998) 'Purchasing prison health care services', *Prison Service Journal* 115 (January): 40–43.

Barraclough, B.M. and Hughes, J. (1987) *Suicide: Clinical and Epidemiological Studies*, London: Croom Helm.

Bean, P. (1976) *Rehabilitation and Deviance*, London: Routledge & Kegan Paul.

Beck, U. (1992) *The Risk Society: Towards a New Modernity*, London: Sage.

Beirne, P. (1988) 'Heredity versus environment: A reconsideration of Charles Goring's *The English Convict* (1913)' *British Journal of Criminology* 28(3): 315–39.

Bhui, K., Brown, P., Hardie, T., Watson, P. and Parrott, J. (1998) 'African-Caribbean men remanded to Brixton prison', *British Journal of Psychiatry* 172: 337–44.

Biles, D. and Mulligan, G. (1973) 'Mad or bad? The enduring dilemma', *British Journal of Criminology* 13: 275–9.

Birmingham, L. (2001) 'Screening prisoners for psychiatric illness: Who benefits?' *Psychiatric Bulletin* 25: 462–4.

Birmingham, L. (2002) 'Detaining dangerous people with mental disorders: New legal framework is open for consultation', *British Medical Journal* 325: 2–3.

Birmingham, L. (2003) 'The mental health of prisoners', *Advances in Psychiatric Treatment* 9: 191–201.

Birmingham, L. (2004) 'Mental disorder and prisons', *Psychiatric Bulletin* 28: 393–7.

Birmingham, L., Mason, D. and Grubin, D. (1996) 'Prevalence of mental disorder in remand prisoners: Consecutive case study', *British Medical Journal* 313: 1521–4.

Birmingham, L., Mason, D. and Grubin, D. (1997) 'Health screening at first reception into prison', *Journal of Forensic Psychiatry* 8(2): 435–9.

Birmingham, L., Mason, D. and Grubin, D. (1998) 'A follow-up study of mentally disordered men remanded to prison', *Criminal Behaviour and Mental Health* 8: 202–13.

Birmingham, L., Mason, D. and Grubin, D. (1999) 'The psychiatric implications of visible tattoos in an adult male prison population', *Journal of Forensic Psychiatry* 10(3): 687–95.

Birmingham, L., Gray, J., Mason, D. and Grubin, D. (2000) 'Mental illness at reception into prison', *Criminal Behaviour and Mental Health* 10: 77–87.

Bland, J., Mezey, G. and Dolan, B. (1999) 'Special women, special needs: A descriptive study of female special hospital patients', *Journal of Forensic Psychiatry* 10(1): 34–45.

Bluglass, R. (1966) 'A psychiatric study of Scottish sentenced prisoners', unpublished PhD thesis, University of St Andrews.

Boast, N. and Chesterman, P. (1995) 'Black people and secure psychiatric facilities: Patterns of processing and the role of stereotypes', *British Journal of Criminology* 35: 218–35.

Bolger, L. (1992) 'Prevalence of personality disorder in a women's prison', MSc Dissertation, London: Birkbeck College, University of London.

Bottoms, A. (1977) 'Reflections on the renaissance of dangerousness', *Howard Journal of Penology and Crime Prevention* 16: 70–96.

Bottoms, A. (1995) 'The philosophy and politics of punishment and sentencing', in C.M.V. Clarkson and R. Morgan (eds) *The Politics of Sentencing Reform*, Oxford: Clarendon Press.

Bourdieu, P. (1996) 'Towards a reflexive sociology: A workshop with Pierre Bourdieu', in S. Turner (ed), *Social Theory and Sociology: The Classics and Beyond*, Oxford: Blackwell.

Bowden, P. (1978a) 'Men remanded into custody for medical reports: The selection for treatment', *British Journal of Psychiatry* 132: 320–31.

Bowden, P. (1978b) 'Men remanded into custody for medical reports: The outcome of the treatment recommendation', *British Journal of Psychiatry* 132: 332–8.

Bowden, P. (2000) 'Review of *The Future Organisation of Prison Health Care*', *Journal of Forensic Psychiatry* 11(2): 473–6.

Box, S. (1987) *Recession, Crime and Punishment*, London: Tavistock.

Braithwaite, J. (1999) 'Restorative justice: Assessing optimistic and pessimistic accounts', in M. Tonry (ed), *Crime and Justice: A Review of Research*, Chicago: Chicago University Press.

British Medical Association (2001) *Prison Medicine: A Crisis Waiting to Break*, London: British Medical Association.

Brody, S.R. (1976) *The Effectiveness of Sentencing*, London: HMSO.

Brooke, D., Taylor, C., Gunn, J. and Maden, A. (1996) 'Point prevalence of mental disorder in unconvicted prisoners in England and Wales', *British Medical Journal* 313: 1524–7.

Brown, P., Bhui, K., Hardie, T., Parrott, J. and Watson, J. (1996) 'Prison based psychiatrists and the needs of mentally disordered remand prisoners', *European Psychiatry* 11: 283.

Browne, D. (1991) *Black People, Mental Health and the Courts: An Exploratory Study into the Psychiatric Remand Process as it Affects Black Defendants at Magistrates' Court*, London: NACRO.

Browne, D. (1996) 'The black experience of mental health law', in T. Heller, J. Reynolds, R. Gomm, R. Muston and S. Pattison (eds), *Mental Health Matters: A Reader*, London: Macmillan.

Browne, D., Francis, E. and Crowe, I. (1993) 'The needs of ethnic minorities', in W. Watson and A. Grounds (eds), *The Mentally Disordered Offender in an Era of Community Care*, Cambridge: Cambridge University Press.

Buchanan, A. and Leese, M. (2001) 'Detention of people with dangerous severe personality disorders: A systematic review', *The Lancet* 358 (8 December): 1955–9.

Bullard, H. (1994) 'Health care for prisoners today', *Prison Service Journal* 95: 22–5.

Burchell, G. (1991) 'Peculiar interests: Civil society and governing "the system of natural liberty" ', in G. Burchell, C. Gordon and P. Miller (eds), *The Foucault Effect: Studies in Governmentality*, Hemel Hempstead: Harvester Wheatsheaf.

Burchell, G., Gordon, C. and Miller, P. (eds) (1991) *The Foucault Effect: Studies in Governmentality*, Hemel Hempstead: Harvester Wheatsheaf.

Burney, E. and Pearson, G. (1995) 'Mentally disordered offenders: Finding a focus for diversion', *Howard Journal of Criminal Justice* 34(4): 291–313.

Busfield, J. (1983) 'Gender, mental illness and psychiatry', in M. Evans and C. Ungerson (eds), *Sexual Divisions: patterns and processes*, London: Tavistock.

Bynoe, I. (1992) *Treatment, Care and Security: Waiting for Change*, London: MIND.

Candy, J. (1985) 'The relationship of the Prison Medical Service to the National Health Service', in Prison Reform Trust (ed), *Prison Medicine: Ideas on Health Care in Penal Establishments*, London: Prison Reform Trust.

Carlen, P. (1983) *Women's Imprisonment: A Study in Social Control*, London: Routledge & Kegan Paul.

Carlen, P. (1985a) *Criminal Women*, Oxford: Polity Press.

Carlen, P. (1985b) 'Law, psychiatry and women's imprisonment: A sociological view', *British Journal of Psychiatry* 146: 618–21.

Carlen, P. (1986) 'Psychiatry in prisons: Promises, premises, practices and politics', in: P. Miller and N. Rose (eds), *The Power of Psychiatry*, Cambridge: Polity Press.

Casale, S. (1989) *Women Inside: The Experience of Women Remand Prisoners in Holloway*, London: Civil Liberties Trust.

Castel, R. (1991) 'From dangerousness to risk', in G. Burchell, C. Gordon and P. Miller (eds), *The Foucault Effect: Studies in Governmentality*, Hemel Hempstead: Harvester Wheatsheaf.

Cavadino, M. and Dignan, J. (1997) *The Penal System: An Introduction*, 2nd edn, London: Sage.

Chesler, P. (1974) *Women and Madness*, London: Allen Lane.

Chiswick, D. (1996) 'Sentencing mentally disordered offenders: A new law to "protect the public" will block beds in secure units', *British Medical Journal* 313: 1497–8.

Clements, J. (2000) 'Assessment of Race Relations at HMP Brixton', HM Prison Service web site (www.hmprisonservice.gov.uk/filestore/202_206.pdf)

Clemmer, D. (1940) *The Prison Community*, New York: Holt, Rinehart and Winston.

Cohen, S. (1972) *Folk Devils and Moral Panics*, London: Paladin.

Cohen, S. (1985) *Visions of Social Control*, Cambridge: Polity Press.

Cohen, S. (2001) *States of Denial: Knowing about Atrocities and Suffering*, Cambridge: Polity Press.

Cohen, S. and Taylor, L. (1972) *Psychological Survival: The Experience of Long-Term Imprisonment*, Harmondsworth: Penguin.

Coid, J. (1984) 'How many psychiatric patients in prison?' *British Journal of Psychiatry* 145: 78–86.

Coid, J. (1988) 'Mentally abnormal prisoners on remand: I and II', *British Medical Journal* 296: 1779–84.

Coid, J. (1991) 'Psychiatric profiles of difficult/disruptive prisoners', in A.K. Bottomley and W. Hay (eds), *Special Units for Difficult Prisoners*, Hull: Centre for Criminology and Criminal Justice, University of Hull.

Coid, J. (1996) 'Diagnostic classification and aetiology of psychopathic disorder: An overview and future research', in *Understanding the Enigma: Summary of the Anglo-Dutch Conference on Personality Disorder and Offending*, London: Special Hospitals Service Authority.

Coid, J. and Maden, T. (2003) 'Should psychiatrists protect the public? A new risk reduction strategy, supporting criminal justice, could be effective', *British Medical Journal* 326: 407.

Coid, J., Robertson, G. and Gunn, J. (1991) 'A psychiatric study of inmates in Parkhurst Special Unit', in R. Walmsley (ed), *Managing Difficult Prisoners: The Parkhurst Special Unit*, Home Office Research Study No 122, London: HMSO.

Cookson, H. (1977) 'A survey of self-injury in a closed prison for women', *British Journal of Criminology* 17: 332–46.

Cooper, D., Denig-Smitherman, P., Doherty, D., Hynes, P., Oldham, W., Stephen, W., Topp, D., Trafford, P. (1991) 'New prison health service', *British Medical Journal* 302: 52–3.

Cope, R. and Ndegwa, D. (1990) 'Ethnic differences in admission to a regional secure unit', *Journal of Forensic Psychiatry* 3: 343–78.

Corbett, K. and Westwood, T. (2005) ' "Dangerous and severe personality disorder": A psychiatric manifestation of the risk society', *Critical Public Health* 15(2): 121–33.

Council of Europe (1998) *Recommendation of the Committee of Ministers to Member States Concerning the Ethical and Organisational Aspects of Health Care in Prison*, Recommendation No R 98(7). Strasbourg: Council of Europe.

Crawford, A. (1997) *The Local Governance of Crime: Appeals to Partnerships and Community*, Oxford: Clarendon.

Crawford, A. (2003) ' "Contractual governance" of deviant behaviour', *Journal of Law and Society* 30(4): 479–505.

Cullen, E. (1997) *Grendon and Future Therapeutic Communities in Prison*, London: Prison Reform Trust.

Cullen, J.E. (1985) 'Prediction and treatment of self-injury by female young offenders', in D. Farrington and R. Tarling (eds), *Prediction in Criminology*, Albany: State University of New York Press.

Dean, M. (1994) *Critical and Effective Histories: Foucault's Methods and Historical Sociology*, London: Routledge.

Dell, S., Grounds, A., James, K. and Robertson, G. (1991) *Mentally Disordered Remand Prisoners*, Report to the Home Office.

Dell, S., Robertson, G., James, K. and Grounds, A. (1993) 'Remands and Psychiatric Assessments in Holloway Prison', *British Journal of Psychiatry* 163: 634–44.

Department of Health/Home Office (2000) *Reforming the Mental Health Act: Part II: High risk patients*, London: The Stationery Office.

Department of Health/Home Office/Prison Service (2005) *Dangerous and Severe Personality Disorder (DSPD): High Secure Services: Planning and Delivery Guide*, London: Home Office.

Department of Health/Prison Service/National Assembly for Wales (2001) *Changing the Outlook: A Strategy for Developing and Modernising Mental Health Services in Prisons*, London: Department of Health.

Department of Health and Social Security (DHSS) (1974) *Revised Report of the Working Party on Security in NHS Psychiatric Hospitals*, London: DHSS (The Glancy Report)

DHSS/Home Office (1986) *Offenders Suffering from Psychopathic Disorder: Joint Consultation Document*, London: HMSO.

Dobash, R.P, Dobash, R.E. and Gutteridge, S. (1986) *The Imprisonment of Women*, London: Basil Blackwell.

Dolan, B. and Mitchell, E. (1994) 'Personality disorders, psychological and behavioural characteristics of women in the medical units of HMP Holloway: A comparison with women in specialist NHS treatment', *Criminal Behaviour and Mental Health* 4(2): 130–42.

Dooley, E. (1990) 'Prison suicide in England and Wales, 1972–87' *British Journal of Psychiatry* 156: 40–45.

Douglas, M. (1992) *Risk and Blame: Essays in Cultural Theory*, London: Routledge.

Downes, D. (1988) *Contrasts in Tolerance: Post-War Penal Policy in The Netherlands and England and Wales*, Oxford: Clarendon Press.

Downes, D. and Morgan, R. (1997) 'Dumping the "hostages to fortune"? The politics of law and order in post-war Britain', in M. Maguire, R. Morgan and R. Reiner (eds), *The Oxford Handbook of Criminology*, 2nd edn, Oxford: Clarendon Press.

Downes, D. and Morgan, R. (2002) 'The skeletons in the cupboard: The politics of law and order at the turn of the millennium' in: M. Maguire, R. Morgan and R. Reiner (eds), *The Oxford Handbook of Criminology*, 3rd edn, Oxford: Clarendon Press.

Dunbabin, J. (2002) *Captivity and Imprisonment in Medieval Europe, 1000–1300*, Basingstoke: Palgrave Macmillan.

Duke, K. (2003) *Drugs, Prisons and Policy-Making*, Basingstoke: Palgrave Macmillan.

Earthrowl, M., O'Grady, J. and Birmingham, L. (2003) 'Providing treatment to prisoners with mental disorders: Development of a policy. Selective literature review and expert consultation exercise', *British Journal of Psychiatry* 182: 299–302.

East, W.N. (1949) *Society and the Criminal*, London: HMSO.

East, W.N. and Hubert, W.H. de B. (1939) *The Psychological Treatment of Crime*, London: HMSO.

Eastman, N. (1993) 'Forensic psychiatric services in Britain: A current review', *International Journal of Law and Psychiatry* 16: 1–26.

Eastman, N. (1996) 'Hybrid Orders: an analysis of their likely effects on sentencing practice and on forensic psychiatric practice and services', *Journal of Forensic Psychiatry* 7: 481–94.

Eastman, N. (1999) 'Public health psychiatry or crime prevention?' *British Medical Journal* 318: 549–51.

Eastman, N. and Peay, J. (1998) 'Sentencing Psychopaths: Is the "Hospital and Limitation Direction" an ill-considered hybrid?' *Criminal Law Review* 93–108.

Edwards, B., Gunn, J., Kilgour, J. and Smith, R. (1985) 'Cooperation between the Prison Medical Service and the NHS: A conversation', *British Medical Journal* 291: 1698–9.

Epps, P. (1951) 'A preliminary survey of 300 female delinquents in Borstal institutions', *British Journal of Delinquency* 1: 187–97.

Epps, P. (1954) 'A further survey of female delinquents undergoing Borstal training', *British Journal of Delinquency* 4: 270–1.

Ericson, R. (1994) 'The division of expert knowledge in policing and security', *British Journal of Sociology* 45: 149–75.

Ericson, R. (2005) 'Governing through risk and uncertainty', *Economy and Society* 34(4): 659–72.

Evershed, S. (1991) 'Special unit, C wing, HMP Parkhurst', in K. Herbst and J. Gunn (eds) *The Mentally Disordered Offender*, Oxford: Butterworth-Heinemann.

Eysenck, S. and Eysenck, H. (1973) 'The personality of female prisoners', *British Journal of Psychiatry* 122: 693.

Farnham, F. and James, D. (2001) ' "Dangerousness" and dangerous law', *The Lancet* 358: 1926.

Farrall, S. and Bowling, B. (1999) 'Structuration, human development and desistance from crime', *British Journal of Criminology* 39(2): 253–68.

Faulk, M. (1976) 'A psychiatric study of men serving a sentence in Winchester Prison', *Medicine, Science and the Law* 16: 244–61.

Fazel, S. and Danesh, J. (2002) 'Serious mental disorder in 23 000 prisoners: A systematic review of 62 surveys', *The Lancet* 359: 545–50.

Feeley, M. and Simon, J. (1992) 'The new penology: notes on the emerging strategy of corrections and its implications', *Criminology* 30: 449–74.

Feeley, M. and Simon, J. (1994) 'Actuarial justice: The emerging new criminal law', in D. Nelken (ed), *The Futures of Criminology*, London: Sage.

Fernando, S. (1988) *Race and Culture in Psychiatry*, London: Croom Helm.

Fernando, S. (1991) *Mental Health, Race and Culture*, London: Macmillan.

Fido, A. and Al-Labally, M. (1993) 'Presence of psychiatric morbidity in prison population in Kuwait', *Annals of Clinical Psychiatry* 5: 107–10.

Floud, J. (1982) 'Dangerousness and criminal justice', *British Journal of Criminology* 22(3): 213–28.

Forrester, A. (2002) 'Preventive detention, public protection and mental health', *Journal of Forensic Psychiatry* 13(2): 329–44.

Forsythe, W.J. (1991) *Penal Discipline, Reformatory Projects and the English Prison Commission 1895–1939*, Exeter: University of Exeter Press.

Forsythe, W.J. (1993) 'Women prisoners and women penal officials 1840–1921', *British Journal of Criminology* 33(4): 525–40.

Forsythe, W.J. (1995) 'The Garland thesis and the origins of modern English prison discipline', *Howard Journal* 34(3): 259–73.

Foster, C. and Plowden, F. (1996) *The State under Stress: Can the Hollow State be Good Government?* Buckingham: Open University Press.

Foucault, M. (1967) *Madness and Civilization: A History of Insanity in the Age of Reason*, London: Routledge.

Foucault, M. (1972) *The Archaeology of Knowledge*, London: Tavistock.

Foucault, M. (1977) *Discipline and Punish: The Birth of the Prison*, London: Allen Lane.

Foucault, M. (1978) 'About the concept of the "dangerous individual" in 19th-century legal psychiatry', *International Journal of Law and Psychiatry* 1: 1–18.

Foucault, M. (1982) 'Afterword: The subject and power' in: H. Dreyfus and P. Rabinow (eds), *Michel Foucault: beyond Structuralism and Hermeneutics*, Brighton: Harvester.

Foucault, M. (1983) 'Structuralism and post-structuralism: An interview with Michel Foucault', *Telos* 55: 195–211.

Foucault, M. (1991a) 'Questions of method', in G. Burchell, C. Gordon and P. Miller (eds), *The Foucault Effect: Studies in Governmentality*, Hemel Hempstead: Harvester Wheatsheaf.

Foucault, M. (1991b) 'Governmentality', in G. Burchell, C. Gordon and P. Miller (eds), *The Foucault Effect: Studies in Governmentality*, Hemel Hempstead: Harvester Wheatsheaf.

Fox, L.W. (1934) *The Modern English Prison*, London: Routledge and Kegan Paul.

Frigon, S. (1995) 'A genealogy of women's madness', in: R.E. Dobash, R.P. Dobash and L. Noaks (eds), *Gender and Crime*, Cardiff: University of Wales Press.

Gallo, E. and Ruggiero, V. (1991) 'The "Immaterial" prison: Custody as a factory for the manufacture of handicaps', *International Journal of the Sociology of Law* 19: 273–91.

Gamble, A. (1988) *The Free Economy and the Strong State: The Politics of Thatcherism*, London: Macmillan.

Garland, D. (1981) 'The birth of the welfare sanction', *British Journal of Law and Society* 8(1): 29–45.

Garland, D. (1983) 'Durkheim's theory of punishment: A critique', in D. Garland and P. Young (eds), *The Power to Punish*, Aldershot: Gower.

Garland, D. (1985) *Punishment and Welfare: A History of Penal Strategies*, Aldershot: Gower.

Garland, D. (1990a) *Punishment and Modern Society: A Study in Social Theory*, Oxford: Clarendon Press.

Garland, D. (1990b) 'Frameworks of enquiry in the sociology of punishment', *British Journal of Sociology* 41(1): 1–15.

Garland, D. (1995) 'Penal modernism and postmodernism', in: T. Blomberg and S. Cohen (eds), *Punishment and Social Control*, New York: Aldine de Gruyter.

Garland, D. (1996) 'The limits of the sovereign state', *British Journal of Criminology* 36(4): 445–71.

Garland, D. (1997a) 'Of crime and criminals: The development of criminology in Britain' in: M. Maguire, R. Morgan and R. Reiner (eds), *The Oxford Handbook of Criminology*, 2nd edn, Oxford: Oxford University Press.

Garland, D. (1997b) ' "Governmentality" and the problem of crime: Foucault, criminology, sociology', *Theoretical Criminology* 1(2): 173–214.

Garland, D. (2000) 'The culture of high crime societies: Some preconditions of recent "law and order" policies', *British Journal of Criminology* 40(3): 347–75.

Garland, D. (2001) *The Culture of Control: Crime and Social Order in Contemporary Society*, Oxford: Oxford University Press.

Garland, D. (2003) 'The rise of risk', in R. Ericson and A. Doyle (eds), *Risk and Morality*, Toronto: University of Toronto Press.

Garland, D. and Young, P. (1983) 'Towards a social analysis of penality', in D. Garland and P. Young (eds), *The Power to Punish*, Aldershot: Gower.

Genders, E. and Player, E. (1989) *Race Relations in Prison*, Oxford: Clarendon Press.

Genders, E. and Player, E. (1995) *Grendon: A Study of a Therapeutic Prison*, Oxford: Clarendon Press.

Ghubash, R. and El-Rufaie, O. (1997) 'Psychiatric morbidity among sentenced male prisoners in Dubai: Transcultural perspectives', *Journal of Forensic Psychiatry* 8: 440–46.

Gibbens, T. (1967) *Psychiatric Studies of Borstal Lads*, Maudsley Monograph No 11, Oxford: Oxford University Press.

Gibbens, T. (1971) 'Female offenders', *British Journal of Hospital Medicine* 279.

Gibson, J. (1971) *John Howard and Elizabeth Fry*, London: Methuen.

Giddens, A. (1984) *The Constitution of Society*, Cambridge: Polity Press.

Giddens, A. (2000) *The Third Way and its Critics*, Cambridge: Polity Press.

Gladstone Committee (1895) *Report of the Departmental Committee on Prisons*, PP 1895, lvi.

Gledhill, K. (2000) 'Managing dangerous people with severe personality disorder', *Journal of Forensic Psychiatry* 11(2): 439–47.

Goffman, E. (1961) *Asylums: Essays on the Social Situation of Mental Patients and Other Inmates*, Garden City, NY: Doubleday Anchor.

Gordon, C. (1986) 'Psychiatry and the problem of democracy', in P. Miller and N. Rose (eds), *The Power of Psychiatry*, Cambridge: Polity Press.

Goring, C. (1913) *The English Convict: A Statistical Study*, London: HMSO.

Gorsuch, N. (1998) 'Unmet need among disturbed female offenders', *Journal of Forensic Psychiatry* 9(3): 556–70.

Gray, J. (1997) *Endgames: Questions in Late Modern Political Thought*, Cambridge: Polity Press.

Gray, W.J. (1973) 'The English prison medical service: its historical background and more recent developments', in G. Wolstenholme and M. O'Connor (eds), *Medical Care of Prisoners and Detainees*, London: Associated Scientific Publishers.

Grounds, A. (1990) 'Transfers of sentenced prisoners to hospital', [1990] *Criminal Law Review* 544–51.

Grounds, A. (1991a) 'The mentally disordered in prison', *Prison Service Journal* 80: 29–40.

Grounds, A. (1991b) 'The transfer of sentenced prisoners to hospital 1960–1983', *British Journal of Criminology* 31(1): 54–71.

Grounds, A. (1994) 'Mentally disordered offenders', in E. Player and M. Jenkins (eds), *Prisons after Woolf: Reform through Riot*, London: Routledge.

Gunn, J. (1985) 'Psychiatry and the Prison Medical Service', in L. Gostin (ed), *Secure Provision: A Review of Special Services for the Mentally Ill and Mentally Handicapped in England and Wales*, London: Tavistock.

Gunn, J. (2000) 'Future directions for treatment in forensic psychiatry', *British Journal of Psychiatry* 176: 332–8.

Gunn, J., Dell, S. and Way, C. (1978) *Psychiatric Aspects of Imprisonment*, London: Academic Press.

Gunn, J. and Felthous, A. (2000) 'Politics and personality disorder: The demise of psychiatry', *Current Opinion in Psychiatry* 13(6): 545–7.

Gunn, J., Maden, T. and Swinton, M. (1991) *Mentally Disordered Prisoners*, London: Home Office.

Gutting, G. (1994) 'Foucault and the history of madness', in G. Gutting (ed), *A Cambridge Companion to Foucault*, Cambridge: Cambridge University Press.

Guy, W. (1869) 'On insanity and crime', *Journal of the Statistical Society* 32: 162–90.

Habermas, J. (1976) *Legitimation Crisis*, London: Heinemann.

Habermas, J. (1987) *The Philosophical Discourse of Modernity: Twelve Lectures*, Lawrence, F. (trans), Cambridge: Polity Press.

Haddock, A., Snowden, P.R., Dolan, M., Parker, J. and Rees, H. (2001) 'Managing dangerous people with severe personality disorder: A survey of forensic psychiatrists' opinions', *Psychiatric Bulletin* 25: 293–6.

Harding, T. and Zimmerman, E. (1989) 'Psychiatric symptoms, cognitive stress and vulnerability factors: A study in a remand prison', *British Journal of Psychiatry* 155: 36–43.

Health Advisory Committee for the Prison Service (1997) *The Provision of Mental Health Care in Prisons*, London: Prison Service.

Heather, N. (1977) 'Personal illness in "lifers" and the effects of long-term indeterminate sentences', *British Journal of Criminology* 17(4): 378–86.

Heidensohn, F. (1975) 'The imprisonment of females', in S. McConville (ed), *The Use of Imprisonment*, London: Routledge and Kegan Paul.

Heidensohn, F. (1994) 'From being to knowing: Some reflections on the study of gender in contemporary society', *Women and Criminal Justice* 6(1): 13–37.

Heidensohn, F. (1996) *Women and Crime*, 2nd edn, Basingstoke: Macmillan.

Heidensohn, F. (1997) 'Gender and crime', in M. Maguire, R. Morgan and R. Reiner (eds), *The Oxford Handbook of Criminology*, 2nd edn, Oxford: Clarendon Press.

Heidensohn, F. (2002) 'Gender and crime', in M. Maguire, R. Morgan and R. Reiner (eds), *The Oxford Handbook of Criminology*, 3rd edn, Oxford: Clarendon Press.

Held, D. and Thompson, J. (eds) (1989) *Social Theory of Modern Societies: Anthony Giddens and His Critics*, Cambridge: Cambridge University Press.

HM Chief Inspector of Prisons (1985) *Report of an Inspection of HM Prison Holloway*, London: Home Office.

HM Chief Inspector of Prisons (1990) *Suicide and Self-Harm in Prison Service Establishments in England and Wales*, Cm 1383, London: HMSO.

HM Chief Inspector of Prisons (1996) *Patient or Prisoner?* London: Home Office.

Hobsbawm, E. (1994) *Age of Extremes: The Short Twentieth Century 1914–1991*, London: Abacus.

Home Affairs Committee (2000) *First Report: Managing Dangerous People with Severe Personality Disorder*, London: The Stationery Office.

Home Office (1964) *Report of the Working Party on the Organization of the Prison Medical Service*, London: HMSO.

Home Office (1985) *First Report of the Advisory Committee on the Therapeutic Regime at Grendon*, London: Home Office.

Home Office (1990a) *Report on an Efficiency Scrutiny of the Prison Medical Service*, London: Home Office.

Home Office (1990b) *Crime, Justice and Protecting the Public*, London: HMSO.

Home Office (1991) *Custody, Care and Justice*, London: HMSO.

Home Office (2005) *Dangerous and Severe Personality Disordered (DSPD) Programme – Key Points*, London: Home Office.

Home Office/Department of Health (1999) *Managing Dangerous People with Severe Personality Disorder: Proposals for Policy Development*, London: Home Office.

Home Office/DHSS (1975) *Report of the Committee on Mentally Abnormal Offenders*, Cmnd 6244, London: HMSO. (The Butler Report)

Home Office/DHSS (1987) *Report of the Interdepartmental Working Group of Home Office and DHSS Officials on Mentally Disturbed Offenders in the Prison System in England and Wales*, London: Home Office/DHSS.

House, A. (1990) 'Prison suicides', *British Journal of Psychiatry* 156: 586–7.

House of Commons Social Services Select Committee (1986) *Third Report, Session 1985–6, Prison Medical Service*, London: HMSO.

Howard, J. (1777) *The State of the Prisons in England and Wales*, Warrington: W. Eyres.

Howe, A. (1994) *Punish and Critique: Towards a Feminist Analysis of Penality*, London: Routledge.

Hudson, B. (1998) 'Punishment and governance', *Social and Legal Studies* 7(4): 553–9.

Hudson, B. (2003) 'Detaining dangerous offenders: Dangerous confusions and dangerous politics', *Criminal Justice Matters* 51: 14–15.

Hutton, W. (1995) *The State We're In*, London: Jonathan Cape.

Ignatieff, M. (1978) *A Just Measure of Pain: The Penitentiary in the Industrial Revolution*, London: Macmillan.

Ignatieff, M. (1983) 'State, civil society and total institutions: A critique of recent social histories of punishment', in: S. Cohen and A. Scull (eds), *Social Control and the State*, London: Martin Robertson.

Isherwood, S. and Parrott, J. (2002) 'Audit of transfers under the Mental Health Act from prison – the impact of organizational change', *Psychiatric Bulletin* 26: 368–70.

James, D. (1999) 'Court diversion at 10 years: Can it work, does it work and has it a future?' *Journal of Forensic Psychiatry* 10: 507–24.

Jones, H. (1992) *Revolving Doors: Report of the Telethon Inquiry into the Relationship between Mental Health, Homelessness and Criminal Justice*, London: NACRO.

Joseph, P. (1992) *Psychiatric Assessment at the Magistrates' Court*, London: Home Office/Department of Health.

Kesteven, S. (2002) *Women Who Challenge: Women Offenders and Mental Health Issues*, London: NACRO.

Keyes, S., Scott, S., Truman, C. (1996) *People with Mental Health Problems in Contact with the Criminal Justice System: Report of a Service Mapping Exercise in Camden and Islington*, London: Revolving Doors Agency.

Kilgour, J. (1987) 'Medical care at Brixton Prison', *The Lancet* 2: 1216.

Laing, J. (1995) 'The mentally disordered suspect at the police station', *Criminal Law Review* 371–81.

Laing, R.D. (1960) *The Divided Self: An Existential Study in Sanity and Madness*, Harmondsworth: Penguin.

Lancet, The (1987) 'Government's response on Prison Medical Service', *The Lancet* 1: 783–4.

Laurance, J. (1987) 'Mentally ill boost prison numbers rise', *New Society*, (1 May) 5.

Leacock, V. and Sparks, R. (2002) 'Riskiness and at-risk-ness: Some ambiguous features of the current penal landscape', in N. Gray, J. Laing and L. Noaks (eds), *Criminal Justice, Mental Health and the Politics of Risk*, London: Cavendish.

Learmont, J. (1995) *Review of Prison Service Security in England and Wales and the Escape from Parkhurst Prison on Tuesday 3rd January 1995*, London: HMSO.

Leech, M. (1993) 'Prison medicine: A patient's perspective', *British Medical Journal* 306: 1550.

Lewis, A. (1974) 'Psychopathic personality: A most elusive category', *Psychological Medicine* 4: 133–40.

Lewis, D. (1996) 'Free the servants', *Guardian*, 13 May, 9.

Lewis, D. (1997) *Hidden Agendas: Politics, Law and Disorder*, London: Hamish Hamilton.

Liebling, A. (1992) *Suicides in Prison*, London: Routledge.

Livingston, M. (1997) 'A review of the literature on self-injurious behaviour amongst prisoners', in G. Towl (ed), *Suicide and Self-Injury in Prisons*, Issues in Criminological and Legal Psychology No 28, Leicester: British Psychological Society.

Lloyd, C. (1990) *Suicide and Self-Injury in Prison: A Literature Review*, Home Office Research Study No 115, London: HMSO.

Loader, I. and Sparks, R. (2002) 'Contemporary landscapes of crime, order, and control: Governance, risk and globalization', in M. Maguire, R. Morgan and R. Reiner (eds), *The Oxford Handbook of Criminology*, 3rd edn, Oxford: Clarendon Press.

Long, C. and Midgley, M. (1992) 'On the closeness of the concepts of the criminal and the mentally ill in the nineteenth century: Yesterday's opinions reflected today', *Journal of Forensic Psychiatry* 3(1): 63–78.

Longford, F. (1992) *Prisoner or Patient*, London: Chapmans.

McCallum, D. (2001) *Personality and Dangerousness: Genealogies of Antisocial Personality Disorder*, Cambridge: Cambridge University Press.

McDonald, M. (1981) *Mystical Bedlam: Madness, Anxiety and Healing in Seventeenth Century England*, Cambridge: Cambridge University Press.

Mackay, R.D. and Machin, D. (2000) 'The operation of section 48 of the Mental Health Act 1983: An empirical study of the transfer of remand prisoners to hospital', *British Journal of Criminology* 40: 727–45.

Maden, T. (1996) *Women, Prisons and Psychiatry: Mental Disorder Behind Bars*, London: Butterworth-Heinemann.

Maden, T. (2003) 'Invited commentary on *The Mental Health of Prisoners*', *Advances in Psychiatric Treatment* 9: 200–01.

Maden, T., Swinton, M. and Gunn, J. (1994) 'A criminological and psychiatric survey of women serving a prison sentence', *British Journal of Criminology* 34(2): 172–91.

Mandaraka-Sheppard, A. (1986) *The Dynamics of Aggression in Women's Prisons in England*, Aldershot: Gower.

Mannheim, H. (1939) *The Dilemma of Penal Reform*, London: George Allen and Unwin.

Marshall, P. (1997) *A Reconviction Study of HMP Grendon Therapeutic Community*, Research Findings No 53, London: Home Office.

Martinson, R. (1974) 'What works? Questions and answers about prison reform', *Public Interest* 35: 22–54.

Matthews, R. (1999) *Doing Time: An Introduction to the Sociology of Imprisonment*, London: Macmillan.

Matthews, R. and Young, J. (1992) 'Reflections on realism', in J. Young and R. Matthews (eds), *Rethinking Criminology: The Realist Debate*, London: Sage.

Mayhew, H. and Binney, J. (1862) *The Criminal Prisons of London and Scenes of Prison Life*, London: Charles Griffin.

Medlicott, D. (1999) 'Surviving in the time machine: Suicidal prisoners and the pains of prison time', *Time and Society* 8(2): 211–30.

Melossi, D. (1985) 'Punishment and social action: Changing vocabularies of punitive motive within a political business cycle', *Current Perspectives in Social Theory* 6: 169–97.

Melossi, D. (1993) 'Gazette of morality and social whip: Punishment, hegemony and the case of the USA, 1970–92', *Social and Legal Studies* 2: 259–79.

Melossi, D. and Pavarini, M. (1981) *The Prison and the Factory: Origins of the Penitentiary System*, Basingstoke: Macmillan.

Mercer, K. (1986) 'Racism and transcultural psychiatry', in P. Miller and N. Rose (eds), *The Power of Psychiatry*, Cambridge: Polity Press.

Mitchison, S., Rix, K., Renvoize, E. and Schweiger, M. (1994) 'Recorded psychiatric morbidity in a large prison for male remanded and sentenced prisoners', *Medicine, Science and the Law* 34(4): 324–30.

Monahan, J. (1992) 'Mental disorder and violent behaviour: Perceptions and evidence', *American Psychologist* 47: 511–21.

Monahan, J., Steadman, H., Silver, E., Appelbaum, P., Robbins, P., Mulvey, E., Roth, L., Grisso, T. and Banks, S. (2001) *Rethinking Risk Assessment: The MacArthur Study of Mental Disorder and Violence*, New York: Oxford University Press.

Moran, R. (1985) 'The origins of insanity as a special verdict: The trial for treason of James Hadfield (1800)', *Law and Society Review* 19: 487–519.

Morgan, R. (1997) 'Imprisonment: Current concerns and a brief history since 1945', in M. Maguire, R. Morgan and R. Reiner (eds), *The Oxford Handbook of Criminology*, 2nd edn, Oxford: Clarendon Press.

Morgan, R. (2002) 'Imprisonment: A brief history, the contemporary scene and likely prospects', in: M. Maguire, R. Morgan and R. Reiner (eds), *The Oxford Handbook of Criminology*, 3rd edn, Oxford: Clarendon Press.

Morris, A. (1987) *Women, Crime and Criminal Justice*, Oxford: Basil Blackwell.

Morris, T. and Morris, P. (1963) *Pentonville: A Sociological Study of an English Prison*, London: Routledge.

Mountbatten, Lord (1966) *Report of the Inquiry into Prison Escapes and Security*, London: HMSO.

Muijen, M. (1996) 'Scare in the community: Britain in moral panic', in T. Heller, J. Reynolds, R. Gomm, R. Muston and S. Pattison (eds), *Mental Health Matters: A Reader*, Basingstoke: Macmillan.

Mullen, P. (1999) 'Dangerous people with severe personality disorder: British proposals for managing them are glaringly wrong – and unethical', *British Medical Journal* 319: 1146–7.

Muncie, J. (1996) 'Prison histories: Reform, repression and rehabilitation', in E. McLaughlin and J. Muncie (eds), *Controlling Crime*, London: Sage.

Murphy, E. (1996) 'The past and future of special hospitals', *Journal of Mental Health* 5(5): 475–82.

Murphy, E. (2003) 'The administration of insanity in England 1800 to 1870', in R. Porter and D. Wright (eds), *The Confinement of the Insane: International Perspectives, 1800–1965*, Cambridge: Cambridge University Press.

NACRO (1993) *Mentally Disturbed Prisoners at Winson Green: A Study of Staff and Prisoner Perceptions of the Problem at HMP Birmingham*, London: NACRO.

Needham-Bennett, H. (1995) 'Waiting for a disaster to happen', *British Medical Journal* 311: 516.

Newburn, T. and Jones, T. (2005) 'Symbolic politics and penal populism: The long shadow of Willie Horton', *Crime, Media, Culture* 1(1): 72–87.

O'Brien, M., Mortimer, L., Singleton, N. and Meltzer, H. (2001) *Psychiatric Morbidity among Women Prisoners in England and Wales*, London: ONS.

O'Malley, P. (1992) 'Risk, power and crime prevention', *Economy and Society* 21: 252–75.

O'Malley, P. (1999) 'Volatile and contradictory punishment', *Theoretical Criminology* 3(2): 175–96.

O'Malley, P. (2000) 'Risk societies and the government of crime', in M. Brown and J. Pratt (eds), *Dangerous Offenders: Punishment and Social Order*, London: Routledge.

O'Malley, P. (2001) 'Governmentality', in E. McLaughlin and J. Muncie (eds), *The SAGE Dictionary of Criminology*, London: Sage.

O'Malley, P. (2004) *Risk, Uncertainty and Government*, London: GlassHouse Press.

Orr, J. (1978) 'The imprisonment of mentally disordered offenders', *British Journal of Psychiatry* 133: 194–9.

Outen, F. (2003) 'A victim of its own success? Psychiatry and pre-crime interventions', *Safer Society* 17: 6–8.

Pailthorpe, G. (1932) *Studies in the Psychology of Delinquency*, London: HMSO.

Parkinson, C. (1981) *The Right Approach to Mental Health*, London: Conservative Party Political Centre.

Parsons, S., Walker, L. and Grubin, D. (2001) 'Prevalence of mental disorder in female remand prisons', *Journal of Forensic Psychiatry* 12(1): 194–202.

Pearson, G. (1975) *The Deviant Imagination: Psychiatry, Social Work and Social Change*, London: Macmillan.

Pearson, G. (1999) 'Madness and moral panics', in N. Eastman and J. Peay (eds), *Law Without Enforcement: Integrating Mental Health and Justice*, Oxford: Hart.

Peay, J. (1988) 'Offenders suffering from psychopathic disorder: The rise and demise of a consultation document', *British Journal of Criminology* 28: 67–81.

Peay, J. (1997) 'Mentally disordered offenders', in M. Maguire, R. Morgan and R. Reiner (eds), *The Oxford Handbook of Criminology*, 2nd edn, Oxford: Oxford University Press.

Peay, J. (2002) 'Mentally disordered offenders, mental health and crime', in M. Maguire, R. Morgan and R. Reiner (eds), *The Oxford Handbook of Criminology*, 3rd edn, Oxford: Clarendon Press.

Peay, J. (2003a) 'Working with concepts of "dangerousness" in the context of mental health law', *Criminal Justice Matters* 51: 18–19.

Peay, J. (2003b) *Decisions and Dilemmas: Working with Mental Health Law*, Oxford: Hart Publishing.

Penrose, L.S. (1939) 'Mental disease and crime: Outline of a comparative study of European statistics', *British Journal of Medical Psychology* 18: 39–41.

Phillips, C. and Bowling, B. (2002) 'Racism, ethnicity, crime, and criminal justice', in M. Maguire, R. Morgan and R. Reiner (eds), *The Oxford Handbook of Criminology*, 3rd edn, Oxford: Oxford University Press.

Phillips, M. (1986) *A Study of Suicides and Attempted Suicides at HMP Brixton 1973–83*, Department of Psychological Services Report, Series I No 24.

Pilling, J. (1992) 'Back to basics: Relationships in the Prison Service', Eve Savile Memorial Lecture, London: ISTD.

Player, E. (1994) 'Women's prisons after Woolf', in E. Player and M. Jenkins (eds), *Prisons after Woolf: Reform through Riot*, London: Routledge.

Player, E. and Jenkins, M. (1994) 'Introduction', in E. Player and M. Jenkins (eds), *Prisons after Woolf: Reform through Riot*, London: Routledge.

Polidano, C. (1999) 'The bureaucrat who fell under a bus: Ministerial responsibility, executive agencies and the Derek Lewis affair in Britain', *Governance* 12(2): 201–29.

Porter, R. (1987) *Mind Forg'd Manacles: A History of Madness in England from the Restoration to the Regency*, London: Athlone.

Porter, R. (1990) 'Foucault's Great Confinement', *History of the Human Sciences* 3: 47–54.

Porter, R. (2003) 'Introduction', in R. Porter and D. Wright (eds), *The Confinement of the Insane: International Perspectives, 1800–1965*, Cambridge: Cambridge University Press.

Pratt, J. (1997) *Governing the Dangerous: Dangerousness, Law and Social Change*, Sydney: Federation Press.

Pratt, J. (1998) 'Towards the "decivilizing" of punishment?' *Social and Legal Studies* 7(4): 487–515.

Pratt, J. (1999) 'Norbert Elias and the civilized prison', *British Journal of Sociology* 50(2): 271–96.

Pratt, J. (2000a) 'The return of the wheelbarrow men; Or, the arrival of postmodern penality?' *British Journal of Criminology* 40: 127–45.

Pratt, J. (2000b) 'Dangerousness and modern society', in M. Brown and J. Pratt (eds), *Dangerous Offenders: Punishment and Social Order*, London: Routledge.

Prins, H. (1980) 'Mad or bad: Thoughts on the equivocal relationship between mental disorder and criminality', *International Journal of Law and Psychiatry* 3: 421–33.

Prins, H., Backer-Holst, T., Francis, E. and Keitch, I. (1993) *Report of the Committee of Inquiry into the Death in Broadmoor Hospital of Orville Blackwood and a Review of the Deaths of Two Other Afro-Caribbean Patients: Big, Black and Dangerous?* London: Special Hospitals Service Authority.

Prison Reform Trust (2005) *Troubled Inside: Responding to the Mental Health Needs of Men in Prison*, London: Prison Reform Trust.

Prison Service (1985) *Holloway Project Review Committee Report*, London: Prison Service.

Prison Service/NHSE (1999) *The Future Organisation of Prison Health Care*, London: Home Office/Department of Health.

Pugh, R. (1968) *Imprisonment in Medieval England*, Cambridge: Cambridge University Press.

Rabinow, P. (ed) (1984) *The Foucault Reader*, London: Penguin.

Radzinowicz, L. (1978) 'John Howard', in J. Freeman (ed), *Prisons: Past and Future*, London: Heinemann.

Radzinowicz, L. and Hood, R. (1986) *The Emergence of Penal Policy in Victorian and Edwardian England*, Vol 5 of *A History of English Criminal Law*, Oxford: Clarendon Press.

Ramsay, M. (1977) 'John Howard and the discovery of the prison', *Howard Journal* 16: 1–16.

Rasch, W. (1981) 'The effects of indeterminate detention: A study of men sentenced to life imprisonment', *International Journal of Law and Psychiatry* 4: 417–31.

Reed, J. (1992) *Review of Health and Social Services for Mentally Disordered Offenders and Others Requiring Similar Services: Services for People from Black and Ethnic Minorities Groups: Issues of Race and Culture. A Discussion Paper*, London: HMSO.

Reed, J. (1993) *Review of Health and Social Services for Mentally Disordered Offenders and Others Requiring Similar Services*, Vol 2, *Service Needs*, London: HMSO. ('The Reed Review')

Reed, J. (1994) *Report of the Department of Health and Home Office Working Group on Psychopathic Disorder*, London: HMSO.

Reed, J. (2002) 'Delivering psychiatric care to prisoners: Problems and solutions', *Advances in Psychiatric Treatment* 8: 117–27.

Reed, J. (2003) 'Mental health care in prisons', *British Journal of Psychiatry* 182: 287–8.

Reed, J. and Lyne, M. (1997) 'The quality of health care in prison: Results of a year's programme of semi-structured inspections', *British Medical Journal* 315: 1420–24.

Reichman, N. (1986) 'Managing crime risks: Towards an insurance based model of social control', *Research in Law, Deviance and Social Control* 8: 151–72.

Resodihardjo, S. (2004) 'Discourse and funnelling: How discourse affected Howard's leeway during the 1994–5 crisis', *Journal for Crime, Conflict and the Media* 1(3): 15–27.

Revolving Doors Agency (2002) 'Reed in the new Millennium', *The Circular* Issue 25: 2.

Ritchie, J., Dick, D. and Lingham, R. (1994) *The Report of the Inquiry into the Care and Treatment of Christopher Clunis*, London: HMSO.

Robertson, G. and Gunn, J. (1987) 'A ten-year follow-up of men discharged from Grendon Prison', *British Journal of Psychiatry* 151: 674–8.

Robertson, G., Pearson, R. and Gibb, R. (1995) *The Mentally Disordered and the Police*, Research Findings No 21, London: Home Office.

Robinson, C., Patten, J. and Kerr, W. (1965) 'A psychiatric assessment of criminal offenders', *Medicine, Science and the Law* 5: 140–6.

Rock, P. (1988) 'Micro-sociology and power: A natural history of research on policy-making', in N. Fielding (ed), *Actions and Structure: Research Methods and Social Theory*, London: Sage.

Rock, P. (1995) 'The opening stages of criminal justice policy making', *British Journal of Criminology* 35(1): 1–16.

Rock, P. (1996) *Reconstructing a Women's Prison: The Holloway Redevelopment Project 1968–1988*, Oxford: Clarendon Press.

Roper, W.F. (1951) 'A comparative study of the Wakefield Prison population in 1948: Parts I and II', *British Journal of Delinquency* 1: 15–28; 243–70.

Rose, M. S. (1987) 'Conditions in Brixton Prison Hospital Block', *The Lancet* 2: 915.

Rose, N. (1985) *The Psychological Complex: Psychology, Politics and Society in England, 1869–1939*, London: Routledge & Kegan Paul.

Rose, N. (1986) 'Psychiatry: the discipline of mental health', in P. Miller and N. Rose (eds), *The Power of Psychiatry*, Cambridge: Polity Press.

Rose, N. (1990) 'Of madness itself: *Histoire de la folie* and the object of psychiatric history', *History of the Human Sciences* 3(3): 373–80.

Rose, N. (1993) 'Government, authority and expertise in advanced liberalism', *Economy and Society* 22(3): 283–99.

Rose, N. (1996a) 'Psychiatry as a political science: Advanced liberalism and the administration of risk', *History of the Human Sciences* 9(2): 1–23.

Rose, N. (1996b) 'Governing "advanced" liberal democracies', in A. Barry, T. Osborne and N. Rose (eds), *Foucault and Political Reason*, Chicago: Chicago University Press.

Rose, N. (1996c) 'The death of the social? Re-figuring the territory of government', *Economy and Society* 25(3): 327–56.

Rose, N. (1998) 'Governing risky individuals: The role of psychiatry in new regimes of control', *Psychiatry, Psychology and Law* 5: 177–95.

Rose, N. (1999a) *Powers of Freedom: Reframing Political Thought*, Cambridge: Cambridge University Press.

Rose, N. (1999b) *Governing the Soul: The Shaping of the Private Self*, 2nd edn, London: Free Association.

Rose, N. (2000) 'Government and control', in D. Garland and R. Sparks (eds), *Criminology and Social Theory*, Oxford: Oxford University Press.

Rose, N. and Miller, P. (1992) 'Political power beyond the state: Problematics of government', *British Journal of Sociology* 43(2): 172–205.

Royal College of Psychiatrists (1979) 'The College's evidence to the prison services enquiry', *Bulletin of the Royal College of Psychiatrists*, May: 81–4.

Rusche, G. and Kirchheimer, O. (1939) *Punishment and Social Structure*, New York: Columbia University Press.

Russell, J. and Lipsedge, M. (1987) 'Medical care at Brixton Prison', *The Lancet* 2: 1216.

Sapsford, R.J. (1978) 'Life-sentenced prisoners: Psychological changes during sentence', *British Journal of Criminology* 18: 128–45.

Scull, A. (1977) *Decarceration: Community Treatment and the Deviant*, Englewood Cliffs, NJ: Prentice-Hall.

Scull, A. (1993) *The Most Solitary of Afflictions: Madness and Society in Britain 1700–1900*, London: Yale University Press.

Selby, M. (1991) 'HMP Grendon – The care of acute psychiatric patients: A pragmatic solution', in K. Herbst and J. Gunn (eds), *The Mentally Disordered Offender*, Oxford: Butterworth-Heinemann.

Shaw, J., Tomenson, B., Creed, F. and Perry, A. (2001) 'Loss of contact with psychiatric services in people diverted from the criminal justice system', *Journal of Forensic Psychiatry* 12: 203–10.

Shaw, S. (1985) 'Introduction: The case for change in prison medicine', in Prison Reform Trust (ed), *Prison Medicine: Ideas on Health Care in Penal Establishments*, London: Prison Reform Trust.

Shaw, S. (1992) 'Prisons', in E. Stockdale and S. Casale (eds), *Criminal Justice under Stress*, London: Blackstone.

Shaw, S. and Sampson, A. (1991) 'Thro' cells of madness: The imprisonment of mentally ill people', in K. Herbst and J. Gunn (eds), *The Mentally Disordered Offender*, Oxford: Butterworth-Heinemann.

Showalter, E. (1985) *The Female Malady: Women, Madness and English Culture, 1830–1980*, New York: Vintage.

Sim, J. (1990) *Medical Power in Prisons: The Prison Medical Service in England 1774–1989*, Buckingham: Open University Press.

Sim, J. (1994a) 'Reforming the penal wasteland', in E. Player and M. Jenkins (eds), *Prisons after Woolf: Reform through Riot* London: Routledge, 31–45.

Sim, J. (1994b) 'Prison medicine and social justice', *Prison Service Journal* 95: 30–38.

Sim, J. (2002) 'The future of prison health care: a critical analysis', *Critical Social Policy* 22(2): 300–23.

Simon, J. (1987) 'The emergence of a risk society: Insurance, law and the state', *Socialist Review* 95: 61–89.

Simon, J. (1988) 'The ideological effects of actuarial practices', *Law and Society Review* 22: 771–800.

Simon, J. (1993) *Poor Discipline*, Chicago, IL: University of Chicago Press.

Simon, J. (1998) 'Managing the monstrous: Sex offenders and the new penology', *Psychology, Public Policy and Law* 4: 452–67.

Singleton, N., Meltzer, H. and Gatward, R. with Coid, J. and Deasy, D. (1998) *Psychiatric Morbidity among Prisoners in England and Wales*, London: The Stationery Office.

Sked, A. and Cook, C. (1993) *Post-War Britain: A Political History*, 4th edn, London: Penguin.

Smart, C. (1976) *Women, Crime and Criminology: A Feminist Critique*, London: Routledge & Kegan Paul.

Smith, A. (1962) *Women in Prison*, London: Stevens & Sons.

Smith, C. (2000) ' "Healthy Prisons": A Contradiction in Terms?' *Howard Journal of Criminal Justice* 39(4): 339–53.

Smith, L. (2003) 'Dangerous and severe personality disorder: Difficulties in assessment', *Criminal Justice Matters* 51: 16–17.

Smith, R. (1981) 'The boundary between insanity and criminal responsibility in nineteenth-century England', in A. Scull (ed), *Madhouses, Mad-Doctors and Madmen: The Social History of Psychiatry in the Victorian Era*, Pennsylvania: University of Pennsylvania Press.

Smith, R. (1984) *Prison Health Care*, London: British Medical Association.

Smith, R. (1990) 'Arise the new prison health service', *British Medical Journal* 301: 892–3.

Snell, H.K. (1962) 'HM Prison, Grendon', *British Medical Journal* 2: 789–92.

Snider, L. (2003) 'Constituting the punishable woman: Atavistic man incarcerates postmodern woman', *British Journal of Criminology* 43: 354–78.

Sparks, R. (1994) 'Can prisons be legitimate? Penal politics, privatization, and the timeliness of an old idea', *British Journal of Criminology* 34 Special Issue: 14–28.

Sparks, R. (1996) 'Penal "austerity": The doctrine of less eligibility reborn?' in R. Matthews and P. Francis (eds), *Prisons 2000: An International Perspective on the Current State and Future of Imprisonment*, London: Macmillan.

Sparks, R. (1997) 'Recent social theory and the study of crime and punishment', in M. Maguire, R. Morgan and R. Reiner (eds), *The Oxford Handbook of Criminology*, 2nd edn, Oxford: Clarendon Press.

Sparks, R. (2000a) 'Perspectives on risk and penal politics', in T. Hope and R. Sparks (eds), *Crime, Risk and Insecurity: Law and Order in Everyday Life and Political Discourse*, London: Routledge.

Sparks, R. (2000b) 'Risk and blame in criminal justice controversies: British press coverage and official discourse on prison security (1993–6)', in M. Brown and J. Pratt (eds), *Dangerous Offenders: Punishment and Social Order*, London: Routledge.

Sparks, R. (2001a) ' "Bringin' it all back home": Populism, media coverage and the dynamics of locality and globality in the politics of crime control', in K. Stenson and R. Sullivan (eds), *Crime, Risk and Justice: The Politics of Crime Control in Liberal Democracies*, Cullompton: Willan.

Sparks, R. (2001b) 'Degrees of estrangement: The cultural theory of risk and comparative penology', *Theoretical Criminology* 5(2): 159–76.

Sparks, R. (2003) 'States of insecurity: Punishment, populism and contemporary political culture', in S. McConville (ed), *The Use of Punishment*, Cullompton: Willan.

Sparks, R., Bottoms, A. and Hay, W. (1996) *Prisons and the Problem of Order*, Oxford: Clarendon Press.

Spierenburg, P. (1991) *The Prison Experience: Disciplinary Institutions and Their Inmates in Early Modern Europe*, New Brunswick, NJ: Rutgers University Press.

Stafford, P. (1999) *Defining Gender Issues . . . Redefining Women's Services*, London: Women In Special Hospitals (WISH).

Stanko, E. and Hobdell, K. (1993) 'Assault on men: Masculinity and male victimization', *British Journal of Criminology* 33: 400–15.

Stenson, K. (2005) 'Sovereignty, biopolitics and the local government of crime in Britain', *Theoretical Criminology* 9(3): 265–87.

Stern, V. (1993) *Bricks of Shame: Britain's Prisons*, updated 2nd edn, Harmondsworth: Penguin.

Stewart, C. and Shine, J. (1984) 'Disturbed women in Holloway', unpublished report, Psychology Department, HMP Holloway.

Swyer, B. and Lart, R. (1996) 'Prisoners' mental health problems: Screening needs and accessing services', *Probation Journal* 43(4): 205–10.

Sykes, G. (1958) *The Society of Captives*, Princeton, NJ: Princeton University Press.

Talbot, C. (1996) 'The Prison Service: A framework of irresponsibility?' *Public Money and Management* (January–March) 5–7.

Taylor, P.J. (1986) 'Psychiatric disorder in London's life-sentenced offenders', *British Journal of Criminology* 26(1): 63–78.

Taylor, R. (2000) *A Seven-Year Reconviction Study of HMP Grendon Therapeutic Community*, Research Findings No 115, London: Home Office.

Tooth, G.C. and Brooke, E.M. (1961) 'Trends in the mental hospital population and their effect on future planning', *The Lancet* 1: 710.

Topp, D. (1977) 'The doctor in prison', *Medicine, Science and the Law* 17(4): 261–64.

Topp, D. (1979) 'Suicide in prison', *British Journal of Psychiatry* 134: 24–7.

Turner, T. and Tofler, D. (1986) 'Indicators of psychiatric disorder among women admitted to prison', *British Medical Journal* 292: 651.

Vaughan, B. (2001) 'Handle with care: On the use of structuration theory within criminology', *British Journal of Criminology* 41: 185–200.

Vaughan, P., Kelly, M. and Pullen, N. (2001) 'The working practices of the police in relation to mentally disordered offenders and diversion services', *Medicine, Science and the Law* 41: 13–20.

Verdun Jones, S. (1989) 'Sentencing the partly mad and partly bad: The case of the Hospital Order in England', *International Journal of Law and Psychiatry* 12: 1–27.

Voruz, V. (2005) 'The politics of *The Culture of Control*: undoing genealogy', *Economy and Society* 34(1): 154–72.

Walker, N. (1968) *Crime and Insanity in England*, Vol 1, *The Historical Perspective*, Edinburgh: Edinburgh University Press.

Walker, N. (1983) 'Side-effects of incarceration', *British Journal of Criminology* 23(1): 61–71.

Walker, N. and McCabe, S. (1973) *Crime and Insanity in England*, Vol 2, *New Solutions and New Problems*, Edinburgh: Edinburgh University Press.

Wall, S., Hotopf, M., Wessely, S. and Churchill, R. (1999) 'Trends in the use of the Mental Health Act, 1984–96', *British Medical Journal* 318: 1520–1.

Ward, D.A. and Kassebaum, G.G. (1965) *Women's Prison*, London: Weidenfeld.

Watt, F., Tomison, A. and Torpy, D. (1993) 'The prevalence of psychiatric disorder in a male remand prison: A pilot study', *Journal of Forensic Psychiatry* 4(1): 75–83.

West, D.J. (1963) *The Habitual Prisoner*, London: Macmillan.

Wiener, M.J. (1990) *Reconstructing the Criminal: Culture, Law and Policy in England, 1830–1914*, Cambridge: Cambridge University Press.

Wilczynski, A. (1997) 'Mad or bad? Child killers, gender and the courts', *British Journal of Criminology* 37: 419–36.

Wilkins, J. and Coid, J. (1991) 'Self-mutilation in female remanded prisoners I: An indicator of severe psychopathology', *Criminal Behaviour and Mental Health* 1: 247–67.

Wilson, S. (2004) 'The principle of equivalence and the future of mental health care in prisons', *British Journal of Psychiatry* 184: 5–7.

Windlesham, Lord (1993) *Responses to Crime*, Vol 2, *Penal Policy in the Making*, Oxford: Clarendon Press.

Wise, J. (1996) 'News: NHS takeover of prison health service proposed', *British Medical Journal* 313: 1099.

Woodcock, J. (1994) *The Escape from Whitemoor Prison on Friday 9th September 1994*, London: HMSO.

Woodside, M. (1962) 'Instability in women prisoners', *The Lancet* 2: 928–30.

Wool, R. (1996) 'The future contribution of the prison service', in *Understanding the Enigma: Summary of the Anglo-Dutch Conference on Personality Disorder and Offending*, London: Special Hospitals Service Authority.

Woolf, H. and Tumim, S. (1991) *Prison Disturbances April 1990*, Cm 1456, London: HMSO.

Young, J. (1999) *The Exclusive Society: Social Exclusion, Crime and Difference in Late Modernity*, London: Sage.

Young, J. (2002) 'Searching for a new criminology of everyday life: Review of *The Culture of Control* by David Garland', *British Journal of Criminology* 42: 228–43.

Young, J. (2004) 'Crime and the dialectics of inclusion/exclusion: Some comments on Yar and Penna', *British Journal of Criminology* 44: 550–61.

Zedner, L. (1991) *Women, Crime and Custody in Victorian England*, Oxford: Clarendon Press.

Zedner, L. (1995) 'Wayward sisters: The prison for women', in N. Morris and D. Rothman (eds), *The Oxford History of the Prison: The Practice of Punishment in Western Society*, Oxford: Oxford University Press.

Zedner, L. (2002) 'Dangers of dystopias in penal theory', *Oxford Journal of Legal Studies* 22(2): 341–66.

Index

Page numbers in *italics* refer to tables, *passim* indicates numerous mentions within page range.